THE TSAR'S LOYAL GERMANS

The Riga German Community:
Social Change and the Nationality Question, 1855–1905

By ANDERS HENRIKSSON

EAST EUROPEAN MONOGRAPHS, BOULDER
DISTRIBUTED BY COLUMBIA UNIVERSITY PRESS, NEW YORK

1983

EAST EUROPEAN MONOGRAPHS, NO. CXXXI

To Ann

CONTENTS

ACKNOWLEDGEMENTS

I am pleased to acknowledge my appreciation to the many contributions made to this project by friends, teachers and colleagues. My work on the Riga German community first took shape as a doctoral dissertation at the University of Toronto. I owe a major debt of gratitude to John L.H. Keep, who supervised the dissertation and later read the book manuscript. His perceptive comments on the manuscript have helped in no small way to shape its form and style. Thanks are also due Harvey L. Dyck, who first encouraged me to pursue my interest in the history of the Baltic region; Peter Brock, who has contributed a great deal to my understanding of eastern Europe's complicated nationality relationshps; Peter Scheibert, who lent me much assistance and insightful advice during my research stay in Germany; and Patricia Grimsted, who shared with me her extensive knowledge of Baltic archival materials. I want especially to thank my family for their encouragement and support and my wife, Ann, without whose patient understanding and willingness to make sacrifices this work could not have been undertaken. Research for this book has been carried out in numerous libraries and institutions in Europe and North America; but I would particularly like to express my gratitude for the assistance afforded me by the staffs of the Hoover Institution on War, Revolution and Peace at Stanford University, the J.G. Herder-Institut in Marburg and the Helsinki University Library. Finally, I wish to thank the Canada Council, the Deutscher Akademischer Austauschdienst and the University of Toronto Centre for Russian and East European Studies for their generous grants of financial support.

A Note on Dates, Transliteration and Measures

All dates follow the Julian calendar, which was used in Russia until 1917. Transliteration of Russian words and names is based on the Library of Congress system, with the exception of a few prominent

vii

names which have accepted English spellings (hence, for example, "Witte" rather than "Viitte"). The Russian *pud* is the equivalent of 36.11 pounds. The value of the ruble fluctuated in relation to western currencies during the period 1855–1905, but in 1900 one ruble was worth approximately fifty American cents.

PREFACE

In the history of late nineteenth-century Russia and eastern Europe two themes stand out with particular clarity. One is the growing attraction which political nationalism held both for governments confronted with the task of ruling multi-national states and for the area's numerous minority groups. A central feature of regional politics was the clash between nationalist governments, bent on centralization and assimilation, and equally nationalistic minorities seeking to defend and to assert themselves against the centre. The other salient theme is the rapid, intensive economic modernization of what were relatively underdeveloped societies. This period witnessed the extension of the industrial revolution to eastern Europe. Industrialization brought fundamental social change. Traditional elites were faced with unfamiliar challenges and forced to compete with groups and classes in society which drew their strength from the new industries. Hand in hand with industrial development came urbanization, as millions of peasants sought to escape rural poverty by migrating to the cities, where they found employment as factory labourers. My purpose in this volume is to examine the inter-relationship between social change and nationality conflict.

The Russian Empire, like its Austro-Hungarian and Ottoman neighbours, was a multi-national state. Centuries of imperial expansion had brought a wide variety of national minorities under Russian rule. By the late nineteenth century less than half the population was Great Russian. The Baltic provinces of Kurland, Livland and Estland typified the national diversity of the empire's western borderlands. In Kurland and southern Livland the peasantry and the bulk of the urban lower classes were Latvian. In northern Livland and Estland they were Estonian. The rural nobility and clergy together with the upper and middle urban classes throughout the three provinces were German. Most of the larger Baltic towns also had Russian and Jewish minorities. Political nationalism was to play a major role in shaping the relationship between the Russian state and the local comunities and among the various nationalities which inhabited the Baltic region.

At the heart of Livland province lay Riga, its capital. By far the largest and most important city in the Baltic provinces and the fifth largest in the Russian Empire,* Riga experienced profound social and economic changes during the late nineteenth century. In the space of a few decades the city was transformed from a commercial centre of a hundred thousand into a great industrial metropolis whose population was fast approaching the half-million mark.

The German community in Riga presents a revealing case study of the interplay between social and national interests. The Germans were a pre-industrial social elite who had dominated Riga's political, economic and cultural life since the Middle Ages. Industrialization constituted a very real challenge to their social position, forcing them to make serious adjustments or face eventual ruin. They also found themselves attacked on two fronts as a national minority. On the one hand they were confronted with the aggressively anti-German nationalism of a small, but vocal and well organized Latvian bourgeoisie; and on the other hand they became the objects of government policies aimed first at administrative centralization at the expense of indigenous German local institutions and finally at Russification.

The bulk of the secondary literature on this subject contends that the Germans in Riga, like so many eastern European minorities, responded to the challenge of alien nationalism by developing a counter-nationalism of their own. This argument does not reflect the realities of the period 1855–1905. Most of the historians who subscribe to this school of thought (the most important among them being Reinhard Wittram) are themselves Baltic Germans, who view the pre-1905 period through the prism of their own experiences in the revolutions of 1905 and 1917, World War I and the subsequent establishment of an independent Latvian republic. Prior to the Revolution of 1905 the Germans of Riga (and elsewhere in the Baltic provinces) rejected political nationalism. Most of them did not even possess a clear or well developed national consciousness. The explanation for this lies in the manner in which the Riga German community adapted to social change, an aspect of nineteenth-century Riga which Wittram and others either ignore or dismiss too lightly. In the end, the social and economic environment proved to be the determining factor in the German perception of their local Latvian rivals and of their position within the multi-national empire.

---

*Only St. Petersburg, Moscow, Warsaw and Odessa surpassed Riga in population.

Chapter 1

NATIONALITY AND SOCIETY IN MID-NINETEENTH CENTURY RIGA

Travelers who visited Riga during the middle decades of the last century almost invariably describe it as a German city. The walled old town, the skyline dominated by tall, narrow church steeples and the winding streets lined with closely packed rows of stone buildings were characteristically north German. In 1867 the first systematic municipal census revealed the population of 102,590 to be 42.8 per cent German, 25.1 per cent Russian, 23.5 per cent Latvian and 5.1 per cent Jewish; but the German community completely dominated the city.[1] German was the main language of business and of cultural life. It was the sole language of government.

Much of the responsibility for municipal government and for the regulation of the local economy rested with the two guilds, whose role as public authorities had endured since the fourteenth century. The membership of the merchant, or St. Mary's, guild and the artisan, or St. John's, guild was overwhelmingly German. Approximately seven hundred and fifty guild merchants, who exercised a virtual monopoly on commerce and industry and who dominated local politics, formed the pinnacle of Riga society. The German guild artisans, while neither as affluent nor as powerful as the merchants, also constituted a privileged, corporate class that wielded considerable political and economic power. Embracing thirty-seven trades from wainwright to clock maker, the guild regulated all craft production in the city. Full guild membership, restricted to certified master craftsmen, was held by seven hundred and twenty-one men in 1861. Certified *(zünftige)* journeymen and apprentices, who worked for guild masters and who could hope one day to achieve master status themselves, numbered 2,398 in the same year. Non-certified *(unzünftige)* artisans were allowed to ply their trades only at the tolerance of the guild.[2] Members of the free professions, known in the Baltic provinces as "literati", formed another distinct element in the German community.[3] The literati were not a corporate estate like the merchants and artisans, but they comprised a clearly defined group with

1

certain specific privileges, including the right to join the merchant guild. Members of the legal profession were also eligible to serve in the magistracy, the executive organ of municipal government. Most of the literati were educated at nearby Dorpat University, a German-language institution established in 1802 by Tsar Alexander I; and membership in the *Fraternitas Rigensis,* a Dorpat fraternity for Riga students, often served as a social and professional bond that underlined the cohesiveness of the literati as a social group. Many Germans pursued more humble occupations. Very few of them were to be found among the poorest urban classes, but a not inconsiderable number belonged to the *Kleinbürgertum,* a lower middle class of shopkeepers, clerks, minor civil servants, non-certified artisans and servants.[4]

In contrast to their German neighbours the Latvian population was almost wholly lower class. Most were unskilled labourers and domestic servants.[5] The thin upper layer of Latvian society was formed by a handful of shopkeepers and clerks and by the practitioners of the so-called "Latvian trades", a group of nineteen semi-skilled occupations that possessed a loose corporate organization endowed with a degree of self-regulatory authority.[6] Upward social mobility in a relatively static society ruled by corporate, self-governing classes is normally difficult and infrequent, but this does not fully explain the absence of Latvian upper and middle classes. When upward mobility did occur it was nearly always accompanied by total Germanization. Latvian served as the language of the lower social orders and German as that of the upper. When an individual acquired a higher social status he also acquired German language and nationality as a matter of course. The main avenue through which upwardly mobile Latvians underwent Germanization was gradual absorption into the *Kleinbürgertum.* At the end of a process that might last two or three generations, the successful scion of a humble Latvian family could perhaps gain admission to the artisan guild or even enter the ranks of the literati. By this time he would have become fully assimilated into the German community. The line of demarcation between German and Latvian in Riga was at best indistinct. Many of those who claimed German as their "customary language" in the 1867 census spoke Latvian as children and had Latvian-speaking parents. The transition from Latvian to German nationality did not present much difficulty. A foreigner who visited Riga in the 1840's commented that, "The ease with which the Latvians . . . take on German nationality is astounding."[7] Most urban Latvians were forced by circumstances to be bi-lingual; and both Germans and Latvians were predominantly Lutheran, a factor that facilitated inter-marriage.

Concentrated in the sprawling Moscow suburb, the Riga Russian minority exhibited a higher degree of social diversity than did the Latvians. More than one-fifth of them were soldiers posted to the local garrison, and as such were not permanent members of the community. The Russian community was also split along religious lines at all social levels. A majority (61.9 per cent) of the civilian Russian population were Orthodox. Nearly all of the rest were Old Believers whose ancestors had fled Russian persecution in the seventeenth century, when Riga was under Swedish rule.[8] The two Russian communities had little to do with one another. A scattering of civil servants and affluent merchants formed the upper layers of Russian society. Some of the wealthiest Russian merchants managed to gain entry to the merchant guild. They were the only non-Germans with a voice in municipal government, but they never played an active role in guild affairs. No Russian ever held guild office.[9] Many more Russians engaged in petty trade or worked as non-certified artisans; but most were unskilled labourers, many of whom were peasant *otkhodniki* who drifted back and forth seasonally between Riga and their villages in neighbouring Vitebsk province.[10]

The only other nationality represented in significant numbers in Riga were Jews, although Riga lay outside the Jewish Pale of Settlement. Denied the right to membership in the guilds and forbidden until 1858 to own real property in the city, the Jews formed an underprivileged minority of petty merchants and tradesmen.[11]

The mid-nineteenth century Riga economy was based on commerce. Situated on the Baltic seacoast at the mouth of the Dvina river, the city was positioned astride a major artery of east-west trade and had been a commercial centre for centuries. In terms of the value of goods imported and exported, Riga was the third most important Russian port during this period.[12] Riga's largely German merchantry amassed fortunes exporting Russian timber, flax, hemp, linseed oil, grain and other raw materials that were purchased in nearby Vitebsk and Smolensk provinces and floated down the Dvina on wooden barges. The import trade, while less in volume and worth, was nonetheless substantial, the chief imports being footstuffs for local consumption and raw materials and partially fabricated goods that supplied the needs of Riga industry.

Industrialization came late to the Russian Empire. Riga's industrial complex had only begun to develop by the middle of the nineteenth century. Chamber of Commerce statistics reveal that in 1864 there were ninety "factories" with a labour force of 5,670; but many of these "factories" were only small workshops with as few as three or four employees.[13] As a manufacturing centre Riga was easily surpassed by

Moscow and St. Petersburg. Riga had nevertheless experienced a slow, steady industrial development throughout the first half of the nineteenth century. Between 1834 and 1854 the number of "factories" in the city had nearly tripled and the industrial labour force quadrupled.[14] Lacking nearby sources of raw materials, Riga's industry, like that of St. Petersburg, was based on the processing of import and export commodities. Since industry was so closely allied to commerce, it is not surprising that it was almost entirely controlled by the local German merchants, who invested mercantile capital in industrial ventures. The most important local industry was textile manufacturing, which employed over two thousand workers in twenty-one plants.[15] The cotton textile industry, which spun thread from imported raw cotton, was led by the Pychlau mill, one of Riga's largest and most modern manufacturing concerns. In the 1860's it employed more than five hundred workers. Two large firms, E.D. Holm and G.A. Thilo, specialized in weaving English woollen yarn into cloth for sale on the domestic market. Linen manufacturing still faced stiff competition from the rural cottage industry, but the early 1860's witnessed the establishment of two fully mechanized linen manufacturing concerns in Riga, the Baltic Linen Manufacturing Company and the Altona Corporation, both of which spun Russian and Baltic Flax into linen cloth for export. The Pychlau, Thilo and Holm mills were the property of local German merchant families; and the Baltic Linen Manufacturing Company was a joint-stock company founded by a consortium of Riga German merchants. Only the Altona Corporation, organized by the British entrepreneur Henry Robinson, made use of capital drawn from outside Riga.[16]

Other significant local industries included wood processing and cigar making. Two steam-powered sawmills processed Russian timber into wood products for export market. The larger of the two, Armitstead, Mitchell and Company, was owned by British investors, but its competitor, Wöhrmann and Son, belonged to the Wöhrmanns, one of Riga's most prominent German merchant families.[17] The cigar making industry had developed in response to a tariff system that placed prohibitively high duties on Cuban cigars and low duties on unprocessed American tobacco. In 1864 Riga boasted eight cigar making factories with a combined labour force of nearly one thousand. Most of the factories, including the four largest, were owned by local German tobacco importers.[18]

Machine building, later to figure as one of the leading branches of industry in Riga, had just begun to develop in the middle of the nineteenth century. The only two firms then engaged in machine building, Wöhrmann and Son and Rosenkranz and Company, were quite small. The former had been set up by the Wöhrmann family to provide machinery for their sawmill, and the latter, which also assembled machines for local industry, had been founded by a former Wöhrmann employee.[19] The remainder of Riga industry included a number of small food processing plants, breweries, distilleries and factories producing household goods for the local market. Virtually all of these small-scale operations belonged to Riga German merchants. Unlike their German counterparts, the city's leading Russian merchants did not display much interest in the diversion of mercantile capital into industry. The only important industrial enterprise in Russian hands was a porcelain and chinaware factory owned by the Kuznetsovs, a local Old Believer family.[20]

The provision of effective local government presented serious difficulties for the imperial Russian state. Confronted with a vast land area, a large and diverse population, a shortage of competent administrative personnel and a lack of experience with self-government even on the part of the privileged classes, successive Russian rulers found themselves engaged throughout the eighteenth and early nineteenth centuries in an all but futile search for a workable system of local government. The weakest link in the entire administrative structure was at the municipal level. The eighteenth century alone witnessed three major efforts directed at the restructuring of city government, none of which was conspicuous by its success.

Unlike much of western and central Europe, Russia did not possess urban classes endowed with corporate rights and long experience with the duties of self-government. The concept of government as a mutually binding contract between ruler and ruled had no place in the Russian constitutional and legal tradition. Ultimate political power was concentrated in the hands of the tsar. Russian subjects were granted various privileges, but could not invoke legal rights against the will of the sovereign. Attempts by Russian rulers to effect municipal reform by remodeling municipal institutions to resemble those of the west met with repeated failure, because they captured only the form, not the substance, of the European models. The lack of political experience among the Russian urban classes and the fundamental unwillingness of Russian sovereigns to alienate political and legal authority undermined the reforms from the beginning. The municipal institutions established by the eighteenth century reforms were in reality little more than devices for regulating the fiscal and service obligations owed to the state by the urban population. Membership in a Russian guild, for example, was a juridical expression of one's status vis-a-vis obligations to the state, not a claim to a share in the rights and duties of a corporate class. Since service in municipal government brought them no gain, townsmen generally did their best to avoid it. The failure of municipal government was so complete that government inspectors discovered during the 1820's that the organs of administration did not even exist in many provincial cities.[21] Administrative and judicial power in most cities fell by default to the provincial governors.

In light of this situation it is understandable that when Russia expanded westward to incorporate Poland, Finland and the Baltic provinces, the tsars felt it wise to leave the indigenous institutions of urban government there intact.[22] Relations between the Russian state and the organs of local government in the Baltic provinces were based on the Capitulations of 1710, concluded by Peter the Great with the Riga estates and with the Livland and Estland provincial diets. The Capitulations guaranteed estate self-government, granted the Lutheran church a privileged position under the patronage of local authorities and declared German to be the language of all instances of government, including crown offices, within the Baltic provinces. The Capitulations were re-confirmed in the 1721 Treaty of Nystadt and by every Russian ruler, with the exception of Peter III and the infant Ivan VI, from Peter I through Alexander II.

The Riga estate system, modelled on those of the German Hansa towns, had its origins in a charter granted by the Bishop of Riga in 1226. It provided the city with government by politicized social corporations. Guild members and men who served in the magistracy all held Riga citizenship, a status that conferred the rights and responsibilities of self-government on its holders. The criterion for membership in one of the three estates was occupational. The artisan guild was restricted to master craftsmen. The merchant guild admitted merchants, literati, artists and master goldsmiths. The magistracy *(Rath)* drew half its twenty members from the merchant guild. The other half were *"Rechtsgelehrte"* magistrates, selected from the ranks of legally trained literati. Executive authority rested with the magistracy, which was composed of sixteen magistrates *(Rathsherren)* and four burgomasters *(Bürgermeister)*. A chief burgomaster *(wortführender Bürgermeister)* was elected annually by the four burgomasters to preside over the magistracy and act as chief municipal executive officer. The magistracy was responsible for the day-to-day administration of the city and the dispensation of civil and criminal justice through seven lower courts. The full magistracy acted as an appellate instance, although final appeals could be directed to the Senate in St. Petersburg. The magistracy was also patron of the Riga Lutheran Consistory and ran an extensive city educational system that included fourteen elementary schools, a middle school, a girls' secondary school, and the ancient Riga Cathedral

School, which was converted into a technical gymnasium in 1861. The language of instruction throughout the system was German. Riga also possessed a provincially supported German-language gymnasium; and the state maintained two Russian-language schools, one elementary and one middle, in the city.

The two guilds supervised trade and commerce. Each was governed by a bench of elders *(Aeltestenbank)*, thirty strong in the artisan guild and forty strong in the merchant guild. The executive officer of each guild, the alderman *(Ältermann)*, was elected by the bench of elders for a two-year term. The guilds wielded political, as well as economic, power. Guild representatives sat together with magistrates on the city treasury board, the military quartering board and several municipal inspectorates. Before making any major decision the magistracy was legally bound to consult the guilds.

The estates system involved self-government, but it was hardly democratic. Citizens of the estates accounted for a mere 1.5 per cent of the city population. Citizenship was furthermore not a status available on demand even to those who met the occupational requirements. The estates were empowered to select as members adult males resident in Riga who, besides meeting the occupational requirements, were Christian, Russian subjects, free (*i.e.,* not serfs) and of "irreproachable character."[23] Within the estates authority was largely in the hands of the senior officers. The citizenry at large played a relatively limited role in government. Burgomasters and magistrates held office for life and were elected by the magistracy itself. Normally they were recruited from the ranks of the merchant guild officers and from lawyers who had served for years in the magistracy chancery or in the municipal court system. Nearly all of the men chosen to serve as magistrates belonged to a small circle of wealthy patrician families.[24] Guild aldermen and elders had to be confirmed in office by the magistracy, and plenary guild assemblies could be summoned only with the consent of the chief burgomaster. Disputes between the magistracy and the guilds were submitted to a special arbitration court composed of two representatives from each estate. Guild elders were elected for life terms by a plenary session of the guild, but only the bench of elders could nominate candidates. Not all citizens were even eligible to hold guild office. Only members of the brotherhoods, inner circles in each guild which chose their members from the citizenry at large, could serve as officers. The ordinary citizen's sole means of exerting political influence was the submission of petitions to the bench of elders through a special official known as the *Dockmann* when the guild met in plenary session. These assemblies normally took place twice a year, at Michaelmas and Shrovetide.

Their unique form of self-government notwithstanding, the Riga

Germans, as Russian subjects, were liable to most of the same fiscal and service obligations as inhabitants of other Russian cities. All Russian laws and administrative regulations had full force in Riga unless the provincial law code specified otherwise.[25] All Russian subjects who were permanent legal residents in Riga belonged to the Riga tax community. This was a legal personality which provided the juridical framework for the levying of state taxes, the issuance of internal passports and military conscription. The tax community was also responsible for the welfare of its members if they became ill or indigent. In order that these obligations might be assessed, Riga's tax community was subdivided into the legal categories which applied to all urban Russians. These categories were simply superimposed upon the corporate class structure. Members of the tax community were accordingly segregated into merchants of the first and second "guilds", artisans, *meshchane*, workers and servants. A Riga merchant, for example, might belong to the St. Mary's guild as a participant in corporate self-government and to the first merchant guild of the tax community with respect to his state service and fiscal obligations. Merchants, together with nobles and honoured citizens, did not pay the head tax and were free from military conscription and corporal punishment. Artisans were subject to the head tax, but so long as they were *zünftige* were not liable to either conscription or corporal punishment. This was a privilege not accorded to artisans in the cities of European Russia.

The imperial government, while granting the Riga Germans a latitude of self-government unheard of in Russia proper, retained important supervisory powers in Riga. These were exercised by the Baltic governor-general and the governor of Livland province, both of whom resided in the city. Verdicts reached in the city courts, elections to the magistracy and the municipal budget were all subject to approval by the governor-general; and police powers were shared between the governor-general and the magistracy. The imperial government seldom made use of its right to interfere with estate self-government in Riga. Russian rulers were content to leave the local administration there in the hands of a privileged German elite, who like themselves had a vested interest in the maintenance of social stability and public order.

Chapter 2

FROM *STILLEBEN* TO REFORM

The first half of the nineteenth century was a period of political stagnation in the Baltic provinces. The Germans in Riga complacently carried on living in the manner of generations past in an atmosphere of drowsy indifference to the world beyond the city walls. This was an age contemptuously dismissed by the more active politicians of the 1860's as the *"livländisches Stilleben"*.[1]

The tranquil *Stilleben* came to an end in 1855 when the rigidly conservative Tsar Nicholas I was succeeded by his son Alexander II. Humiliating defeat at the hands of the western powers in the Crimean War had made the need for change in the immense but backward Russian Empire manifestly apparent. Alexander had no choice but to implement a series of sweeping reforms. The Russian serfs were emancipated, a judicial system featuring jury trials and an independent judiciary was established, the educational system was improved, the military and the civil service were overhauled and a limited form of self-government was introduced in most of European Russia.

The government's commitment to reform produced a stir of excitement in educated circles, and a relaxation of censorship permitted a lively public debate on the question of Russia's future. Before long the new spirit began to make itself felt in the Baltic, and the question of reform emerged as the dominant topic on the local political agenda. By the end of the 1850's there came into being a peculiarly Baltic German liberal reform programme that claimed an important following among the urban merchants and literati as well as the rural nobility.

A vigourous political press soon appeared as the champion of the new liberalism. In 1859 the journal *Baltische Monatschrift* was founded in Riga by Magistrate Alexander Faltin and Theodor Bötticher, a noble from Kurland. They were joined in 1862 by Riga City Librarian Georg Berkholz, who rapidly established himself as one of the leading figures in the liberal movement. The first issue of the journal carried a laudatory article on the reforms being planned for European Russia;[2] and subsequent numbers devoted much space to hopeful essays calling for

9

parallel reforms in the Baltic. The Riga daily press also took up the liberal cause. Two young literati, Julius Eckardt and John Baerens, acquired the century-old *Rigasche Zeitung* and transformed it into an aggressive advocate of reform. Eckardt and Baerens promised the public that they would, "endeavour to offer an open word on all true political and economic progress."[3] A second liberal daily, the *Zeitung für Stadt und Land,* began to appear in 1867 under the editorship of Riga literatus Gustav Keuchel. In a retrospective look taken at these developments a decade later, Eckardt wrote that, "The young Russian press had given the impetus for the awakening of publicistic life in Riga, Dorpat and Reval . . . one believed then that the time had come when an analogous regeneration of Baltic provincial life was possible. In this sense reform plans emerged that touched upon almost every facet of public life, and that really ran parallel to the endeavour to reshape Russian administration, Russian justice, etc."[4]

In its perception of individual freedom as the highest good, Baltic liberalism stood squarely in the mainstream of nineteenth century European liberal thought. This principle lay at the foundation of a liberal reform programme which called for the elimination of estates' privileges, civil equality, the creation of an independent judiciary and the gradual extension of self-government to all responsible citizens. Like many continental liberals, the Baltic Germans admired the British constitution and wished to emulate it. As Berkholz argued in 1863, "Where does the secret lie? In the freedom for individual development that the English institutions guarantee . . . England has no monopoly on this discovery. The machinery is there for anyone with clear vision to see. It is only a matter of summoning the courage to decide to achieve the same success by the same methods."[5]

Liberalism in the Baltic was moderate and cautious. Its proponents in Riga were established merchants and professional people who had a stake in the maintenance of public order and who mistrusted the political judgement of the poorer classes. They stressed that all men should be equal before the law and were optimistic believers in the blessings of popular education, but they did not wish to allow the poor and uneducated masses to have a voice in self-government: "Only better educated individuals serve themselves with freedom . . . the more poorly educated easily confuse freedom with lawlessness."[6] Municipal and provincial self-government was to be the preserve of the propertied and educated.

Although it was inspired by the Russian reform movement, Baltic German liberalism bore a different character from its Russian counterpart. This can be traced to the nature of the Baltic constitutional tradition. In Russia the realization of liberal goals like self-government and civic equality presupposed the creation of new political and legal forms. In contrast, the Baltic provinces possessed a long tradition of self-government by politicized social corporations. The Baltic provinces, moreover, were seen by their German upper classes as a *Rechtsstaat,* in which the written law was the supreme political and legal authority. The Russian government had generally respected this notion and gave it an important additional confirmation as recently as 1845 with the codification of Baltic law. Liberalism could ostensibly achieve its goals in the Baltic by the reform of already extant forms and institutions. The creation of entirely new ones was not necessary.

A central feature of Baltic liberalism was the conviction that reform would have to be based upon the existing Baltic political and legal system as defined by the rights and privileges granted to the estates in the Capitulations of 1710:

> These privileges contain a nucleus, the proper understanding of which can now, after 160 years, propel the people to greater freedom and morality than all the reforms that the humanity and enlightenment of the monarch provide for the remainder of the empire.[7]

Alien forms imposed by monarchical fiat could not, in liberal German eyes, be successful. New laws and institutions would have to be organic continuations of what had gone before. Even more importantly, the imposition of such reforms by the ruler would constitute a serious violation of the Baltic *Rechtsstaat,* and the Baltic liberals placed a high value on the notion of due process of law.

In the early 1860's it appeared that the Baltic Germans would be able to bring about reform on their own terms. By granting concessions to Finland and Poland, the tsar demonstrated his awareness of the special position of the national minorities. A series of popular Baltic governors-general, including General Alexander Suvorov (1848–1861), Baron Wilhelm Lieven (1861–1864) and Count Peter Shuvalov (1864–1866), were instrumental in encouraging liberal hopes and often acted as spokesmen for Baltic interests at the imperial court.[8]

Liberalism in Riga was strictly an affair of the German community. Political articulateness did not then extend far beyond the German ruling classes; but in the nationally diverse Riga environment any comprehensive political movement had to address itself to the nationality question. The German liberals had to come to terms both with the Russian state and with the city's large non-German population.

Baltic Germans traditionally defined their collective identity in terms of estate and region. Class and geographical barriers within the German minority were quite rigid. Each of the three provinces was a world unto itself. The German townspeople, furthermore, had little to do with the nobility, even though many nobles spent the winter season in the provincial capitals.[9] Within the cities merchants and literati did not intermarry or mingle socially with artisans and *Kleinbürger*.[10] Nationality was not perceived as a primary determinant of collective identity, but rather as a subsidiary function of social class. The upper classes were German and the lower were Latvian and Estonian. The identification of social class with nationality was so strong that an alteration in social class usually occasioned a change of nationality. The weak national consciousness of the Baltic Germans was recorded by a somewhat perplexed visitor from Germany, who wrote in a Leipzig journal in 1848 that, "National consciousness, which after long struggle has become so powerful in Germany, is completely foreign to the Germans of the Baltic provinces."[11]

A collective identity based on estate membership could naturally have no place in a liberal programme that advocated civic equality. Consequently, the liberals strove to replace the traditional determinants of collective identity with a sense of membership in a unitary Baltic community:

> If we really wish to arouse ourselves from estates particularism . . . and to create a Baltic community we must be fully indifferent to estate and region, be it Livland, Estland or Kurland, Riga, Reval or Mitau.[12]

The very word "Baltic" in reference to the three provinces was first brought into common usage by the liberals in the late 1850's. It was not co-incidental that they chose to title their leading journal *"Baltische Monatschrift"*.

This Baltic community was to encompass all of the people in the area, Latvians and Estonians as well as Germans. The liberals spurned nationality as a determinant of collective identity. Their Baltic community was to be supranational, a single people composed of different ethnic groups. Ernst von der Brüggen, who in 1869 succeeded Berkholz as chief editor of the *Baltische Monatschrift*, captured the essence of this attitude when he wrote that, "Fate has permitted us to develop as a single people composed of different ethnic groups, different in language and social position."[13] This ethnically and linguistically diverse Baltic people was united by a common history and a common culture which were essentially German.[14] The language of the ruling classes, of government and of higher education had always been German, and the Baltic political, cultural and religious tradition was a German one.

Latvian and Estonian had yet to become literary languages, and were still merely the idioms of peasant cultures that never exerted any influence beyond the lower classes. In the estimation of the German liberals the Estonians and Latvians were not distinct nationalities. They were only the lower social strata in a culturally German society. This made them German in every way save language:

> The substance of their religion had been moulded into a German form by Lutheranism and Herrnhuterism, they have lived for centuries within a German legal framework, and their entire literature consists of translations or imitations of German products.[15]

Any attempt to elevate these peasant cultures to a higher level would be doomed to failure, because, "A linguistic splinter of a few hundred thousand, be they the cleverest men, can not equal what can be achieved by the intellectual and material resourcs of forty million who speak the same language."[16]

The liberals nonetheless emphatically rejected linguistic Germaniza-tion, for, as Berkholz declared, "next to religious persecution there is nothing more inhuman and odious than coercion to use a foreign language."[17] To Germanize the lower classes would be to violate their civil rights as individuals; and, although the liberals did not think the Latvian and Estonian languages appropriate media for government or even secondary education, they did advocate expanded use of them in elementary schools, in the court system and at the lower levels of public administration.[18]

The liberals approached the relationship between Germans and Lat-vians in Riga in a manner consistent with this ideology. They saw the city's Latvian community as a group of lower classes who could not be clearly differentiated in a cultural sense from the Germans. When a Russian newspaper claimed that Riga had a Latvian minority twenty thousand strong, the *Rigasche Zeitung* characteristically retorted that, "It would be interesting to know how Mr. Lamanskii has concluded that 20,000 Latvians live in Riga. In our opinion it is impossible to draw an exact boundary between these people and the Riga Germans."[19]

The nationality question in Riga was further complicated by the presence of a large and socially diverse Russian community. The Rus-sians did not fit into the indigenous Baltic pattern of nationality rela-tionships; and the liberal movement was at odds with itself as to how to deal with them. Some liberals, including Faltin, Eckardt and Baerens, were willing to make concessions to the local Russians as a national group, guaranteeing them representation in the city government and making Russian an official language.[20] Most others were reluctant to grant favours to any group on the grounds of nationality, becuase this would give members of that group a special status incompatible with a system predicated upon the principle of equal rights for all individual citizens. In the words of merchant guild alderman Schnakenburg, "There are no Russians here, only Riga citizens."[21] This kind of argument was completely in line with liberal philosophy. The interests of the group, be it national or other, were secondary to those of the individual.

Political nationalism was anathema to the liberals. Berkholz sternly denounced it, warning that, "All Pan-Slavism, Pan-Germanism, Pan-Finnism, as soon as it seeks to overstep the limits of language study, mythology and antiquarianism, truly belongs in the realm of higher stupidity."[22] For him nationalists were "nationality swindlers" who "have only two ideas in their heads: ethnic origin and language, and who do not understand how to deal with other aspects of life."[23] Several years later von der Brüggen added in agreement that, "Our era is a most singular one. Everyone wants to shut himself off within his own people, and erroneously to advocate nationality, rather than culture, as the most important goal in the development of his people."[24]

The attitude notwithstanding, the Riga Germans had to face challenges from both Russian and Latvian political nationalism. Russian nationalists were basically intolerant of national diversity within the empire, which they envisioned as a monolithic Russian nation-state. In their eyes the cultural and linguistic Russification of minorities was a desirable goal, and the fact that groups like the Baltic Germans were allowed to maintain non-Russian forms of local government was utterly intolerable. In 1863 a bloody, but unsuccessful Polish revolt against Russian rule drew the attention of the nationalist Russian press to the western borderlands. Led by Mikhail Katkov's *Russkii vestnik* and *Moskovskie vedomosti*, as well as Ivan Aksakov's Slavophile newspaper *Den'*, this press inundated its public with tales of plots hatched by minority groups and revolutionaries designed to topple the monarchy and dismember the empire. The Baltic Germans were favourite targets for xenophobic tirades accusing them of harbouring secret desires to break with Russia and throw in their lot with Bismarck's Prussia.[25]

In reality nothing could have been farther from the truth. The Baltic Germans were steadfastly loyal. Katkov's attacks caused an angry Berkholz to write that, "The Kurlanders, Estlanders and Livlanders have always been good Russians—perhaps even the best of all."[26] Separatism in the cause of national solidarity with other Germans was unthinkable for people whose national consciousness was weak and who actively rejected political nationalism. The liberals stood for an autonomous Baltic region within a liberalized Russia. As Eckardt explained, "We wanted to be a part of the edifice of a transformed Russia, albeit as a uniquely carved building block."[27]

The nationalist press nonetheless turned an important segment of Russian public opinion against the Baltic Germans and put pressure on the imperial government to Russify the Baltic area on security grounds. Russian nationalism was also not without influence in Riga itself,where many of the local Russians turned to it as a vent for their frustration at life on the periphery of a German-dominated society. They actively campaigned for a Russian role in city government and, in 1867, founded a newspaper entitled *Rizhskii vestnil*, whose programme closely resembled that of Katkov's publications.[28]

The middle decades of the last century also witnessed a trend toward the development of political nationalism among the smaller nationalities of central and eastern Europe. The Latvians were no exception to this. Beginning in the 1850's, after a series of agrarian reforms made upward social mobility somewhat easier for the Latvian peasantry, growing numbers of young Latvians managed to gain admission to Dorpat University. There many of them made the conscious decision to retain their Latvian nationality rather than submit to Germanization. This new Latvian intelligentsia soon formulated a Latvian nationalism that challenged the traditional assumptions and argued that, "The Latvians are nothing more and nothing less than a nation, which has been consigned by long oppression to lowly stations in life."[29]

Latvian nationalism was not monolithic. Atis Kronvalds, a publicist and educator who was among the most prominent early nationalists, strove mainly to better Latvian education and to raise Latvian culture to a higher plane. He quite naturally sought to place Latvian-German relations on a new footing, but he and his collaborators were not anti-German.[30] Other nationalists were bitterly hostile toward the Baltic Germans, whom they viewed as oppressors and outside intruders in a Latvian country, which would have to be reclaimed by its rightful owners through complete Latvianization and perhaps even expulsion of the Germans. The chief representative of this school was the journalist Krisjanis Valdemars, who created a forum for his views by founding a Latvian newspaper, the *Petersburgas avises* (St. *Petersburg Gazette*), in the imperial capital in 1862. There Valdemars became acquainted with Katkov and wrote several articles for the latter's newspapers calling for Russian help in the Latvian struggle against the Germans.[31]

The most important manifestation of Latvian nationalism in Riga was the Riga Latvian Union, founded in 1868 by a group of Latvian intellectuals and professional people. This organization, whose members represented all shades of opinion within the nationalist movement, sponsored Latvian cultural events, maintained a Latvian-language theatre, published a literary journal and administered a scholarship program for Latvian students.

The Riga Germans did not understand Latvian nationalism. They could not even bring themselves to take it seriously. This is not surprising given their views of Latvian nationhood, their own lack of national awareness and their disavowal of political nationalism. Gustav Keuchel, chief editor of the *Zietung für Stadt und Land,* flatly declared that the Latvians were not a nation because they had no educated classes:

> There are no educated Latvians. Those who are educated and call themselves Latvian only deceive themselves . . . To be both Latvian and educated is an impossibility.[32]

Berkholz dismissed Latvian nationalism as a temporary symptom of social inequality that would vanish with the fulfillment of the liberal programme:

> Once education, economic well-being and political equality have permitted our lower classes to develop far enough so that they are generly conscious of their solidarity with the other classes and with provincial institutions, agitation in the name of race will die out.[33]

If the Latvian movement gave the Germans any cause for concern, it was not on its own merits, but because of its connections with men like Katkov.

The ultimate political goal of the German liberals was the fusion of the three Baltic diets into an autonomous Baltic legislature elected by all propertied and educated men. Any concrete move in this direction would have to be made by the diets themselves, and the urban Germans had no share in the workings of these bodies, which represented only the provincial nobility.

Within Riga itself, however, there was much to capture the atention of reform-minded liberals. The city's medieval system of public administration was badly in need of overhaul, if only on the grounds that it was no longer able to cope efficiently with the management of a growing city. The twenty members of the magistracy were overburdened with responsibilities in administration, justice, education, law enforcement and church affairs. There was already a serious backlog of cases before the municipal courts that was threatening to become progressively worse. Some governmental functions were shared with the two guilds; but the heavy work load of the magistracy, which had to meet six days per week, placed harsh demands on the merchant magistrates, who had to divide their attention between public service and private business responsibilties.

Developments in St. Petersburg made the need for municipal administrative reform all the more urgent. The imperial government was readying a municipal reform of its own, and past experience showed the Riga Germans that such reforms were not always without effect in the Baltic provinces. Catherine II simply abolished the estates system in the Baltic cities for a time and replaced it with the administrative apparatus provided by the Russian municipal Charter of 1785. The old institutions were restored in 1797 by Tsar Paul, but as recently as the 1840's another threat to Riga's indigenous form of government had materialized. The tsar and his ministers were considering a major restructuring of city government; and in 1842 a special commission was despatched to Riga to investigate the possibility of municipal reform there. After three years of deliberation the commission produced a reform scheme that involved a complete dismantling of the traditional administrative system. The proposal was never implemented. Governor-General E.A. Golovin, a supporter of the commission's efforts, was replaced in 1848 by Alexaner Suvorov, who reported to Tsar Nicholas that it was, "incredible that a system which has functioned for hundreds of years could be completely without merit."[34] Even in Russia itself reform was limited to St. Petersburg, where a new administrative system was introduced in 1846.

The imperial government turned its attention away from the improvement of city administration until the 1860's. The 1846 St. Petersburg reform was extended to Moscow in 1862 and to Odessa in 1863. In April, 1862 provincial governors were instructed by the Ministry of Internal Affairs to set up committees to discuss the question of a general municipal reform, thus inaugurating the process that was to lead to the statute on municipal self-government of 1870.

Concern lest the tsar introduce changes in Riga that would prove contradictory to local constitutional tradition combined with the very real need for municipal reform to rouse Riga's leading citizens from their political *Stilleben*. The local press eagerly endorsed the idea of constitutional reform. Berkholz warned that the city fathers should seize the initiative before change could be imposed from without, and called for an extension of self-government beyond the narrow boundaries of the estates:

The real drawback [of the estates system] lies in the false limitation of the urban community, which consists only of the two corporations of the merchants and artisans, while all the remaining inhabitants, even if they possess city property and pay high taxes, are not called upon to participate.[35]

In October, 1861 *Rigasche Zeitung* editor Eckardt advocated municipal reform which could be achieved, "without violation of the honourable edifice of our constitution."[36] A month later the newspaper published the text of a public lecture delivered by a young lawyer named Robert Büngner. Büngner echoed the fear that if Riga did not begin to reform itself its constitutional tradition would fall victim to the imperial government's "ever present efforts at centralization."[37] Even the normally apolitical weekly *Rigasche Stadtblätter* appealed for a broadening of the municipal franchise and a separation of justice from administration.[38]

These demands for constitutional reform were characteristic of Baltic liberalism. They centred around the extension of self-government to all propertied men and the establishment of a judicial system that would provide adequate protection of individual civil liberties. Above all, the partisans of reform insisted that any beneficial change would have to take place within the framework of Riga's own constitutional tradition.

The appeals of the press did not fall on deaf ears in the city government. A reform party emerged within the estates under the leadership of Burgomaster Otto Müller and Magistrates Alexander Faltin and Gustav Hernmarck. These three were among the most able men in the city government. It is noteworthy that they were *homines novi* in Riga who had not been born into the conservative, particularist milieu of the local patriciate. Müller was the son of an impecunious pastor from rural Kurland, Faltin's family were immigrants from Prussia and Hernmarck, a native of Stockholm, came to Riga as a teenaged boy. Both Faltin and Müller were Dorpat-trained lawyers who had risen through a series of junior positions in the city judicial and administrative system before winning election as *Rechtsgelehrte* magistrates. Müller, who earned a reputation as a man impatient with the obsolete structures and outworn rules of the estates system, became one of the youngest men to be elected in modern times to the office of burgomaster. Faltin's career exhibits more diversity. Besides serving in the magistracy and maintaining a private law practice, he was founder and editor of the *Baltische Monatschrift* and sat on the board of directors of the Riga-Dünaburg Railroad Corporation. Hernmarck, who had served as president of the Chamber of Commerce, as a merchant guild elder, and after 1854 as a magistrate, had been a force for progress and modernization throughout his career as a public official. He had campaigned for the reform of Riga's medieval trade laws, the improvement of the city's harbour facilities, the installation of the first telegraph line in the Russian Empire (Riga-Bolderaa) and the construction of the first railroad link to Riga. More of a practical businessman than a politician, Hernmarck had come to feel that the prosperity of the local business community required a thoroughgoing renovation of city government.[39]

The more conservative members of the magistracy were hesitant to change the old, familiar ways of doing things, but the reform party eventually prevailed thanks to support from the local press and to mounting pressure for reform applied by the merchant guild elders, who, like Hernmarck, had come to believe that material prosperity and political change were inseparable.[40] After a couple of false starts a committee composed of Hernmarck, Faltin, the two guild aldermen and two legal experts tabled a series of reform proposals in 1863. Included in them were the separation of justice from administration and the reorganization of the citizenry so as to permit enfranchisement of propertied men who did not qualify for estate membership. The committee suggested the creation of a "citizens' guild" whose membership would encompass the hitherto disenfranchised. The members of the three guilds would then elect a municipal legislature. The magistracy, which would choose its members from among candidates nominated by the legislature, would continue as city executive and would exercise a virtual veto power over the decisions of the legislature.[41]

In May, 1865 the estates set up a thirty-member commission for the preparation of a definitive constitutional reform based on the 1863 proposals. The commission's task was restricted to the political and administrative sphere. In 1864 Governor-General Lieven, acting on the advice of the imperial Council of State, had summoned representatives of the various Baltic estates to a Central Justice Commission in Dorpat for the purpose of working out a reform of the entire Baltic judicial system. The separation of justice from administration, already agreed upon as a basis for constitutional reform in Riga, was henceforth the responsibility of the justice commission in Dorpat.

The final draft of the Riga constitutional reform plan, submitted to Governor-General Shuvalov in July, 1865, followed most of the general guidelines set down in 1863, but in several ways the final plan was more liberal. The property qualifications for enfranchisement were slightly lower; and the final plan abandoned the idea of creating a third guild in favour of a unitary, corporate citizenry. The magistracy would remain as city executive, but was to forfeit veto power over the municipal legislature.[42] A central feature of the plan was its conformity with local constitutional tradition. Berkholz praised it for this quality when he wrote in the *Baltische Monatschrift* that, "We would not like to leap into the unknown with a single bound, and thereby kill the communal

spirit, which is always of a traditional nature."⁴³ Similar feelings were
expressed by John Baerens in the *Rigasche Zeitung:*

> The new constitution will in large part consist of survivals from the old, and a
> centuries-long past, whose successes are still in evidence today, will prove
> itself stronger than a short-sighted endeavour that would confuse appear-
> ance with substance and the past with the obsolete.⁴⁴

The most important survival of the estates system in the 1865 plan was
its recognition of the Riga citizenry as a corporate entity. The reform
plan in effect replaced the old separate self-governing social corporations of merchants and artisans with a single one of propertied citizens.
Citizenship was not to be the prerogative of any adult male who
happened to live in Riga and to meet the property qualifications. It was
to be a status granted upon application to those resident in the city for at
least one year and who were deemed to be of "irreproachable character".⁴⁵ The rights and duties of the citizenry as a corporate body were
made very clear by a clause in the plan requiring the municipal legislature to account for its conduct before a biennial plenary assembly of the
citizenry. This assembly was the lineal descendant of the biennial plenary guild assembly. The corporate nature of local government was a
feature of the estates system which the German liberals felt to be
particularly worthy of preservation. They believed that a corporate
citizenry would be endowed with "community spirit" *(Gemeinsinn)* and
would function in such a way as to permit all of its members to have a
direct influence on government and to experience the full weight of
public responsibility. Membership in the governing corporation could
be expanded to embrace an ever broader spectrum of society as popular
education gradually bestowed a sense of civic responsibility and political maturity upon the population as a whole.

The success of any reform was naturally predicated upon the
approval of the imperial government. The promoters of reform in Riga
were justifiably optimistic about their chances. Governors-General
Suvorov, Lieven and Shuvalov had always supported their efforts; and
in 1862, when the Riga reform project got under way, Lieven agreed
that reform had become "an urgent requirement for the common
good."⁴⁶

The hopes of the reform party were soon disappointed. Late in 1865
Governor-General Shuvalov pronounced the estates' reform plan unacceptable. He found it too conservative. His major objection was to the
delegation of executive authority to a magistracy that would not be
directly elected by the citizenry or even by the municipal legislature. He

also felt that the property qualification for enfranchisement was too high and that "irreproachable character" should be dropped as a criterion for admission to the citizenry. He strongly recommended that measures be taken to bring the Riga Russian minority into a more active role in municipal government than it had played in the past. In order to ensure that the Russians would be represented in the municipal legislature, Shuvalov proposed that elections be held by district rather than on a city-wide basis. The heavily Russian Moscow suburb would be certain to return some Russian candidates. Finally, he contended that Russian should be granted parity with German as an official language of local government.[47]

The estates reform commission agreed to lower the property qualification slightly, to remove the "irreproachable character" requirement for citizenship and to conduct city elections by district. These changes did not go far enough to please Shuvalov, who felt that the property qualification was still too high, that the magistracy remained far too powerful and that Russian legislators should have the right to work in their own language. In spite of Shuvalov's repeated entreaties the Riga estates refused to budge on these issues, and the governor-general's only option was to send the Riga reform plan to the Ministry of Internal Affairs without approving it.

The wheels of the imperial bureaucracy turned slowly. Judgement on the plan was not forthcoming until February, 1868. Interior Minister P.A. Valuev came to the same conclusion as the Baltic governor-general. The plan was too conservative and did not fully serve the interests of the Riga Russians. He nonetheless praised Riga's tradition of corporate self-government and assured the estates that the implementation in Riga of a reform alien to that tradition could "hardly be termed sensible."[48]

Under pressure from the imperial government, the estates finally agreed to make the magistracy subordinate to the municipal legislature. The suggestions of newly appointed Baltic Governor-General Peter Albedinskii (1866–1870) that the property qualification be lowered and that Russian be made an official language were, however, ignored. Albedinskii, like Shuvalov before him, consequently found himself unable to support the reform plan as it stood.

Late in 1868 the imperial government changed its approach to municipal reform in Riga. In spite of its recent assurances to the contrary, the Ministry of Internal Affairs abruptly informed the Riga estates that their proposal for reform was entirely unacceptable. Reform in the Baltic cities would be based on the plan then being worked out for the cities of European Russia.

The unwillingness of the Riga estates to compromise on the specifics of municipal reform did not enhance their chances of success, but this does not fully explain the imperial government's change of heart. The rejection of the Riga plan coincided with the replacement of Valuev by A.E. Timashev as Minister of Internal Affairs. Valuev, whose mother was a Baltic German and who had once served as governor of Kurland province, was familiar with Baltic affairs and sympathetic to the Baltic liberal programme.[49] Timashev, on the other hand, could not see any point in allowing the Riga Germans to have their own special set of local administrative institutions different from those about to be introduced in the cities of European Russia. One of his chief subordinates in the Ministry was later to recall him remarking that, "So long as I am Minister of Internal Affairs, the Baltic provinces will in no way be accorded special institutions of their own."[50]

Apart from this, the general political atmosphere in Russia was changing. A revolutionary movement, impatient with the slow pace of government-sponsored reforms, arose and showed itself capable of violence. In 1866 the tsar himself narrowly escaped assassination at the hands of a terrorist. There was serious unrest among equally impatient and unhappy members of some national minorities, and the Polish revolt of 1863 cast a pall over the relationship between Russian and non-Russian. The government began to worry as much about security as reform.

Alexander II and his chief advisors were not Russian nationalists after the manner of Katkov. In 1867 the tsar went so far as to tell representatives of the Baltic nobility that, "I spit upon this press which tries to put you on the same level as the Poles. I respect your nationality and will be as faithful to it as you. I have always maintained that it is ridiculous to criticize someone because of his origins."[51] Four years later an official report entitled "The Baltic Question from the Government Point of View" categorically rejected nationalist demands for Russification of the area, arguing that the Baltic Germans were loyal and dutiful Russian subjects.[52] Nonetheless, given its ever present security concerns and the anti-German mood of much of the educated public,[53] the government was now less inclined than it had been in the early 1860's to let the Riga Germans have their own way in the matter of reform.

The greatest real threat to the aspirations of the Riga liberals, however, emanated from the ongoing reform projects of the imperial government. Ironically, it was the promise of change and renewal held out by these reforms that had first inspired the development and spread of liberalism among the Riga Germans. The estates system of local government had been left intact in the Baltic provinces chiefly because the imperial government did not have a suitable replacement for it. Local government in pre-reform European Russia was far too ineffective to be considered as a useful model for the Baltic. After the introduction of the judicial, police and administrative reforms of the 1860's this was no longer true. The imperial government gradually came to the conclusion by the late 1860's that it was more efficient to extend these reforms to the Baltic provinces than to permit the Baltic Germans to effect reforms of their own.[54]

The first sign of what lay in store for the Baltic had come in June, 1867, when the tsar, in violation of the Capitulations of 1710, approved a recommendation of the Committee of Ministers that Russian replace German as the official language of crown offices in the Baltic provinces. This was not an act of Russification for its own sake, but a means to improve governmental efficiency through uniformity. Other measures followed over the space of several years. The Russian military conscription reform of 1874 was implemented without delay in the Baltic provinces. The new conscription boards were placed under the partial control of the various Baltic estates, but the reform brought with it the forfeiture of certain special privileges enjoyed by upper and middle class Baltic Germans vis-a-vis military service. An important step toward the administrative unification of the Baltic region with European Russia was taken in January, 1876, when the tsar abolished the Baltic governor-generalship. Henceforth the three provinces stood in the same relationship to the central authorities as provinces in Russia proper. Finally, in the spring of 1880, the tsar decreed that the institution of justice of the peace, as created in the 1864 Russian judicial reform, would be introduced in the Baltic. In Riga this meant that jurisdiction in petty civil and criminal cases was transferred from the magistracy to justices salaried by the new duma, or municipal assembly, established under the provisions of the Russian municipal reform statute.

Of all the various reform measures enacted by the imperial government, the most important for the Riga Germans was the restructuring of municipal government. The decision made in 1868 by the Ministry of Internal Affairs to bring Riga's municipal government into conformity with that in Russian cities received final approval in the *ukaz* of 16 June 1870 proclaiming the implementation of a municipal reform in forty-five cities throughout the empire. The *ukaz* did not order the immediate or unqualified introduction of reform in Riga, but it promised eventual implementation there.

After the rejection of its reform project, the Riga estates reform commission had been charged by the Ministry of Internal Affairs with the task of drawing up a new project that, while taking local needs into account, would adhere as closely as possible to the terms of the general municipal reform then under preparation in St. Petersburg.[55] The estates commission completed its assigned task in 1870, producing a revised project that attempted to reconcile local tradition with the Russian municipal statute. In most respects the Riga project was identical to the Russian statute. There were only two important differences. The estates commission insisted that the magistracy continue as city executive, and that Riga should retain a corporate citizenry.[56]

The spring of 1874 saw the establishment of a new commission to deal with the introduction of the 1870 municipal reform statute in the Baltic cities. The commission was chaired by Minister of Internal Affairs Timashev and included representatives from the ministries of justice and finance, the Baltic governor-general, the three Baltic governors and the chief burgomasters of Riga, Reval and Mitau. It was apparent from the outset that the estates commission's attempt to reconcile local tradition with the 1870 statute stood little chance of success. Timashev was unsympathetic; and at the opening session of his commission the representatives of the imperial government stressed that allowing the Baltic cities to make major alterations in the statute in order to accommodate local customs would be tantamount to conceding that every city in the empire should have its own special municipal constitution.[57] The commission therefore decided to proceed on the premise that, "The fundamental principles of the [1870] statute must be fully preserved. A few changes may be permissible in those individual cases where full application of one or another article does not suit local conditions."[58] By this the commission meant minor alterations in the statute like those in force in St. Petersburg, Moscow and Odessa, not concessions to historic principle like those envisioned in the proposal submitted by the Riga estates. The three chief burgomasters objected strenuously to this, but there was very little that they could do to change the direction of the commission's work. Wilhelm Greiffenhagen, the chief burgomaster of Reval, bitterly recalled in his memoirs that, "The distinguished gentlemen who sat on the commission simply tossed the reform proposals made by the Baltic cities into the waste basket."[59]

The commission's labours came to an end in December, 1875, when Timashev submitted its proposals to the Council of State. Local constitutional tradition was not taken into acount, although two significant alterations were made in the municipal statute to render it more suitable for the Baltic cities. German, as well as Russian, was recognized as an official language of city government; and the franchise for municipal elections was extended to "those persons considered by local custom to be 'literati'.'[60] The commission felt that it would have been impractical not to have allowed German as an official language, and that granting the vote to literati would widen the pool of responsible persons available for service in the city government.[61] The proposals were approved and became law in an *ukaz* of 26 March 1877.

The enactment of this reform marked the culmination of more than fifteen years' work on various municipal reform projects by the Riga estates and by the imperial government. It also represented the ultimate failure of the liberals to achieve their political goals in Riga. The disappointment and frustration occasioned by this failure were to have a deep and lasting effect on the Riga German community.

The liberal movement among the Riga Germans was not confined to constitutional issues. It had an economic programme as well; and in this sphere it was far more successful. The businessmen and professional people who made up the liberal party stood to profit from commercial and industrial development. Like contemporary liberals elsewhere in Europe, they were firm believers in the benefits of material progress, which they thought could best be ensured by free enterprise. This conviction had the virtue of compatibility with the liberal stress on individual freedom. Competition in the marketplace free from outside intervention was perceived as a basic individual civil right akin to freedom of assembly and speech. The liberal economic *credo* was neatly summed up by H. von Stein, chief of the Riga Statistical Commission, who wrote in the *Baltische Monatschrift* that, "Just as Riga was the point of departure for the dissemination of western culture in the Baltic provinces during the thirteenth century and in the sixteenth century was the leader in the struggle for the ecclesiastical reformation in our provinces, we must now take upon ourselves the honourable mission of the industrial reformation of the nineteenth century."[62]

Advocates of free enterprise had their work cut out for them in mid-nineteenth century Riga. Commerce and manufacturing were still subject to guild regulations, and local commercial law had not been revised since 1765. Even this law was little more than a codification of earlier statutes and regulations, many of which were survivals from the days of the Hanseatic League. The realization of the liberal economic programme would require a thorough reform of commercial law and a freeing of the marketplace from guild intervention.

Economic reform got under way several years earlier than reform in other areas, as even the conservative government of Nicholas I realized that Riga's archaic commercial laws were an obstacle to local prosperity. In 1849 a special commission was convened by the Committee of Ministers to revise Riga's commercial law. This led to a series of reforms that gradually did away with some of the more restrictive regulations, including the 1861 repeal of the ancient Hanseatic rule that "a guest may not trade with a guest," and a piecemeal removal of complicated and obsolete quality controls on export goods.[63]

Free competition in craft production and in some areas of manufacturing was inhibited by artisan guild regulations. The most important of these was the *Zunftzwang*, which required all craftsmen in the city to belong to the guild. Other rules limited the number of employees permitted to masters, restricted the adoption of new production techniques and prohibited shops devoted to more than one trade. The liberals found this situation intolerable. They did not aim at the demise of the guild, which they saw as a setter of quality production standards, but they believed that the future of craft manufacture lay in co-operative associations and credit societies like those pioneered by Schultze-Delitzsch in Germany. To this end liberal merchants and literati assisted artisans in setting up several craft-manufacturing co-operatives, an educational association and a credit union.[64] Not all artisans were willing to dispense with the old ways. The guild restrictions were, after all, designed to protect artisans from ruinous competition with wealthier producers. Only after overcoming stubborn resistance by conservative elders did the guild issue a new set of craft regulations in 1861. These rationalized the relationship between masters and employees, permitted the creation of multi-craft workshops and facilitated the adoption of new techniques. Five years later the *Zunftzwang* was abolished by imperial decree.

Another barrier to economic progress was the short supply of people with technical and managerial expertise. This the liberals sought to redress through education. As early as 1857 a group of merchants and municipal officials, among them Otto Müller and Gustav Hernmarck, proposed to the Chamber of Commerce that a technical institute be established in the city. This project gained the support of Governor-General Suvorov and came to fruition in 1861 with the founding of the Baltic Polytechnical Institute. Financed by the Riga estates, the Chamber of Commerce and the three Baltic provincial diets, the institute offered post-secondary level instruction in engineering, business administration, applied sciences and agronomy. Its first director was Otto Müller. The establishment of this school was one of the most important and most enduring achievements of the liberal era in Riga. It was to have a profound effect on the Riga Germans, for it provided them with the skills necessary for their gradual transformation from a pre-industrial urban elite into industrial entrepreneurs, technicians and corporate executives.

Chapter 3

CONSTITUTIONAL CRISIS AND THE POLITICS OF RETRENCHMENT

The extension of Russian administrative and legal reforms to the Baltic region spelled disaster for the German liberals. In many respects the reforms were compatible with the liberal programme; but the rub lay in the liberal belief that successful reform had to be based on local constitutional tradition. The liberals viewed the imposition of Russian laws and institutions as a violation of the Baltic *Rechtsstaat*. This meant a constitutional crisis of major proportions. In Julius Eckardt's words, "That institutions, which had existed for seven hundred years and which had just begun to demonstrate their potential for rejuvenation, should be condemned to a forcible and sudden death, seemed incomprehensible to those who had grown up with them and whose life's work had been the quest for their regeneration."[1]

The Riga Germans nurtured a concept of legality which was fundamentally different from that held by the imperial government. In the Baltic provinces, as in the west, the law was regarded as the supreme and final authority. This is the very essence of the *Rechtsstaat*. Russia had a different legal and constitutional tradition. There supreme authority resided in the will of the sovereign, who could change or even violate the written law as he saw fit. The clash between these two conflicting concepts of legality underlay many of the difficulties which were to arise between the Riga Germans and the imperial government during the late nineteenth century.

Liberal frustration was compounded by the ongoing campaign waged by the Russian nationalist press against the Baltic Germans as a national minority. In spite of the imperial government's open disavowal of sympathy for the nationalists, the chorus of demands for Russification in the Baltic gave the Baltic Germans cause for trepidation over what the future might bring. Matters were made even worse by the inability of the Riga press to respond fully to nationalist accusations. The press in Moscow and St. Peersburg was not subject to pre-publication censorship, whereas the Riga press was severely handi-

27

capped by censorship that became more restrictive after the replacement of Count Shuvalov as governor-general by Peter Albedinskii, who was less sympathetic to the local Germans than his predecessors.[2]

In this atmosphere of disappointment and apprehension liberalism began to lose its appeal. The process was hastened by the departure of many of its chief advocates from the local scene. Eckardt, embittered by the imperial government's changing attitude toward the local reform programme, emigrated to Germany in May, 1867.[3] In 1869 two more liberal journalists abandoned the local political arena. A frustrated Georg Berkholz quit his post with the *Baltische Monatschrift;* and John Baerens moved to St. Petersburg, where he unsuccessfully tried to set up a German-language newspaper. The liberals also suffered losses in the city government. Otto Müller died in 1867; and two years later Gustav Hernmarck followed Eckardt into emigration in Germany.

As liberalism declined, a new conservatism began to gather support. At the forefront of this trend stood Carl Schirren, a Dorpat University history professor. In the liberal heyday of the early 1860's Schirren had been a lonely figure on the right. He feared even then that the reform movement would only serve to incite the tsar and his ministers to impose alien laws and institutions in the Baltic provinces. The nationalist press campaign against Baltic German traditions particularly frightened Schirren, who saw it as the harbinger of future trouble.

In time it became apparent that Schirren's forebodings could not easily be dismissed. They took on an especially heightened relevance in 1868, when Russian nationalist agitation reached a fever pitch with the publication in Prague of the first volume of Iuri Samarin's *Borderlands of Russia.*[4] Typically, Samarin claimed that the Baltic Germans were seeking to detach their provinces from Russia, and that they were bent on the ruthless Germanization of the Latvians and Estonians, who rightly belonged in the Russian cultural orbit. This grave danger could only be thwarted by the complete Russification of the Baltic provinces. As a first step the privileges granted to the Baltic estates in the Capitulations of 1710 would have to be revoked by the tsar, whose word was above any written law. There was nothing in Samarin's basic thesis that had not already appeared at least once in the nationalist press, but *Borderlands of Russia* represented the first cogent, thorough articulation of the Russian nationalist position on the Baltic question.

Schirren, infuriated by Samarin's book, felt that the time had come to challenge the Russian nationalists openly. In May, 1869 he published a pamphlet entitled *Livland's Answer to Mr. Iuri Samarin.* Schirren shared the liberals' respect for the Baltic *Rechtsstaat* and their perception of Russia as a nationally and regionally differentiated empire in which each region should be governed according to its own customs. *Livland's Answer* was an eloquent defense of these beliefs against both the Russian nationalist concept of the empire as a Russian nation state and the imperial govenrnment's drive to violate the Baltic *Rechtsstaat* in the interest of administrative uniformity. Schirren believed that the imperial government was legally bound to recognize the rights and privileges granted to the Baltic estates by the Capitulations of 1710:

> The decendants of [Peter I] possess these provinces, as he did, by accord. The accord binds the provinces to their sceptre and them to the conditions set forth in the accord.[5]

The Capitulations, in turn, formed the basis of the Baltic *Rechtsstaat:*

> The tsar swore to uphold more than a collection of special rights held by corporations and estates. The Capitulations . . . guarantee to the Baltic provinces as a whole and to all their inhabitants that they are and will remain provinces of the Russian Empire which have their own administration and their own laws.[6]

When the tsar imposed alien institutions in the Baltic provinces he was breaking the law. For Schirren, Samarin and other Russian nationalists were guilty of a double crime. Not only did they advocate that the law be broken, but they also wished to establish, "The lordship of race . . . in the name of imperial unity."[7] Like the liberals, Schirren felt that nationality was unacceptable as a principle of government. Addressing Samarin directly, Schirren concluded that, "You wish to call yourself 'Russian', and that is praiseworthy in one who is born as such; but above the Russian stands the human being and above the masses stands the state . . . You recognize no political principle, no governmental or social order. You know only one Russian church, one Russian people, one alphabet and racial instinct. You are grey."[8] To a conservative like Schirren, nationalism was associated with mob rule, and Samarin's ideas were a threat to social stability. Accordingly, Russian nationalism was a threat to the welfare of the empire and the throne. The Baltic Germans, in contrast to Samarin, were good Russian subjects, whose "loyalty stands unshaken."[9]

Schirren met the challenge of Russian nationalism and administrative centralization by asserting what he perceived to be the legal rights of the Baltic provinces. He did not try to counter either challenge by adopting any form of German nationalism. He described Livland as a "German province of the Russian Empire by culture, treaty and name," and he asserted that the Capitulations guaranteed the preservation of the "German-Protestant culture" and the "German nation" in the Baltic provinces;[10] but *Livland's Answer* stands as a defense of the Baltic *Rechtsstaat* rather than the Baltic Germans as a national group. German nationalism was every bit as objectionable to Schirren as the Russian variety.

The government promptly banned Schirren's pamphlet, but not before its author, who chanced to be the university censor, arranged its brief appearance in the Dorpat bookstores, where it sold out immediately and then was passed from hand to hand. The effect of *Livland's Answer* on Baltic German public opinion was electric. After reading it Berkholz could only exclaim, "What a book! I have never experienced from any other such an immediate and general effect."[11] The historian Theodor Schiemann, then a student in Dorpat, later recalled that, "I, like most Dorpat students, sat through the whole night in order to read it. Today it is difficult to imagine how profound its effect upon us was."[12]

Schirren was soon deprived of his chair at the university and forced into exile in Germany; but his work was to become the focal point of an emerging conservative consensus among the Germans in Riga.[13] In response to the constitutional crisis engendered by the violation of the *Rechtsstaat,* the Germans abandoned all thought of reform and adopted a policy of political retrenchment. What remained of the estates system was to be defended at all cost.

The appeal of conservatism had a social, as well as a constitutional, side. Schirren had been wary of reform not only because it might endanger the Baltic *Rechtsstaat,* but also because he opposed the extension of self-government beyond the traditional ruling classes. Even the liberals had cautioned that only the propertied and educated should enjoy the right of self-government. The municipal reform of 1877 enfranchised a broader segment of the local population than the German political leadership thought wise. From their standpoint the imperial government had imposed a reform which, besides being illegal, seemed to threaten the political position of the ruling classes. Defense of the remnants of the estates system was unquestionably motivated by class interest as well as by the desire to preserve the *Rechtsstaat* framework in which municipal government had traditionally operated.

The political setbacks of the late 1860's and 1870's had dramatically narrowed the gap between the conservative and liberal positions. Both found the government-imposed reforms objectionable on legal and social grounds. Berkholz, who in 1863 had dismissed Schirren as a "reactionary",[14] observed in 1869 that, "The position developed by

Schirren has resolved all of our provincial political differences with a single stroke."[15] This facilitated the gradual rightward inclination of public opinion, a process clearly reflected in the transformation of the local German-language press from liberal to conservative. Riga acquired its first openly conservative newspaper in 1878, with the establishment of the *Neue Zeitung für Stadt und Land*. The following year conservative journalist Richard Ruetz took over the editorship of the *Zeitung für Stadt und Land* from the liberal Baron Edmund Heyking; and in the spring of 1879 Georg Berkholz returned briefly to public life as chief editor of the *Rigasche Zeitung*. Berkholz had evolved into a conservative. In one of his first editorials he declared that, "The liberals of 1864 and 1865 must now be conservatives."[16] The metamorphosis of the press was completed late in 1879 with the replacement of Baron Heyking as chief editor of the *Baltische Monatschrift* by Friedrich Bienemann, a conservative whose political motto was "honourable fixity."[17]

The Riga German community had entered a period when its relationship to the imperial government, to the new forms of municipal administration and to the other nationalities in Riga was guided by a conservative political philosophy whose first principle was the rigid defense of all that remained of the estates system.

After 1877 the focus of political life in Riga shifted to the new institutions established under the provisions of the Russian municipal statute. Most of the administrative authority held by the estates was transferred to a seventy-two member municipal duma elected for a four-year term by all adult males who either owned city property, held first guild merchant status in the local tax community or could qualify as literati. The magistracy was replaced as the executive organ of municipal government by an executive board composed of a mayor, a vice-mayor and five councilmen, all elected by the duma.

The character of municipal politics was altered substantially by the extension of the franchise to a broader segment of local society. Self-government under the estates system had been the preserve of a privileged group of about fifteen hundred. The franchise for duma elections, while still a limited one, was liberal enough to quadruple that number.[18] In this way the new institutions created a forum for the politicization of the nationality question. The estates system had placed municipal government almost exclusively in the hands of the Riga Germans, who dominated the occupational categories encompassed by the estates. The new system gave a voice in government to a significant number of non-Germans.

Demographic changes that Riga was experiencing at this time lent particular importance to the broadening of self-government. A provincial census taken in 1881 revealed that the city's population had grown by a dramatic sixty-five per cent since the last census had been conducted in 1867. There had been a heavy influx of peasants from the Latvian-speaking areas of Livland and Kurland provinces.[19] A series of agrarian reforms passed by the Baltic diets had encouraged the bifurcation of the peasantry into a relatively prosperous class of propertied, independent farmers and a poorer class of landless and small-holding peasants. This, coupled with new internal passport regulations that facilitated peasant mobility, helped to produce a constant flow of poorer peasants into Riga, where they sought employment in the city's expanding industrial complex. The result was a decline in the size of the Riga German community relative to the Latvians. The percentage of Riga inhabitants claiming German as their "customary language" fell from 42.8 in 1867 to 39.4 in 1881, while the figures for Latvian increased from 23.5 to 29.5 per cent. The later census also inquired after "nationality", which was normally taken to mean mother tongue. Those claiming Latvian "nationality" accounted for 32.8 per cent of the total population. Only 31 per cent claimed German "nationality".[20]

The importance of this development did not rest on sheer numbers alone. Economic growth and prosperity made it much easier for some able and fortunate Latvians to rise out of the lower classes. This process was hastened by a high literacy rate that was truly remarkable for nineteenth century eastern Europe. Thanks to a system of rural elementary schools maintained by the Baltic nobility, the Lutheran church and by the peasant communities themselves, many of the Latvian peasants who migrated to Riga were literate. By the end of the 1870's Riga had the nucleus of an independent Latvian middle class of small businessmen and professional people.[21] Latvian nationalism, with its claim that Latvian speech and customs were not simply marks of lowly status and its hostility toward the entrenched German social and financial elite, found a ready constituency among this new middle class. The focal point of nationalist activity remained the Riga Latvian Union, whose activities expanded to include the publication of the first Latvian-language daily newspaper in the city, the *Rigas lapa (The Riga News)*.[22]

The main nationalist political goal was to win representation in the municipal duma for the Latvians as a national group. In each of the four duma elections held under the provisions of the 1877 reform statute, the Latvian Union sponsored an election committee that nominated a slate of candidates pledged to act in the interests of the Latvian community. The programme of the 1882 committee, a German translation of which was published in full by the *Rigasche Zeitung,* was typical. The text of the programme was almost exclusively devoted to demands for Latvian national representatives in the duma. The only concrete proposal was for the establishment of more Latvian schools.[23]

The proportion of Russians in the Riga population dropped sharply from 25.1 per cent in 1867 to 18.9 per cent in 1881.[24] Nonetheless, under the new system the Russians were also presented with a chance to acquire a greater share in municipal government. Most Russian political activity also bore a nationalist stamp; and the Russian approach to municipal elections was basically no different from that of the Latvians. Prior to each election a Russian election committee nominated a slate of candidates who ran as representatives of the Russian community. Greater representation of non-Germans in the city government was labeled by the nationalist *Rizhskii vestnik* in 1881 as the fundamental issue in any election campaign.[25]

There had always been a Russophile strain in Latvian nationalism, and it seemed to be vindicated by the imperial government's introduction of a reform that gave the Latvians their first real opportunity to participate in city politics. Latvian Russophilia and a common hostility to the German ruling classes drew the Latvians and Russians into alliances in every municipal election from 1878 to 1897. Meeting separately, the Russian and Latvian committees regularly nominated candidates to a joint slate.

The Germans approached municipal politics in a completely different spirit. The new institutions of government were in themselves objectionable to them. Any desirable features which the new system might have possessed were eclipsed by its "illegality". Berkholz captured the mood of the times when he wrote that, "This Riga magistracy that once governed an imperial free city, waged war with the powerful Teutonic Order, represented the city in the Hanseatic League, ruled the city as an independent unit for twenty years after the collapse of the old Livonian state, subjected itself under honourable conditions to Polish rule, and finally agreed to capitulations with Peter the Great—this magistracy shall now have to yield to a 'duma' elected by the politically very uneducated masses! The older a man grows the more conservative he also becomes. My heart lies with the old city constitution like that of the younger Cato, who, succumbing before Caesar, died with the words: 'The gods have decided for the new order of things. Cato decides for the old.' "[26] Whether or not they liked the new system, the Germans were faced with the choice of working within it to preserve their control over municipal government, or boycotting it and thereby ceasing to be a force in local politics. Since the latter course was clearly self-destructive, the conservative Germans opted to strive for maximum continuity, both in terms of style and of personnel, between the old system and the new.

Each municipal election was marked by the organization of a conservative committee for the nomination of candidates who stood for the principle of continuity. The programme of the 1882 committee, for example, stated that, "A healthy development of the city and its administration is only possible under the protection of continuity."[27] The *Neue Zeitung für Stadt und Land* noted in its endorsement of the same committee that, "A sharp break with the past, when it has been a sound and normal one, the dismissal of people who have borne our trust in the past, when they have proved themselves worthy of it, would be a foolish mistake."[28]

The German campaign to ensure continuity in municipal government contrasted sharply with the Latvian-Russian effort to achieve representation as national groups in the duma. The principle of continuity was in effect a defense of the political power of the traditional ruling classes, which were mostly German by nationality. It was not perceived by its advocates as a vehicle for the furtherance of German national interests. In their distaste for political nationalism the conservatives of the 1880's did not differ from the liberals of the 1860's. Like their precursors, the conservatives clung to a perception of the Latvians as lower social strata in a culturally German society. Berkholz, whose 1863 essay "On the Nationality Question" had defined the liberal position on this subject, did not find it necessary to revise his views when he wrote in 1879 that, "The relationship between Latvians and Germans in our provinces is not like that between Germans and Czechs in Bohemia, where all social classes, from the highest to the lowest, can be found in each nationality. There is a Czech nobility, but no Latvian one; and . . . the Latvian intelligentsia is by no means strong enough to offer the kind of cultural leadership that is required by a people overwhelmingly composed of peasants and workers."[29] Alexander Buchholtz, a conservative journalist who suceeded Berkholz as chief editor of the *Rigasche Zeitung* in 1880, simply concluded that, "The Latvians are not a nation, but only a social class—the peasant class of this province."[30]

The Germans saw their conflict with the Latvian and Russian election committees much less in terms of the nationality question than in terms of a social struggle between the largely German ruling classes and the broad masses, led by largely Russian and Latvian lesser property owners enfranchised by the 1877 reform. The *Zeitung für Stadt und Land,* for example, pronounced the Latvian Union, "a workers' association . . . under the patronage of its more highly educated members."[31] A subsequent article contended, much as the liberals had done in the

1860's, that Latvian nationalism was a temporary aberration produced by the lack of political sophistication found among the lower classes.[32] Similarly, the *Rigasche Zeitung* termed the Russian and Latvian election committees a preserve of "nationalist fanatics . . . who prey upon a credulous public," and concluded that their purpose was to sow unrest among the lower classes of the city.[33] In an essay published in the *Baltische Monatschrift*, Chief Burgomaster and duma representative Eduard Hollander expressed his concern that the franchise was now so broad that it, "excited all the bad instincts of the lower classes," who, thanks to their immaturity and credulity, could easily be led astray by nationalist agitators:

> That the great mass of voters is neither mature nor competent enough to assess the qualifications of those who stand for election to municipal office is very obvious and has been made quite clear in the election campaigns of 1878 and 1882. Not even one-tenth of the throngs led into the fray by nationalistic propaganda understood what the election meant. Some voted for the assortment of unfamiliar names on their ballots because they had been told that the rule of the Germans had to be ended, some because they wanted to pay less tax, and some simply because they believed that the law required them to vote.[34]

In their own campaigns the Germans were careful to disavow any national motive. Prior to the 1882 election, for example, the *Rigasche Zeitung* declared that, "It is the duty of each individual duma member to concern himself with the welfare of the whole city, and not merely with the special interests of its German, Latvian or Russian inhabitants. Although the German voters might see fit to elect a purely German duma that would concern itself with the welfare of all and not with that of special interests, they might also vote with pleasure for such Latvian and Russian candidates who share this concern for the entire city. On the other hand, the German voters would be just as unlikely to vote for candidates who stood for specifically German interests as they would be to vote for those who stood for specifically Latvian interests."[35] The *Neue Zeitung für Stadt und Land* urged its readers to vote for candidates on the basis of "personal ability, without reference to religion or nationality;"[36] and Max Tunzelmann, a German lawyer who chaired the 1882 conservative election committee, sounded a similar note when he announced his committee's hopes that, "members of all nationalities and religions co-operate, and that we can avoid a situation in which Germans vote only for Germans, Latvians only for Latvians and Russians only for Russians."[37]

The candidates nominated by the conservative election committees were, in the main, individuals who had served in the estates system. Among the seventy-two candidates on the 1878 slate, for example, were fifty-five representaives of the estates, including the chief burgomaster, two other burgomasters, nine magistrates, the merchant guild alderman, eight merchant guild elders, two artisan guild elders, twenty-three citizens of the merchant guild and nine citizens of the artisan guild.[38] Most of these people were German, but their inclusion on the slate was by reason of class, not nationality. As Tunzelmann explained during the 1882 campaign, "The transition from the old to the new administration had to be accomplished by men who were at least familiar with the old administration. Such men could only be found in the Riga estates; and, as a result, the leadership in the 1878 duma elections emanated from the estates. Given the German character of the estates, a certain national colouration was imprinted upon the election campaign. The two other chief nationalities represented in the Riga electorate, the Latvians and the Russians, erroneously perceived in this circumstance a German design to exclude capable men of other nationalities from the municipal government. Motivated by this belief and also by a feeling of class difference and social alienation, they formed a coalition to contest the election of members of the old German administration."[39] The principle of continuity simply required the election to the duma of the German merchants, literati and artisans who had governed the city in the past.

The conservative election committees did, moreover, make an effort to place some non-Germans on their slates, provided that they were people of means, education or conservative inclination. The 1878 slate included four Russians (all merchants), two Latvians (both officials of the Latvian trades) and one Jew (a merchant); the 1882 slate five Russians (all merchants), four Latvians (a Latvian trades' official, an architect, a lawyer and a physician) and two Jews (both merchants); the 1886 slate five Russians (three merchants and two of undetermined occupation), five Latvians (a Latvian trades' official, two merchants, a physician and a fisherman) and one Jewish merchant; and the 1890 slate six Russians (three merchants, two industrialists and one of undetermined occupation), six Latvians (a Latvian trades' official, a physician, a cab driver, an industrialist and two merchants) and three Jews (all merchants).[40]

In any case, the electoral procedure was such that the votes of the wealthier property owners were given much more weight than those of lesser means. The electorate was split into three classes on the basis of property tax in such a manner that the sum total of tax paid by each electoral class was the equivalent of one-third of all property tax paid by the entire electorate. The first class comprised those who paid the highest taxes and owned the most property, the second class represented a middle group and the third, and largest, class included the lesser property owners. Each class elected one-third of the duma. This system gave an overwhelming advantage to the wealthy Germans, who thoroughly dominated the first two classes. Of the 172 individuals who voted in the first class in 1878, 140 were German; and in the second class Germans accounted for about two-thirds of the eligible voters.[41] The Latvian-Russian coalition never even bothered to enter a list of candidates in the first class. Their only real chance of victory lay in the third class, and even here they were hampered by the inexperience of their constituency. The voters of the first two classes were much more likely to make use of their franchise than those of the third class, most of whom had never voted in any election before 1878.[42] The nationalist leadership could not, moreover, count on the full support of the non-German electorate. The Germanization of upwardly mobile Latvians, while not the universal phenomenon it had once been, was still common in the 1880's. The 1881 census reveals that more than ten per cent of those who claimed Latvian as their native language claimed German as their "customary language".[43] This means that approximately one in ten ethnic Latvians in Riga had undergone Germanization to such a degree that German had become his normal everyday language. Since Germanization was associated with upward social mobility, it is probable that many propertied ethnic Latvians were Germanized to the point where they would be unlikely to support a Latvian nationalist political programme. Complaints made by the Latvian nationalist press to the effect that Germanized ethnic Latvians caused the defeat of the 1886 Russian-Latvian ticket by voting for conservative German candidates lend credence to this hypothesis.[44] Support for the nationalist coalition was also far from unanimous in the Russian community. Some of the wealthier Russian merchants shared the conservative Germans' interest in preserving the *status quo* in local government; and a Russian nationalist programme that identified the interests of the Russian nation with those of the Orthodox church was certainly not appealing to Old Believers. The 1877 reform also gave the franchise to Jews, who by 1881 constituted 11.9 per cent of the city population. The Jews did not organize as an independent political force in this period. Upwardly mobile Jews tended to assimilate linguistically into the German community, and Jewish voters normally lent their support to the candidates of the conservative election committees.[45]

Thanks to the many advantages which they enjoyed, the German conservatives swept to victory in every municipal election. Their triumph was so complete that no candidate nominated by their committee failed to win election to the duma.[46] Municipal government remained in the hands of the traditional German ruling classes. The 1877 reform, in spite of the broader franchise which it introduced, virtually guaranteed that this would happen. The reform in fact strengthened the German position by enabling German nobles who owned city property to participate in municipal government. Most nobles considered bourgeois politics beneath them, but nonetheless many did vote for conservative candidates, and a few played an active role in city government. The triumph of conservative "continuity" is nowhere better illustrated than in the composition of the city executive board. The mayoral office was held in turn by Burgomaster Robert Büngner (1878–1885) and August von Oettingen (1886–1889), a noble who had served as Livland governor from 1862 to 1868. Magistrate Ludwig Kerkovius was vice-mayor from 1878 to 1891; and the ranks of the city councilmen included another burgomaster, two magistrates, the alderman of the merchant guild, three citizens of the merchant guild, a prominent lawyer and a noble.[47]

In relations with the imperial government and in activity designed to encourage local economic growth the conservative municipal government behaved as the representative of the German social elite; but its policy in cultural and educational affairs seems to confirm the conservative claim that they did not wish to govern solely in the interest of the Germans as a national group. The duma voted unanimously in 1886 to grant an annual subsidy to the local Russian theatre; and a year later again voted unanimously to grant similar support to a Latvian theatre maintained by the Latvian Union.[48] More revealing still is the duma's attitude toward non-German city schools. The reformed municipal administration inherited from the estates a city school system that, with the exception of two Russian-lanugage elementary schools founded in the 1870's, was entirely German. By the early 1880's Riga's growing population required more schools. To help meet this demand, the duma established fifteen new elementary schools, three of which were Russian-language ones.[49] A handful of elementary schools were in themselves hardly sufficient to serve the educational needs of the city's large Russian community, but the duma did not bear sole responsibility for the provision of Russian-language schools in Riga. The state and the Orthodox church maintained a network of schools from the elementary to the secondary level that provided the local Russians with the opportunity to acquire an education in their native language. The question of Latvian-language schools was more complicated. The Latvian-language elementary school was a commonplace in rural Livland and

Kurland, but in Riga the only Latvian-language educational facilities were two small private elementary schools with a combined enrollment of less than two hundred pupils.[50] The 1881 census showed that only thirty-seven per cent of school-age Latvian children in Riga attended school at all, and that of these only one in ten went to a Latvian school.[51] Accordingly, the duma voted in 1884 to establish two municipally funded Latvian elementary schools. The German leadership felt that education at this level was most effective when it was in the pupil's native language.[52] Here the conservatives of the 1880's did not differ from the earlier liberals, who had favoured an expansion of Latvian-language elementary education. On the other hand, the Germans felt that the very idea of Latvian middle or secondary schools was nonsense. August Bielenstein, a German pastor who was one of the leading experts of his day on Latvian folklore and language, declared that the use of Latvian as the medium of instruction above the elementary level would always remain a "dream";[53] and the Zeitung für Stadt und Land, while endorsing the duma's decision to build Latvian elementary schools, argued that, "The idea of Latvian middle and secondary schools is absolutely impractical."[54] For the Germans, who still viewed Latvian as a language reserved for the lower classes in a society whose true cultural medium was German, it seemed only natural that Latvians who wanted more than an elementary education should attend a German school. As the Zeitung für Stadt und Land noted in 1884, "No one who wishes to devote himself to an occupation that requires an education beyond the elementary level can achieve this on the basis of the Latvian language alone. Given the prevailing relationships here, a knowledge of the German and Russian languages is of the highest importance for anyone who strives to rise above the very lowest sort of occupation."[55] The duma's refusal to consider the establishment of Latvian higher schools, however short-sighted, stemmed not from any intention to discriminate against Latvians or to subordinate Latvian interests to those of the German community as a national group, but from a conviction of the inherent superiority of the German language as a medium of instruction.

The principle of continuity also found expression in the behaviour of the German-controlled Riga duma toward the imperial government. The German conservatives used their control of the duma to conduct a stubborn defense of every remaining vestige of the estates system. As the Neue Zeitung für Stadt und Land declared in 1880, the basis for relations between the duma and the central authorities should be, "Negotiations based on the given legal structure so far as this is possible; preservation of this legal structure with all permissible means; and loyalty to the old spirit even within the new forms."[56] This defensive campaign provoked a constitutional conflict between the duma and the imperial government that endured for more than a decade.

The manner in which the 1877 reform was implemented in Riga made defense of the estates viable as a policy. The *ukaz* of 26 March 1877 did not eliminate the estates system. It merely superimposed new institutions on top of it. The three estates continued to function as organs of public administration and to exercise authority in all areas not specifically assigned to the new institutions. Particularly significant was the magistracy's continuing role as municipal judicial authority.[57] The guilds continued to play an important role in the supervision of trade and commerce; and the estates retained ownership of some public property as well as control of certain lower administrative organs. Although the public authority of the estates was drastically curtailed, the very fact of their continued existence afforded the conservatives a secure foundation upon which to erect a defense of what remained.

Under the terms of the 1877 reform legislation, the final decision on the separation of administrative competence and on the division of city property between the estates and the duma fell to the Ministry of Internal Affairs. The Riga municipal authorities were required to assist the Ministry. This gave the local German leadership an opportunity to work toward a solution which would be as favourable as possible to the estates.

A report on the division of property and authority was prepared by an estates commission, approved by the duma and submitted to the Ministry in October, 1878. The report argued for the retention by the estates of much city property and of control over the city police, the school system and a wide range of administrative functions.[58] The Ministry, however, did not intend to allow the Riga Germans to prop up the estates system at the expense of the 1877 reform. A ministerial decree issued in 1882 refuted most of the arguments made in the 1878 report and ordered the immediate transfer of property and authority to the duma. The Germans were not prepared to yield without a struggle. The legal ground for resistance on most points was shaky, but in two important matters the Germans opted to contest the decree.

The 1877 reform stipulated that all "municipal" property belonged to the duma, but it was difficult to draw a line between "municipal" property and the private property of one or more of the estates. The city gas and water works presented an especially complicated example of this problem. In the late 1850's the magistracy had been refused permission by the central authorities to build public gas and water works. In order to circumvent this ruling, the three estates had constructed the badly needed facilities as private ventures. According to the 1877 reform, the duma should own and administer the gas and water works; but their status as "municipal" property was questionable since they were legally the private property of the estates. Although the 1878 report claimed them for the estates, the Minister of Internal Affairs demanded that they be turned over to the new administration. These facilities represented a major source of revenue for the estates, and the Germans who controlled the duma did not want to deprive them of it. In order to avoid the complex litigation that a contest over the ownership would doubtlessly entail, the duma voted to buy them from the estates for the princely sum of 377,000 rubles. The city fathers felt that this would compensate the estates for lost revenue, and at the same time satisfy the Ministry.[59]

The duma also defended the right of the magistracy to continue as supervisory authority over craft production. The 1877 legislation clearly stated that this should be a duma function; but the duma argued that the transfer of this authority was impossible, because it was predicated upon the existence of administrative machinery set up under the terms of a Russian artisan craft statute. Since this statute had never been in force in Riga, transfer was physically impossible.

The Ministry's response, made public in June, 1886, was to order that the estates not be compensated for the gas and water works and to reiterate its demand that supervisory authority over artisan crafts be transferred to the duma. The duma still did not give in. It appealed the decision on compensation first to the Livland Board for Municipal Affairs[60] and then to the Senate. The appeals were unsuccessful, and the estates were denied compensation. Appeals regarding craft supervision were likewise overturned, but the Ministry could not force compliance where the machinery for it did not exist, and the magistracy continued to exercise *de facto* authority in this area.

Relations between the Riga administration and the central authorities, already strained by constitutional conflict, were rendered even more acrimonious by the manner in which the latter approached the Riga situation. The imperial government did not behave rationally when it tried to force the Riga duma to do the impossible with regard to artisan craft supervision. It displayed similarly obtuse behaviour when, in 1882, the Riga duma asked the Ministry of Internal Affairs for permission to supplement the obsolete and overburdened facilities of the police fire command with a municipal fire department. After a two-year delay permission was granted. The city purchased equipment, built fire stations, hired technical advisors and even sent people abroad to study foreign fire-fighting systems. In 1887, just as the fire department was ready to begin operation, the Ministry withdrew its permission and ordered the duma to turn the new facilities over to the police fire command, which was under the authority of the provincial governor. Faced with loss of a not inconsiderable capital investment, the duma appealed the case to the Senate. The Senate decided in favour of the Ministry, and Riga lost its new fire department.

Several reasons suggest themselves as explanations for the imperial government's conduct. One is simple incompetence. Livland governor Alexander Baron Uexküll-Guldenbrandt, the government's chief agent in Riga, was sternly criticized in an 1882 senatorial inspection for "lack of independence and consistency."[61] To make matters worse, there were serious personality clashes between the governor and the members of the Riga executive board.[62] The Russian nationalist sympathies of some government officials most certainly also played a role. Many of these men genuinely, if mistakenly, believed that the Germans in the Baltic provinces were dangerous subversives. Viewed from this perspective, it became the duty of imperial officials to keep a tight rein on the activities of local administrations controlled by that minority. Fears were even expressed in some circles that the municipal fire department might serve as a centre for German para-military activity. Finally, the imperial government and the Riga Germans had very different conceptions of the legal framework in which the various disputes took place. The Germans viewed the law as the final arbiter of all disputes. They believed that they could justify their case by proving that the written law was on their side. Russian officials saw matters in a different light. The *Rechtsstaat* traditions of the Baltic provinces were alien and almost incomprehensible to them. In their eyes the law itself did not necessarily possess final or permanent validity. It could be violated or ignored as the tsar and his ministers saw fit.

The Riga Germans saw their difficulties with the central authorities as legal and constitutional ones only. They did not perceive the conflict in national terms as one involving a Russian government and a German minority. This is clearly reflected in the German political literature of the time, the best example of which is a work published anonymously in 1883 in Leipzig by *Rigasche Zeitung* editor Alexander Buchholtz. Unfettered by Russian censorship and protected by anonymity, Buchholtz could express himself freely. The book, titled *Fifty Years of Russian Administration in the Russian Baltic Provinces,* sternly denounced the behaviour of the imperial government toward the Baltic provinces. Buchholtz attacked government policies as illegal and unconstitutional, but he did not ascribe any national content to the matter. His arguments are the same as those advanced fourteen years earlier by Schirren in *Livland's Answer*.

It is also apparent that the constitutional conflict in no way undermined the basic loyalty of the German minority to the Russian Empire. Like the liberals of the 1860's, the conservatives of the 1880's saw Russia as a supranational empire, in which political nationalism could not play a constructive role:

> Every people that wants to guide itself solely by its national spirit will remain stagnant, and, as if by a natural law, slip backward . . . A mixed population is like agitated water that always refreshes itself. A unitary population is like still water that easily stagnates. Many peoples live in the Russian Empire. All of them mutually serve and support one another.[63]

When the German historian Heinrich von Treitschke published an appeal for Baltic separatism in the name of German nationalism, the *Rigasche Zeitung* gave him a stinging rebuff, calling him a fanatic from the same mould as Samarin and declaring that, "We believe that we can speak in the name of all of the Baltic people when we say that in the Russian Baltic provinces there is no political group that favours Treitschke's thoughts and goals regarding separation from Russia . . . The loyalty of the Baltic Germans to the ruling house and to the empire has been proved beyond all question by deeds of blood in Russia's wars and by deeds of the spirit in peace."[64]

For the Riga Germans the heart of the matter was that the imperial government had broken the law, and in so doing had potentially endangered the position of the social elite in their city. The proper response to this was legal action, not disloyalty or even national self-defence.

Chapter 4

RUSSIFICATION AND ITS CONSEQUENCES

When Alexander II fell victim to a terrorist bomb in March, 1881 a new era began in the history of the national minorities. Alexander II had been a sponsor of reform and of relative liberalization. Although he was prepared to violate regional privileges that stood in the way of governmental efficiency, he never advocated Russification for its own sake.

His son and successor, Alexander III, was an arch-conservative who mistrusted his father's reforms and who feared that the national and religious diversity of the empire was in itself a threat to autocratic government. His father's assassination confirmed his apprehensions and steeled his determination to govern the empire with a firm autocratic hand. The new tsar's approach to the minorities was fully shared by his chief advisors, Konstantin Pobedonostsev, Mikhail N. Katkov and Count Dmitri Tolstoi. Pobedonostsev, chief procurator of the Holy Synod and Alexander's closest collaborator during the 1880's, had long felt that the Russian people and the Orthodox faith were by their very nature firm pillars of support for the autocracy, which was itself the product of a specifically Russian historical development. An empire which was uniformly Russian and Orthodox would be the optimum environment for autocratic government. Minorities of any kind were by definition subversive. Concerning the Baltic Germans, Pobedonostsev wrote to the tsar that, "The Baltic provinces are governed by pastors together with barons and gentry, all of whom are fanatical. Fearing nothing and flouting all Russian laws, they engage in illegal activity with impunity."[1]

Katkov's suspicions of minority disloyalty approached paranoia; and his publications had resolutely championed the Russification of the Baltic provinces since the 1860's. He was able to exert a strong and usually decisive influence on Count Tolstoi, who, as Minister of Internal Affairs from 1882 to 1889, had a key role in planning and executing minority policy.

45

The thirteen years of Alexander III's reign were not propitious ones for the empire's many minorities. Minority school systems were Russified, local authorities in many non-Russian areas ceased using the local languages, minority religious groups experienced official harassment and in some cases open persecution and the Jews, special targets of an unabashedly anti-Semitic government, were subjected to discriminatory legislation restricting their access to schools and certain professions.

The Baltic Germans could entertain little hope of escaping at least some measures of Russification. Long the object of Russian nationalist misgivings, they were made to seem all the more threatening by international events. Russian relations with Imperial Germany deteriorated during the 1880's, and any minority suspected of pro-German sympathies, especially one as wealthy, powerful and strategically located as the Baltic Germans, was bound to be deemed worthy of particular attention by men like Alexander III and his advisors.

The shift in the imperial government's policy toward the Baltic Germans became apparent almost immediately after Alexander III assumed power, when he became the first Russian ruler since Peter III in 1762 not to confirm the Capitulations of 1710. Actual Russification did not commence until the mid-1880's; but the groundwork for it was laid by an investigation of conditions in Livland and Kurland conducted in 1882 and 1883 by Senator Nikolai A. Manasein.

Ironically, the inspection was brought about by the Baltic Germans themselves. Livland was troubled by peasant unrest at the beginning of the 1880's, and when the inept governor, Baron Uexküll-Güldenbrandt, failed to deal with it in a manner satisfactory to the local German nobility, the latter complained to the imperial government. The government's response was to send Manasein on his tour of inspection. After a sixteen-month study of Baltic conditions, Manasein submitted a report to the tsar that utterly condemned local administrative and judicial institutions, and that was permeated with Russian nationalist mistrust of the Baltic Germans. Manasein was not simply a reactionary. He was a man with a reputation for comparatively liberal views who blamed the peasant unrest on the shortcomings of local government, which, as he saw it, operated exclusively in the interests of the German upper classes.[2] The Baltic city magistracies, for example, he characterized as incompetent and self-serving:

> The police activity of the majority of magistracies . . . is distinguished by slowness, carelessness, and in large part by the absence of a clear knowledge of the laws among the members of the magistracies, who, chosen by the

townspeople from their own midst, and receiving a very insignificant recompense for the discharge of their service responsibilities, take very little interest in their duties and are diverted from them primarily by private business interests.[3]

The report concluded that the best solution would be to replace the indigenous institutions in town and country with ones patterned on the police and judicial systems in use in European Russia. In order to accommodate further the interests both of the Baltic lower classes and the imperial authorities, Latvian, Estonian and Russian should join German as official languages of local government.[4]

Manasein's nationalism is reflected in his attack on the Baltic educational system. In his judgement the Baltic schools served to emphasize and perpetuate Baltic German distinctiveness from the rest of the empire. He excoriated Dorpat University as a nest of "separatist" feeling. Here the solution was to Russify all schools above the primary level and to place them under the direct supervision of the Ministry of Education.[5]

Finally, he recommended that the best way to break the entrenched power of the German minority would be to reorganize the three provinces into two—a Latvian one in the south and an Estonian one in the north.[6]

The tsar and his ministers did not share Manasein's sympathies for the lower classes. They were far too conservative for that. Manasein's recommendations did, however, seem to confirm their forebodings about the German minority. Hence the Mansein report was to serve as a kind of blueprint for Russification in the Baltic region.

Riga began to feel the full weight of the imperial government's commitment to Russification in May, 1885, when an *ukaz* was pronounced ordering the city military conscription board to use Russian instead of German as its language of business. Robert Büngner, who as mayor of Riga was automatically chairman of the conscription board, was placed in an impossible position. His proficiency in Russian, labeled "notoriously unsatisfactory" by one of his colleagues, was by no means sufficient to permit him to carry out his duties in that language.[7] When Büngner informed the provincial governor of his dilemma, he was told that the law required him to know Russian. An appeal to the Ministry of Internal Affairs brought the suggestion that Büngner resign if he could not perform his duties in Russian. The city government took the matter to the Senate, which ruled that the mayor was indeed required to be proficient in Russian. In desperation, Büngner petitioned the tsar for the right to continue using German. The tsar's reply, which came in August, 1885, was to dismiss Büngner as mayor for "stubborn resistance against the due process of law."[8]

With Büngner's fate decided, Russification proceeded with gathering momentum. An *ukaz* of 14 September 1885 proclaimed Russian to be the sole permissible language of correspondence between local Baltic authorities and agencies of the imperial government, and ordered the introduction of Russian as the language of business in all public institutions under mixed crown and local jurisdiction. In Riga, this meant that the city police, partly controlled by the magistracy and partly by the provincial governor, were to be Russified immediately. In January, 1887 the Riga municipal authorities were compelled henceforth to issue all internal passports and military discharge papers exclusively in Russian.

The introduction of Russian judicial and police institutions had long been discussed by the imperial government. Manasein had urged that this be done, and in 1885 Estland Governor Sergei V. Shakhovskoi, a Russian nationalist whose appointment had been arranged by Pobedonostsev,[9] reported that the need for such a step was becoming ever more pressing. The tsar himself read Shakhovskoi's report, noting in the margin that, "This is long overdue, and will, I hope, soon be arranged."[10] It was. Russian police institutions were introduced in the Baltic provinces in June, 1888; and thirteen months later the court system created in the 1864 Russian judicial reform supplanted the estates' courts. Deprived of its last major field of public responsibility, the Riga magistracy ceased to exist. In many ways the new institutions improved the administration of justice. The old system had been badly in need of overhaul, and the 1864 judicial reform was one of the most successful of Alexander II's reforms; but the government used the reforms as a vehicle for Russification. Russian was made the language of business for the police and the sole language of litigation in the courts. Even Manasein had not wished to go that far.[11]

The Russification programme reached its climax on 9 November 1889, when Russian became the exclusive language of internal business in Baltic municipal administration. This evoked a swift and angry response from the Riga duma. In an emotional speech before the duma, city councilman Max von Oettingen condemned the measure and with it Livland Governor Mikhail A. Zinoviev, who was an enthusiastic advocate of Russification. The imperial government was not prepared to tolerate such effrontery. Von Oettingen was removed from office. Even this was not sufficient to satisfy Zinoviev, who complained that Riga mayor August von Oettingen[12] acted improperly by reading the notice of Max von Oettingen's dismissal in German rather than in Russian and by failing to order the duma to stand while hearing it. The mayor's denial of improper behaviour earned him a formal reprimand from the tsar and loss of official rank *(chin)* won during his service as Livland governor during the 1860's. Disgusted and deeply offended by the affair, Mayor von Oettingen resigned from office.

The government's Russification programme also extended to embrace the Baltic school system, which was certainly the most comprehensive and arguably the finest in the Russian Empire. A far greater proportion of the Baltic population was able to attend school than was the case elsewhere in the empire. In 1885, for example, Livland province boasted one school for every 630 inhabitants. The figure for the empire as a whole was only one for every 2,665. At the end of the nineteenth century the literacy rate in Livland was more than three times the Russian average.[13]

Riga had an extensive municipal school system that was supplemented by the numerous state, private and church-affiliated schools. The language of instruction in most of them was German. The quality and availability of education in Riga was not, however, uppermost in the minds of the men who determined Russian policy toward national minorities. The Manasein report had condemned the Baltic school system as a seedbed of sedition. The Minister of Education, Ivan Delianov, agreed with Mansein's assessment of the situation, and more than once urged the tsar to Russify the Baltic schools, which he considered "foreign to Russia."[14]

In 1883 Mikhail N. Kapustin, a Moscow University law professor, was appointed curator of the Dorpat school district. In Kapustin the Baltic provinces acquired a chief education official who was eager and willing to carry out a comprehensive programme of school Russification. The first hint of what the future held came in May, 1884, when Kapustin issued a circular that proposed to give the study of Russian language and literature primary emphasis in the secondary schools. The proposal was so comprehensive and exacting that it was unfeasible. Kapustin, admitting that the suggested requirements would have to remain an "ideal for the future", was obliged to withdraw the circular before any of its provisions went into effect;[15] but this was only a temporary setback for the forces of Russification. In April, 1886 an undeterred Kapustin declared that, "The chief focus of education in the lowest class must be on the Russian language. The children must be proficient enough to be able to take their second year of instruction entirely in Russian."[16] To this end Russian-language instruction in elementary schools was increased from eight to eleven hours per week, and German-language instruction was reduced from obligatory to optional status. This meant that henceforth parents would have to pay a small fee if their children were to receive instruction in German language and literature. A year later Russian-language instruction was substantially increased in private schools, which had not been affected by the 1886 legislation.

School Russification commenced in earnest later in 1886, when the imperial authorities, acting on Kapustin's recommendation, ordered the state-supported middle school in Riga to substitute Russian for German as the language of instruction beginning with the 1886/1887 school year. In 1887 Delianov proposed to the Council of Ministers that all middle and elementary schools in the Baltic provinces be Russified, because by "supporting the German school in preference to the Russian, the government has led the people to believe that the Estonian/Latvian region is not Russian, that it is part of another, foreign culture."[17] Delianov's proposal was approved, and the 1887/1888 school year saw the beginning of gradual Russification that proceeded class by class from the lowest grade upwards at the rate of one class per year. The use of languages other than Russian was restricted to Lutheran religious instruction. Class by class Russification of boys' secondary schools and all boys' private schools was under way by the fall of 1889. Girls' schools met the same fate a year later. Dorpat University, with the exception of its theological faculty, was Russified in 1893 and the Baltic Polytechnical Institute in 1896. By the middle of the 1890's there was not a single school of any kind in the Baltic provinces which did not use Russian as the sole official language of instruction.

Russification was accompanied by a loss of educational autonomy. Effective control of the Riga municipal school system was taken away from the city government and placed in the hands of the Baltic school district curator, whose office was moved from "separatist" Dorpat to Riga in 1886.

The effects of Russification in Riga were almost wholly negative. The stipulation that government officials carry out their duties in a language which many knew imperfectly or not at all was certainly not conducive to the smooth functioning of that government. The Riga police provide a good illustration of the havoc which Russification could wreak. After 1885 all police business had to be conducted in Russian; but most of the police officials were incapable of doing this, and the police department had to hire translators to render its official paperwork into Russian. The officials who staffed the local courts, which were not Russified until 1889, could not read the Russian correspondence they received from the police, and were obliged to hire translators of their own to deal with it.[18] Russification also impaired the effectiveness of the government's genuine reform measures. The new judicial machinery established in 1889 was in theory more efficient and impartial than the estates' courts, but the requirement that litigants use an unfamiliar language seriously detracted from the benefits it might have brought the local population.

School Russification served no rational purpose in Riga. If there was a problem pertinent to the language of instruction in the local schools it was a lack of facilities for Latvians, not a shortage of them for Russian-speakers. Russification could only diminish the effectiveness and quality of the education dispensed in the schools. In a classroom where a German-speaking instructor was compelled to teach German to German and Latvian pupils through the medium of Russian, the educational process itself had to suffer. Magnus Werbatus, director of the Riga Girls' Secondary School during this period, has described in his memoirs how his son, a student in Riga at the time, could translate entire sentences from Greek to Russian without actually knowing what they meant.[19] The deleterious results of school Russification are clearly documented by a dramatic drop in school attendance and a lowering of the literacy rate.[20]

Hand in hand with Russification went religious persecution. For those who formulated imperial minority policy, Lutheranism was just as pernicious an influence in the Baltic region as German culture. An 1885 trip to Riga gave Pobedonostsev cause for genuine anxiety when he saw first hand the strength of the Lutheran church there and the contrasting weakness of Orthodoxy.[21] On his return to St. Petersburg, the chief procurator launched a campaign to promote Orthodoxy and undermine Lutheranism in the Baltic provinces. The campaign focused chiefly on the Latvian and Estonian Orthodox community, which traced its origin largely to the 1840's, when a government-sponsored drive to convert the Baltic peasantry succeeded in winning more than seventy thousand of them over to the Orthodox fold.[22] Before long the new converts had begun to question the wisdom of their action. The state church never provided adequate personnel or facilities to minister effectively to the needs of the Orthodox peasants, who found themselves isolated and outcast in a Lutheran environment. Reconversion to Lutheranism was expressly forbidden by law, and in the case of mixed Lutheran-Orthodox marriages all children were required to be raised in the Orthodox faith. The situation of the converts had been greatly improved in the 1860's, when Alexander II ceased to enforce these laws; but in 1885 the government began once again to observe the letter of the law. All who had reconverted to Lutheranism, as well as any Lutheran who had an Orthodox parent, were enjoined to return to Orthodoxy. This caused more anguish and distress than any measure aimed at linguistic Russification. Many people attempted to avoid obeying it, and they were often helped in this by sympathetic Lutheran pastors. Since ministering to reconverts was illegal, nearly two hundred German pastors were charged with criminal offences.[23] Not content with the reclamation of reconverts, the government also encouraged the Orthodox church to mount a fresh drive to convert Lutherans, and subjected the Lutheran church to constant harassment. Authorization for the repair and construction of non-Orthodox church facilities, for example, had to come from the local Orthodox authorities; and that authorization was virtually impossible to obtain.

Imperial policies were rendered all the harsher by the behaviour of the Russian officials sent to Riga to enforce them. The quality of the nineteenth-century Russian civil service was poor, and many of the officials who went to Riga to staff the Russified institutions there earned the opprobrium of the local Germans for their dishonesty and incompetence. Others, reflecting government intolerance toward minorities, were purposefully aggressive and arbitrary. School Curator Kapustin certainly belonged to the latter group, as did Mikhail A. Zinoviev, an artillery general who served as Livland governor from 1885 until his death in 1895. Zinoviev's reports to his superiors reveal a man who saw himself as a defender of crown and nation in a hotbed of subversion.[24] In an 1887 speech to the Riga Latvian Union, he described the Riga Germans as "foreigners", whose control of local government threatened state security.[25] The Russification of the Riga duma was originally his idea; and there is evidence that, following Mayor von Oettingen's resignation, he recommended that henceforth the Riga mayor be appointed by the Minister of Internal Affairs.[26]

Zinoviev's most celebrated confrontation with the Riga Germans arose from his conviction that the city's German-language press merited special attention to ensure that it published nothing treasonable. Pronouncing the censorship laws to be insufficiently stringent, he imposed a censorship that was harsh even by the Russian standards of the day. The governor even took it upon himself to double-check much of the material already passed by his own censor.[27] In 1889, as Riga German anger at Russification peaked with Max von Oettingen's denunciation of Zinoviev in the duma, *Rigasche Zeitung* editor Alexander Buchholtz publicly complained that censorship was excessive. Zinoviev responded by forbidding the *Rigasche Zeitung* to carry advertising for an eight-month period, thus effectively striking a financial death blow at the offending newspaper. Certain that he was under police surveillance and fearing arrest, Buchholtz fled to Germany. The *Rigasche Zeitung* folded.

Zinoviev then proceeded to establish a replacement German-language newspaper which would represent a point of view more in tune with official policy. In the fall of 1889 the new newspaper, the *Düna-Zeitung*, began to appear under the editorship of a *Reich*-German citizen named Gustav Pipirs. Claiming that the Baltic Germans were separatists collectively guilty of "naked high treason," the *Düna-Zeitung* supported Russification and argued that in the interest of security the Riga mayor should be appointed by the imperial authorities.[28] When the local Germans boycotted the newspaper and the stores which sold it, two prominent Riga lawyers, Johannes Büngner and Matthias Doss, were administratively banished to European Russia on suspicion of organizing the boycott.

The imperial government's policies toward the German minority in Riga and elsewhere in the Baltic region during the 1880's really benefitted no one. They impaired the efficiency of local government, ravaged what had been a good school system and generally made life difficult for the local people, German and Latvian alike. All of these considerations, however, were of secondary importance to an imperial government obsessed with the notion that its German subjects there were disloyal. Russification, religious persecution and other arbitrary measures were products of a government whose approach to the minority question had become irrational.

When Russification began, the Riga Germans were still absorbed in their constitutional conflict with the imperial government over the fate of the estates; and it was perhaps only natural that their first response to Russification came within the context of this conflict. Perceiving Russification as yet another threat to the continued viability of the Baltic *Rechtsstaat*, they immediately denounced it as "illegal". Werbatus, for example, condemned school Russification as "a forceful violation of historically developed and legally grounded constitutional relationships."[29]

The most cogent expression of this legalistic response to the Russification programme is that contained in the *Russian-Baltic Notes,* a four-volume collection of essays by leading Baltic German public figures published anonymously in Leipzig between 1886 and 1888 under the editorship of Max von Oettingen and the Riga statistician Friedrich Jung-Stilling. The essays attacked virtually every aspect of government policy in the Baltic, from linguistic Russification and religious persecution to the arbitrary and illegal acts of individual officials. The absence of national rhetoric is striking. Russian policy was thoroughly condemned as illegal and destructive, but Russification was never described as an attack on the Germans as a national group. One rather pugnacious essay, "Why and How the Balts Must Struggle", characteristically concluded that the imperial government's aim was to "assimilate the Baltic provinces into the chaos of ancient Russian lawlessness."[30] The author called upon the Balts to defend their legal rights, but said nothing of the interests of the Germans as a national minority. This omission of any call for a German national response was conscious and deliberate. For the authors of these essays nationality was only a "cultural concept" unsuited for political use.[31] Political nationalism could only be destructive in a multi-national empire, as the Russification programme, a crowning example of the "thoughtless deification of the nationality principle that forces the concept of *Rechtsstaat* into the background,"[32] clearly illustrated.

In their hour of adversity the German minority not only continued to exhibit their traditional dislike of nationalism, but also remained steadfastly *kaisertreu*. Werbatus noted that German anger at Russification was tempered by a "thoroughly loyal and *kaisertreu* mentality."[33] Most revealing in this regard is an essay in the *Russian-Baltic Notes* describing the episode of Mayor Büngner's dismissal. True to form, Büngner was not portrayed as a national martyr, but rather as the victim of lawless government. What is particularly noteworthy about the essay is its careful exoneration of the tsar from any blame in the matter. An accusing finger was pointed instead at nationalist officials who somehow misled the sovereign:

> It is highly probable that the tsar was either falsely or incompletely informed about this matter . . . and that he had absolutely no conception of the consequences to which his manner of dealing with it might lead.[34]

Alexander III and his ministers made a grave mistake when they questioned Baltic German loyalty.

Resisting the will of the autocrat was hardly an easy or promising venture, but the Germans in Riga did try to defend themselves against Russification with the same legal tactics employed in the battle for estates' rights. The duma tried to save the German school system by transfering it to private ownership, only to be thwarted by the 1889 ordinance that Russified private schools. In the winter of 1889 local school officials seized upon a legal technicality in the wording of the Russification laws to try to delay Russification in some classes and even to re-introduce German in others. This too was unsuccessful, and earned three school officials disciplinary action for insubordination. Undaunted, the duma tried and ultimately failed in trying to resist takeover of the city gymnasium by the imperial authorities by refusing to vote its formal assent to the measure.

Legal obstacles were a puny defense against a government that did not even respect its own laws. The threat of Russification, moreover, was far more serious in a material sense than the dismantling of the estates. The government-imposed reform of 1877, no matter how objectionable it might have been to the Germans in a constitutional sense, did not in practice weaken or threaten German social, political and cultural dominance in Riga. Russification, on the other hand, had a measurably negative social and economic impact on certain segments of the German minority. Particularly hard hit were the literati. School Russification cost many German teachers their jobs, either because they did not know enough Russian to handle their responsibilities or because the ever suspicious school authorities fired them for "unreliability".[34] The fate of the city gymnasium faculty was typical. Of the twenty-three Germans employed there on the eve of Russification, six were forced to resign because they could not conduct class in Russian.[36] Vacant positions were normally filled with Russians, who comprised half the gymnasium faculty by 1905.[37] Even for many of those who remained in the teaching profession, circumstances were not easy. Friedrich Demme, a mathematics teacher in the small Baltic port city of Libau, has left memoirs describing in detail the traumatic effect of Russification on teachers throughout the Baltic region. As more and more of his colleagues were dismissed for lack of proficiency in Russian or suspected subversion, Demme lived by his wits, memorizing Russian textbooks and mechanically regurgitating them to his classes.[38] German lawyers, compelled to use Russian as the language of litigation and trained in a legal system that was no longer operative after 1889, found themselves in an even less enviable position than the teachers. Judicial reform and Russification also brought the wholesale dismissal of German judges. One year after the changeover, only one of the twenty-seven judges assigned to the Riga district court was German.[39] Members of the legal and teaching professions were not the only ones to suffer. Clergymen risked arrest if they ministered to reconverts, journalists were handcuffed by obsessively vigilant censorship and civil servants, like teachers, were liable to lose their jobs if they could not perform their duties in Russian.

Gradually it became apparent to the hard pressed literati that they could not gain anything through legal action, which was time-consuming and ultimately futile. One option was emigration. Some of the most prominent public figures, among them Alexander Buchholtz, Friedrich Bienemann, *Rigasche Stadtblätter* editor Arend Buchholtz and several high-ranking estates officials, went into exile in Germany. Many others followed them. Half of the teachers dismissed from the city gymnasium during the course of Russification emigrated to Germany; and by the outbreak of World War I there were seventy Baltic Germans, many of them victims of the Russification of Dorpat University and the Baltic Polytechnical Institute, who held professorial chairs in *Reich-* German universities.[40]

Emigration, however appealing or even necessary it might have been to some, was not for everyone. Those who remained in Riga to live with the consequences of Russification had to seek a way to protect themselves. Some of the literati found an answer to their predicament in a form of German nationalism. For people whose livelihood was threatened by the nationalist policies of the Russian government, the idea of self-defense through German national solidarity was an attractive one. This presumed the development of a new sense of collective identity based on nationality rather than on social class and regional origin. As such, it meant a break of major proportions with established local custom, and it was to prove a gradual and hesitant process. The groundwork for this development, however, was being laid by government policies aimed specifically against the Germans as a national group, and, in a different way, by the activities of local Latvian nationalists. The example of Latvian nationalist political organization provided a model of sorts for the Germans. What is more, the slow but steady growth of the Latvian middle class had by the 1890's reached a stage at which the Germans could at least begin seriously to entertain the notion, crucial in itself for the emergence of German national consciousness, that Latvians and Germans were two separate nationalities rather than simply representatives of different social classes.

The first indication of the new German national feeling surfaced in the work of Alexander Buchholtz. In 1888, once more avoiding local censorship by publishing anonymously in Leipzig, he produced a companion volume to his earlier book, *Fifty Years of Russian Administration in the Russian Baltic Provinces.* The new volume, *The German-Protestant Struggle in the Baltic Provinces of Russia,* was, as its title indicates, more national in tone than its predecessor. Buchholtz complained that, "The blows struck against the Baltic school system are in themselves sufficient to destroy the German way of life here, the German nationality. They prevent our children from effectively acquiring German nationality."[41] He was clearly worried about the future of the Germans as a national group. The book was nonetheless not the product of a fully developed German nationalism. It did not openly call for the defense of specifically national interests. Buchholtz focused on the unconstitutionality of the Russification programme and was emphatically *kaisertreu*. He even claimed in the book's introduction to be writing in the spirit of Schirren's *Livland's Answer*.[42]

The emergence of a refined and coherent national consciousness and of a true political nationalism among the Riga Germans had to await the middle of the 1890's. Ironically, the publication which came to serve as the principal organ of the new nationalism was the *Düna-Zeitung*. A German-lanugage Russian nationalist newspaper was not a sound proposition in Riga; and in 1891 it was bought by Knud Horneman, a Dane who had connections with the Empress Maria Fedorovna. In order to render the *Düna-Zeitung* more palatable to the German reading public, Horneman hired Gustav Keuchel as his chief editor. Keuchel, at one time editor of the *Zeitung für Stadt und Land* and of the *Baltische Monatschrift*, was a distinguished veteran journalist, but by 1891 he was near the end of his long career. Effective direction of the *Düna-Zeitung* fell increasingly to Keuchel's young colleague Ernst Seraphim. When Keuchel retired in 1896, Seraphim succeeded him as chief editor. Only twenty-nine when he began to work with the *Düna-Zeitung*, Seraphim was a newcomer to journalism. After graduating from Dorpat University, he spent the years from 1886 to 1891 teaching history at a high school in the northern Livland town of Fellin, where he experienced first hand the demoralizing effects of school Russification.

Under Seraphim's guidance the *Düna-Zeitung* evolved into a German nationalist newspaper. Seraphim himself was the first Riga German publicist to exhibit a clear perception of nationality as the primary determinant of collective identity and to make a distinction between Germans and Latvians on the basis of nationality rather than social class. He stressed that the Baltic Germans possessed a "national individuality," and that they should "hold their language and nationality *(Volkstum)* in honour."[43]

German national consciousness naturally implied concurrent recognition of Latvian nationhood. If the Germans were a nationality rather than an assemblage of social classes, so were the Latvians. Given traditional local attitudes toward the Latvians, this conclusion was not an easy one even for German nationalists to reach; but Seraphim felt obliged to concede national status to the Latvians.[44] Bernhard Hollander, a Riga teacher who shared Seraphim's nationalist views and who was to play an important role in the development of Baltic German nationalism, acknowledged in a letter to the *Düna-Zeitung* that, "We should fully recognize all rightful Latvian demands. We should, for example, cease to wonder why Latvians who achieve higher social status declare their native language to be socially adequate . . . Because we stand by our German nationality, we should certainly not dispute anyone who values his own.["]45

Men like Seraphim and Hollander, of course, went beyond simple cognizance of their nationality to espouse a true political nationalism. This involved the adoption of nationality as the principal basis of political organization. Like the liberals of the 1860's and the conservatives of the 1870's and 1880's, the German nationalists were firm believers in the efficacy of historically developed Baltic laws and institutions. The *Düna-Zeitung* neatly expressed this historicism when it argued that, "Loyalty to history, to our own ways, is the basis of every moral action."[46] The nationalists differed from their predecessors, however, in that they imparted national content to the historically developed forms. Thus Baltic cultural, political and legal traditions were good not only because they were the organic product of centuries of experience, but also becuase they were intrinsically German. In 1901, when Riga celebrated the seven hundredth anniversary of its founding, the *Düna-Zeitung* characteristically noted that the festivities were "a symbol of the capabilities principally of our Baltic German circles."[47]

The overriding concern among German nationalists was that Russification might destroy Riga's German character. They were realistic enough to know that they had small chance of reversing the imperial government's policy. The litigious tactics used in earlier years had shown themselves to be bankrupt by the 1890's. Advocacy of separation from the Russian Empire, another response which might suggest itself, never formed a part of the nationalist programme in this period.

The only course which the nationalists could steer was toward preservation through national solidarity of the German social, economic, political and cultural position *vis-a-vis* the local Latvian and Russian communities. In the words of the *Düna-Zeitung,* "When we take the complicated and special relationships here into consideration, we must become aware that only through the solidification of our position as civic leaders can we Germans protect that very position to which, thanks to history and culture, we have a right."[48] German nationalists admired the strong sense of national cohesiveness displayed by their Latvian counterparts. One anonymous letter to the *Düna-Zeitung* contended that the Germans should emulate the Latvians' "firm solidarity, common drive for progress and self-conscious struggle."[49] In a similar vein, Seraphim exhorted young Germans to observe and learn from the activity of their Latvian contemporaries, because, "in times when national consciousness is stressed by one side even among the very young, it is necessary for self-preservation for those, who in earlier times did not think of national consciousness, to consider developing it."[50]

Seraphim and his fellow nationalists urged Germans to patronize German-owned business establishments as a means of strengthening the economic situation of the German community. They also placed a great deal of emphasis on the need to ensure continued German control of the municipal government. In many of the smaller Baltic cities the influx of Latvians and Estonians from the countryside, higher Latvian and Estonian birth rates and a movement of Germans into Riga all combined to enable Latvians and Estonians to wrest control of the city governments away from the Germans. Given the nature of the social and demographic pattern in Riga, a Latvian takeover there was highly unlikely; but the German nationalists, casting apprehensive glances at the fate of their co-nationals elsewhere, nevertheless felt that precautions had to be taken. The best insurance, in Hollander's words, was "securing German property ownership in the city."[51] Seraphim agreed, and sought to facilitate this by appealing to the rural German nobility to help by investing in urban real estate.[52]

By the late 1890's German nationalism was growing toward maturity in Riga. It had a bright, articulate spokesman in Ernst Seraphim, the *Düna-Zeitung* was a successful newspaper, and a centre of sorts for nationalist activity had formed around a discussion circle which called itself the Kilimanjaro Association. Founded in 1892, the Kilimanjaro Association brought together young literati whose future was seriously jeopardized by Russification and who sought redress in national solidarity. The national movement still, however, lacked a real organizational base. It had shown itself capable of producing earnest rhetoric, but little in the way of concrete action.

This was to change in the opening years of the present century. The chief catalyst of the change was Hans Baron Hahn, a Kurland noble who came to Riga in April, 1902 after several years' residence in South America. Hahn, like many Germans, had been eagerly following the progress of Boer resistance to Britain in South Africa, and brought with him plans for organizing Baltic German financial support for the then flagging Boer effort. In Riga his enthusiasm was directed into another channel by an old acquaintance, Arved von Strandmann. The latter was a man of ability and of exceptional breadth for a Baltic noble. Scion of a wealthy landed family, he had studied law at Dorpat Univeristy, served a term in the Riga duma and was co-founder and director of a Riga-based machine building corporation. He was also involved with the German nationalist movement, and his advice to Hahn was that his efforts would serve a better purpose if he collected money to help the system of underground German private schools which had arisen in the wake of Russification throughout the Baltic provinces. Hahn agreed, and in order to publicize his fund-raising drive in a discreet fashion, for discovery would have meant arrest, he arranged for Bernhard Hollander to write promotional brochures that could be surreptitiously circulated to potential donors. Hollander saw a chance to inject new vigour into the national movement and to set it on a more active course. His pamphlets went beyond an appeal for aid to clandestine schools. They portrayed Baltic German society as one threatened with national extinction, and urged that a comprehensive programme of national self-help be undertaken. Among other things, a scholarship fund was needed to finance the university study of Baltic Germans in German-speaking countries; and private cultural and educational societies should be founded in the Baltic provinces to serve the cause of German civilization and concurrently to provide employment for literati.[53]

Hollander and Hahn had lit a fuse under the local nationalist movement. In October, 1902 the Kilimanjaro Association decided to convoke a general meeting to explore the possibility of establishing an active German nationalist organization in Riga. The meeting took place the following February, and it was attended by about thirty people, mostly literati. The highlight of the evening was a speech delivered by Christian Schroeder, a Riga pastor and Kilimanjaro member who pleaded the case for a nationalist organization that could act on Hollander's recommendations.[54] Schroeder's speech was received enthusiastically, and a committee was immediately set up to investigate ways to do this. It was a delicate task. The imperial government certainly would not allow the establishment of a German nationalist organization whose avowed purpose was to blunt the effects of Russification. The committee did, however, manage to find a clever way out of this difficulty, suggesting that an existing club or organization be converted to serve the nationalist purpose. If this could be arranged, the official permission required to found new organizations would not have to be sought. The most likely candidate for a conversion of this sort was the Euphony Club, a social organization founded in 1797, but nearly defunct by 1903 due to dwindling membership. The nationalists decided to take over the Euphony Club; and by February, 1904 they had transformed it into Riga's first German nationalist organization.

Euphony's statute was soon altered so that it could engage in what were euphemistically termed "cultural and philanthropic activities."[55] In many ways Euphony modeled its activities on those of its Latvian counterpart, the Riga Latvian Union. In the field of education, Euphony maintained a network of clandestine German schools, or "educational circles," in private homes, gave scholarships to German students and, in order to ensure itself of a supply of qualified teachers, sent local people to Germany for pedagogical training. To help keep the municipal duma in German hands, the nationalist club made emergency loans to German property owners who were in danger of disenfranchisement because of tax arrears. On the cultural plane, it sponsored lectures on Baltic German history, *Lieder* concerts, theatrical performances and poetry readings.

With the transformation of the Euphony Club from a social into a quasi-political organization, German nationalist activity acquired considerable scope and variety; but prior to the Revolution of 1905 this activity was largely confined to Riga itself. In theory the nationalist movement was concerned with the interests of the German population in the Baltic provinces as a whole. Nationalists believed that the old regional and class differences had to be overcome for the sake of national solidarity. Their ultimate ideal was to establish a common national collective identity for all Baltic Germans. Seraphim never tired of imploring his co-nationals to forget their old loyalties and antagonisms and to come together in the defence of their ethnic nationality;[56] and the Euphony Club did include several members of the Livland nobility, a group that in the past had shown considerable reluctance to involve itself in the bourgeois social and political life of Riga. Particular concern, moreover, was voiced in nationalist circles regarding the fate of the German communities in the smaller Baltic cities. Nonetheless, the Riga-based nationalist movement never did forge effective links with other Baltic German communities. The movement was still at an embryonic stage, and its leaders had not yet come to grips with the practical problem of broadening their activity to appeal to the Baltic German population as a whole.

Although the nationalists envisioned the formation of a new national consciousness that would weld the German minority in the three Baltic provinces into a cohesive unit, they had no interest in forging a special relationship with the German *Reich*. Above all, they did not advocate separatism or disloyalty to the Russian Empire. They remained unreservedly loyal to the tsar and strove to develop a national collective identity that was Baltic German rather than Pan-German in scope. Several factors account for this. The bonds of common language and cultural heritage notwithstanding, Baltic Germans had always felt themselves to be a group set apart from the Germans of central Europe. Balts who emigrated to Germany during the late nineteenth century found that adjustment to the new environment was difficult; and *Reich*-Germans who lived in Riga found the Baltic milieu equally alien and formed a colony of their own that stood apart from the surrounding local German society.[57] The nature of these differences was perhaps best captured in a 1901 *Rigasche Rundschau** article that compared the relationship between Baltic Germans and *Reich*-Germans to that between South African Boers and the Dutch: "Just as the Boer feels like a foreigner in Holland and suffers there from homesickness for African soil, Baltic Germans become accustomed to Germany with difficulty."[58] Centuries of divergent cultural, social and political development had opened a considerable gulf between the Germans of the Baltic provinces and the citizens of the German *Reich,* and, given this, it was unlikely that even a nationalist Baltic German political programme would be Pan-German.

The potential appeal of Pan-Germanism was further reduced by a Riga German aversion to the political and social environment in Germany. Censorship placed severe limitations on the ability of the Riga press to cover foreign, particularly *Reich*-German, news; but the image of the *Reich* that emerges from occasional oblique references in the press and from the comments of Riga German exiles there is generally not a positive one. Since the end of the 1860's, the political mood of the Riga Germans had been one of sustained conservatism. The nationalists were no exception to this. They were historicists who wished to maintain traditional Baltic administrative and legal forms, which they saw as intrinsically German; and they were socially conservative to the point of finding the 1877 municipal reform too democratic. For people such as these late nineteenth-century Germany was hardly an ideal society. The growth of state power at the expense of traditional, local forms of government that characterized Germany in that period was highly objectionable to them. Universal male suffrage was another frightening aspect of the *Reich*. In 1898 the *Rigasche Rundschau,* itself not the most conservative of the three German-language dailies, published an editorial deploring the baleful influence of the lower classes on government in Germany and praising Russia for having avoided this evil.[59] Seraphim, who proudly identified himself as a conservative as well as a nationalist, laid special stress on the need to keep government in the hands of the propertied classes. The alternative would be to permit the takeover of municipal government by the Latvians.[60]

The salient feature of German nationalism in this period was the restricted nature of its appeal. Nearly all of the people associated with it were literati whose livelihoods were directly threatened by Russification. Nationalists found that their ideas did not stir the vast majority of their co-nationals. Frustrated nationalist spokesmen could belabour

---

*In 1894 the *Zeitung für Stadt und Land* had changed its name to *"Rigasche Rundschau".*

their own community for its "very weakly developed . . . national spirit,"[61] but they did so in vain. The Euphony Club spent much time and energy distributing nationalist literature to the German community at large and even held social gatherings at which German shopkeepers and artisans were encouraged to mingle with the nationalist literati. This too was to no avail. Traditional exclusiveness of caste was still too strong to permit the easy acceptance of a political doctrine that transcended social barriers in the name of an ethnic and linguistic collectivity; and, as Hollander was forced to admit in his memoirs, many local Germans heartily disapproved of nationalist activity because it often circumvented the law and because it involved a degree of disobedience to the tsar.[62] The Euphony Club was never a large organization, and it drew its membership predominantly from the ranks of the threatened literati. Of the twenty-five men who participated in the re-organization of the club in 1904, eighteen were literati (six teachers, five clergymen, three lawyers, a physician and three civil servants). The rest were a mixture of nobles from rural Livland and Riga merchants.*

Years later, in the wake of the 1905 Revolution, nationalist ideas were to gain wider currency in Riga, but at the turn of the century they were the preserve of a vocal and articulate minority whose social and economic position had been directly threatened by Russification.

On balance, the policies pursued by the imperial government toward the Riga Germans during the 1880's were badly conceived and poorly executed. They had been intended to strengthen the hand of the autocracy, but in the end they only served to antagonize a loyal minority group and to foster the growth of a nationalist movement where none had existed before. The Germans remained *kaisertreu,* but they did so in spite of the imperial government's behaviour.

---

*See Appendix III

Chapter 5

INDUSTRIALIZATION

Why did German nationalism fail to attract significant support outside the ranks of the literati? What explains the surprising resiliency of tradition? The appeal of nationalism was, after all, rooted in the socioeconomic threat posed by Russification, religious persecution and arbitrary government. Do social and economic factors also account for the rejection of the nationalism by the Riga German majority? The evidence suggests that this was indeed the case.

The imperial government, fearful lest Russia's backwardness compromise her security, began to encourage industrial development during the late nineteenth century. What started as a slow, gradual, hesitant process in the 1860's and 1870's became a feverish rush toward industrialization in the 1890's. Thousands of industrial enterprises, many of them employing highly sophisticated imported technology, were founded; a railroad network was flung across Russia's vast spaces, uniting producers with markets and raw materials; western investors poured immense sums of money into the Russian economy; industrial entrepreneurs, business executives, engineers and others associated with economic change emerged as an important component in Russian society; and Russia's urban population mushroomed as men and women from peasant villages migrated to the cities in search of work in the new factories.

These changes had a profound impact on Riga and its German elite. At the accession of Alexander II in 1855 Riga was already an important commercial city. Russian industrialization acted as a powerful stimulus to Riga's commercial activity, which expanded both in volume and scope as the nineteenth century wore on. Of central importance for this development was the construction of railroads between the city and its Russian hinterland. The first railroad connection, linking Riga with Dünaburg on the Warsaw-St. Petersburg line, was completed in 1861. Four years later a line was built connecting Dünaburg with Vitebsk, and by 1871 Riga possessed a direct railroad link with Tsaritsyn in the black soil region of southern Russia. A railroad reaching south-west to

65

Mitau, Libau and Kovno was in operation after 1873; direct service between Riga and Moscow began in 1889; and, finally, the completion of the Trans-Siberian railroad after the turn of the century gave Riga access to the markets and resources of the Far East.

The railroad was of incalculable benefit to Riga merchants. Trains could haul a far greater volume of freight than the old river barges, and the railroad functioned all year, whereas river commerce was subject to annual interruption when the Dvina froze during the winter months. The volume of traditional Riga exports like flax and timber increased at a constant rate during the late nineteenth century; and, as the railroads linked Riga to a wider hinterland, new kinds of exports began to play an important role.[1] Although Riga could never hope to rival the Black Sea port of Odessa, the volume of Riga's grain exports rose significantly after the opening of the Riga-Tsaritsyn rail line. When the Trans-Siberian was completed, Riga emerged as a major export centre for Siberian eggs and dairy products.[2] Historically, Riga's import trade had always been greatly overshadowed in volume and value by exports. This pattern continued throughout the late nineteenth century. Imports did increase thanks to the wider market opened up by the railroad and to the growing demand for imported raw materials by Riga industry; but the protectionist policies pursued by the Russian government ultimately placed limits on Riga's role as an import centre.[3]

Hand in hand with commercial prosperity came local industrial development. Mid-nineteenth century Riga was home to a small, but growing, number of industrial enterprises which processed import and export commodities. By the beginning of the twentieth century, Riga had become a great industrial city—a producer of machinery, railroad equipment, steamships, chemical and rubber goods, furniture and even automobiles. Industrial growth accelerated steadily. Chamber of Commerce statistics show that in 1874 Riga possessed 155 "factories", many of them still tiny workshops, employing nearly twelve thousand workers. This represented a major increase from the ninety "factories" with five thousand workers documented for 1864. A survey of local trade, craft production and industry made by the city government in 1884 revealed that by this time there were 117 genuine factories, each with a minimum of twenty-one employees and some with several thousand. Finally, government factory inspection statistics gathered at the turn of the century list 278 factories, each with at least sixteen employees, and a total industrial labour force of 47,242.[4]

Established branches of the import-export commodity processing industry naturally throve when commerce prospered and expanded. The new railroad network provided them with a much larger and more varied supply of raw materials and created a far broader market within the empire for those industries that worked with imported materials. Riga itself became an increasingly lucrative market. Its population nearly tripled during the last thirty years of the nineteenth century, creating a vastly increased demand for personal consumer goods; and the developing local industrial complex itself constituted an important market for machinery and partly finished goods. The wood processing industry was typical. Improved transport opened up wider markets both in Russia and abroad; and population growth, coupled with a construction boom, fueled local demand for all types of wood products, from paper and furniture to construction materials. In 1864 Riga claimed four wood processing establishments with a combined labour force of 748; ten years later there were fourteen employing more than seventeen hundred; and by 1884 there were twenty-nine factories and sawmills manned by 2,483 workers.[5] The tobacco processing industry experienced a similar expansion. The number of tobacco processing firms fluctuated during the late nineteenth century, but the overall labour force grew from approximately nine hundred in 1864 to over two thousand in 1897.[6]

Most other light industries, from food processing to glass making and leather manufacturing, exhibited a similar pattern of development. The only local industry that did not respond positively to the new conditions was textile manufacturing. What in the 1860's had been a thriving industry engaged in spinning and weaving imported cotton and wool fell on hard times in the 1880's due to competition from Moscow-based firms using cheaper domestic raw materials. Several long-established textile mills went bankrupt. Textile production fell by one-half, and the industry's total labour force dropped from over two thousand in 1864 to sixteen hundred in 1884.[7] Not until the 1890's, when the industry experienced an influx of foreign capital, did the situation begin to improve.

The most significant development in Riga's economy during this period was not the growth of established light industry, but rather the emerging pre-eminence of machine fabrication and chemical production. The burgeoning Russian railroad system needed rolling stock, rails and other heavy equipment, and industries of all kinds in Riga and elsewhere in the empire required more and more machinery, tools and chemical products. At mid-century machine fabrication and metallurgy were restricted to a few small workshops employing less than three hundred workers. By 1900 thirty-five factories provided work for more than fifteen thousand men and women.[8] Similarly, the chemical industry grew from a few small firms producing soap, candles, furniture varnish and other items for household consumption into one of the major sectors of the local economy, manufacturing a broad range of chemical products for home and industrial use and employing approximately six thousand workers at the turn of the century.[9]

Industrialization and commercial growth brought social and demographic changes of considerable magnitude. Thousands of peasants migrated from the surrounding countryside into Riga to find work in the factories; and new opportunities in commerce and in service occupations attracted many more. Riga's population shot up from just over one hundred thousand in 1867 to 282,230 in 1897 and 514,451 in 1913.[10] Most of the newcomers were Latvian; and the Germans became a progressively smaller minority in the city.[11]

TABLE 1

RIGA POPULATION BY LANGUAGE, 1867-1897

As a percentage of the total population

Language	1867 "customary language"	1881 "customary language"	1881 "nationality"	1897 "native language"
German	42.8	39.4	31.0	23.8
Latvian	23.5	29.5	32.8	45.0
Russian	25.1	19.6	19.7	16.1
Yiddish[12]	5.1	8.7	12.2	6.0
Other[13]	3.5	2.8	4.3	9.1
Total	100.0	100.0	100.0	100.0

The impact of social and economic change upon the Riga German community, however, cannot be measured solely in demographic terms. Relative numerical decline aside, the Germans benefited substantially from industrial and commercial expansion. The German merchantry was well placed to reap advantage from the growth of foreign trade through the port of Riga. In the 1850's and 1860's nearly all large commercial enterprises were in the hands of wealthy German merchants whose families had dominated local society for generations. Some old and well-established firms, unable to adjust to the new market and supply conditions, went under, but many more prospered; and by the beginning of the twentieth century most of the largest trading firms were still German-owned. The 1883 list of firms registered in Riga shows that 68.7 per cent of all commercial enterprises large enough to pay first guild taxes were owned by persons who can clearly be identified as members of the local German community. Most of the rest were owned either by local Russian and Jewish merchants or by foreigners.[14] The

1891 list reveals much the same pattern. Germans owned 64.6 per cent of the first guild firms, Jews 18.1 per cent and Russians 5.5 per cent.[15] An examination of Chamber of Commerce data on Riga based export firms for the year 1900 yields similar results. Thirty-one of the thirty-seven firms that did more than a half million rubles in business during that year were German-owned.[16]

The wealthy upper layer of German merchants continued to prosper and to dominate the city's commercial life. It is impossible to be as precise concerning the fate of the German lower middle class of shopkeepers and white-collar commercial employees. The censuses group all persons engaged in commerce, from the greatest merchants to the most humble clerks, together under one rubric; but because the upper layer of affluent men was relatively small, the general statistics for commerce can serve as a rough measure of lower middle class fortunes. The Germans had never completely dominated petty trade. According to the 1867 census, only 53.6 per cent of those engaged in all kinds of commerce were German, while 29.3 per cent were Russian, 5.7 per cent Latvian and 11.1 per cent of other nationalities.[17] Shopkeeping and clerical work were occupations to which peasant and other lower class migrants to Riga could aspire. Latvians, for example, gradually came to dominate retail grocery sales, and a large proportion of retail clothing outlets were Jewish-owned by the end of the century.[18] The number of Germans employed in commerce declined in relation to other groups throughout the period. In 1881 they still made up 50.4 per cent of the total, but by 1897 their share had fallen to only 34.7 per cent. Conversely, the figure for Latvians rose from 18.9 per cent in 1881 to 25.2 per cent in 1897.[19] The decline, however, was relative, not absolute. There is no evidence that the German lower middle class, or *Kleinbürger,* fared worse materially. German shopkeepers did have to compete more and more with Latvians who were able to draw upon their co-nationals for easy credit and patronage. Nonetheless, the lower middle class in most European cities, Riga not excepted, tended in the main to profit from urbanization and improvements in transportation and communications. As the local population grew, so did the market for shopkeepers; and the expansion of large commercial firms, while putting some small merchants out of business, meant an increase in the number of available clerical positions.

The German elite was not content to be a passive beneficiary of the commercial prosperity brought by economic modernization. Riga German merchants participated actively in the development of local industry and in the improvement of transportation and communications. As early as the 1840's they began agitating in favour of railroad construction and the improvement of Riga's port facilities. In 1847 the Chamber of Commerce, backed by the merchant guild, proposed the construction of a railroad linking Riga with Warsaw and St. Petersburg via Dünaburg. In spite of energetic support from Governor-General Suvorov, official acceptance of the proposal was delayed first by the imperial government's lack of interest in railroad construction and then by the outbreak of the Crimean War. As soon as the war was over, however, the governor-general and the Chamber of Commerce campaigned with renewed vigour for permission to build the railroad, and finally met with success in the spring of 1858, when a group of Riga German merchants, among them Gustav Hernmarck, were permitted to form the Riga-Dünaburg Railroad Corporation. Approximately one-fifth of the 10.2 million ruble share capital was put up by the German merchants themselves, while the remainder was obtained from British investors attracted to the scheme by Hernmarck.[20] This pattern of railroad promotion and construction, in which the Riga German merchantry, joined in some cases by Baltic nobles, lobbied for government approval of new construction, supplied capital for the formation of railroad companies and acted as agents for the procurement of foreign investment in those companies, was repeated again and again as the railroad network linking Riga to its Russian hinterland grew with the passage of time. By the 1890's, when privately-owned railroads reached their greatest extent in the Riga area, at least ten of the twelve men who sat on the boards of the three principal railroad companies were members of the local German community.[21]

The role played by the Riga Germans in the modernization of transportation and communications was by no means limited to railroads. The Chamber of Commerce actively promoted and financed port construction; the Riga Steamship Corporation, serving Riga, St. Petersburg and other Baltic ports, was established by a group of local German merchants in 1858; and, at the suggestion of the Chamber of Commerce, the imperial government sanctioned the installation in 1852 of telegraph communications between Riga and the coastal town of Bolderaa at the mouth of the Dvina, the first such link in the entire empire.[22]

Riga German merchants and financiers also supplied a large portion of the investment capital, the entrepreneurial drive and the technical expertise which underlay the industrialization of their city. For generations prior to the boom of the late nineteenth century, local merchants had financed export and import commodity processing establishments—sawmills, tanneries, breweries, cigar factories and the like. As these industries expanded and flourished they remained largely under the control of local German interests. Of the twenty-three major sawmills extant in Riga at the turn of the century, at least thirteen were German-owned. Five belonged to local Jewish industrialists, and one each to a Pole, a Russian and a Latvian. The wood processing industry also included three paper mills—Bruhns & Company, the Riga Paper Corporation and Roeder & Knopp—and the Mercury Corporation, which manufactured wooden kegs. All four concerns were owned and managed by members of the local German community.[23] A similar pattern can be discerned in the tobacco, food processing, leather, glass and porcelain industries. By 1900 Riga was home to eight large tobacco and cigar factories, most of which antedated the industrial boom. Among them were A. Bergwitz, established in 1875 by a group of local Germans as Gley & Company and acquired by Friedrich August Bergwitz, another local German, in 1878; F. Kross, founded before 1860 by the German commercial firm of Mey Brothers and taken over by the Riga German entrepreneur Ferdinand Kross during the 1880's; Mündel & Company, founded and still owned by the prominent German Mündel family; A.G. Ruhtenberg, established as early as 1839 and owned by the Ruhtenbergs, another Riga patrician family; Leo Wissor, also owned by Riga German interests; I.V. Gusev and Popov Brothers, both the property of Russian industrialists; and A.S. Maikapar, owned and established by the Jewish entrepreneur Abram Samailov Maikapar.[24] A great many small enterprises were engaged in various kinds of food and beverage processing; and it is impossible to trace the ownership of most of them. The larger firms, whose owners can be identified, included ten breweries, four distilleries, two mineral water bottling plants, three candy and syrup factories, a starch factory and a chicory factory. All of them were owned by Riga Germans with the exception of one brewery, property of the Latvian merchant A. Grünupp, and one of the candy factories, owned by a *Reich*-German.[25] The local glass, chinaware, porcelain and ceramic tile industry was represented by six major producers. The huge Kuznetsov porcelain and chinaware factory belonged to a local Russian Old Believer family, but the other five were owned by Riga German merchants.[26] Finally, of the eight factories and tanneries comprising the leather goods industry, seven were German-owned and one belonged to a Russian merchant.[27] Family or individual factory ownership, as opposed to the joint-stock corporation, was predominant in light industry; and, of the three hundred nineteen manufacturing firms in Riga which were not joint-stock corporations by 1913, two hundred forty-eight were owned by local Germans.[28]

The pattern of family ownership characteristic of light industry was not matched in the developing heavy industrial complex. The production of railroad locomotives, steam turbines, ship engines and other heavy equipment involved costs that were well beyond the means of even the wealthiest merchant families. The new industries required, therefore, fresh sources of capital and new forms of investment. One way of meeting this need was to encourage and solicit foreign participation in local industry. Foreign capital and technical expertise played a major role in Russian industrialization; and Riga was one of several Russian industrial centres which benefited substantially from the foreign presence. The city was, indeed, particularly attractive to foreign investors. As a port, Riga made a natural centre for heavy industries dependent on the availability of imported raw materials and plant equipment. It was far more profitable for foreign companies to build railroad locomotives or marine engines using British- or German-made machinery in Riga than to locate plant facilities deeper in the Russian interior. Foreign companies seeking to set up operations in the Russian Empire also often encountered difficulties arising from the insufficient supply of native technical and managerial personnel. Western European specialists could be, and often were, brought to Russia; but the extensive use of foreign experts presented certain drawbacks. It was expensive, because it took high salaries to lure westerners to Russia; and it was inefficient, because foreign executives often had no idea of how to deal effectively with the local Russian authorities. This problem was far less serious in Riga than in most other Russian industrial centres. There a pool of local managerial and technical personnel, comprised largely of Germans educated at the Baltic Polytechnical Institute, was available. It is also apparent that foreign investors believed the Riga factory labour force to be better trained, more dependable and more disciplined than that which they encountered in European Russia. A study of the Riga railroad car industry released in 1898 by the French banking house Crédit Lyonnais contended that the local labour force of Latvian workers and German foremen was, "vastly superior to its Russian counterpart in both skill and perseverance."[29] Similarly, the German consul in Riga reported to his superiors that, "Most of those who work in the textile industry here are Latvians, who have a reputation for being diligent and hardworking, and who have acquired a far from insignificant education in their community and church schools."[30] The Latvians who made up the bulk of the Riga factory labour force were, unlike Russian workers, on the whole literate, not prone to seasonal migration and, as Protestants, not accustomed to missing considerable numbers of workdays to celebrate religious holidays.

Foreign investment in Riga tended in the main to be concentrated in the machine fabrication, metallurgical, chemical and textile industries. In some cases individual investors or investment groups would buy shares in Riga-based corporations. In other cases western European firms would simply establish affiliates in Riga. Foreign entrepreneurs like Charles Baird in St. Petersburg or John Hughes in the Ukraine, who perceived investment opportunities in Russia, promoted them in their home countries to attract financial backing and then founded their own companies in Russia, were not a major factor on the Riga scene. Investment opportunities of that sort were usually exploited by the local Germans.

An important early example of foreign investment came in response to the demand for railroad rolling stock. During the 1860's the local railroad companies operated with British-made locomotives and cars; but in 1869 the Riga-Dünaburg company awarded a contract for several hundred freight cars to Van den Zypen & Charlier of Cologne-Deutz in the then Prussian Rhineland. The German company saw a golden opportunity open before it. By establishing an affiliate in Riga it could meet the demand there for rolling stock at prices much lower than the foreign competition could offer. In 1874 the Russo-Baltic Wagon Corporation began operation in Riga as an affiliate of Van den Zypen & Charlier with share capital provided exclusively by investors in Germany.[31] Foreign, principally *Reich*-German, involvement in the Riga metallurgical and machine fabrication industry grew progressively more important as Russian tariffs on imported metal wares and machinery became higher and higher. The Russo-Baltic Wagon Corporation was joined by other *Reich*-German affiliates. The Westphalian Wire Industry of Hamm established the Riga Wire Industry, producing wire and nails, as early as 1873; Herminghaus & Voorman set up the Riga Lock Factory as an affiliate venture in 1886; and Klein Brothers of Dalbruch opened a Riga affiliate in 1896 that manufactured pumps, cranes, machine components, engines and other industrial equipment. In other cases, Riga German entrepreneurs promoted schemes that were financed partially by investors in Germany. This pattern was especially common in the tool-making industry. The Sönnecken Saw and File Factory, established in 1879, and the Riga Knife Factory and the Erbe Saw and File Company, both founded in 1887, stand as examples of this.[32] There was also a British presence in the machine fabrication and metallurgical industry. Thomas Firth & Sons, a British investment firm, collaborated with Riga German merchant Ferdinand Meyer to finance the Russo-Baltic File Factory and, after 1900, held a controlling interest in the Salamander Iron Foundry.[33]

Foreign participation also figured prominently in the growth of the Riga chemical and rubberware industry. Provodnik Corporation, a major rubberware and linoleum manufacturer, was established in 1888 with capital largely supplied by French investors; F. Mühlen, a producer of soap and perfume, was affiliated to a Cologne firm; and the Glover Chemical Corporation, which manufactured chemicals for industrial use, drew most of its share capital from Sweden.[34]

The textile industry, which suffered a serious decline in the 1870's and 1880's, was revived during the 1890's by an influx of foreign, mostly British, capital. Some firms founded in the middle of the nineteenth century by local Germans were taken over and reorganized by foreign interests. This was true for the Baltic Linen Manufacturing Corporation, whose share capital was two-thirds *Reich*-German by the turn of the century, Holm & Company (woollen textiles), reorganized in 1900 by *Reich*-German investors, and the Riga Cotton Manufacturing Corporation in Strasdenhof, established in the 1840's by local merchant T. Pychlau and acquired in 1890 by a British investment group which reorganized it as a joint-stock company whose share capital was 67 per cent British, 28 per cent *Reich*-German and 5 per cent local. Foreign investors, sometimes in co-operation with the local Germans, also established new textile concerns, among them the Ilgezeem Woollenware Corporation (British, 1881), the Sassenhof Cotton Spinning and Weaving Corporation (British, 1895) and Textil (British and local German, 1897).[35]

Foreign involvement in other branches of local industry was limited, the only important cases being the Kriegsmann Corporation, a producer of railroad refrigerator car linings established in 1865 by Magistrate A. Kriegsmann but reorganized by Swedish investors in 1895, Sellier & Bellot, an affiliate of an Austrian percussion cap and cartridge manufacturing firm, and the Union Corporation, Riga's only manufacturer of electro-technical equipment. The latter was founded in 1885 by Heinrich Dettman, a local optician with *Reich*-German citizenship, but was restructured in 1898 as a joint-stock affiliate of the Berlin-based Siemens Corporation.[36]

The importance of foreign participation notwithstanding, the role of local German capital and entrepreneurship in heavy industry should not be underestimated. Many Riga Germans invested personal savings in corporate shares, and German-owned commercial firms channeled considerable sums into industry of all kinds.[37] The late nineteenth century also witnesed the development of a local banking system. The three major banks in the city, the Riga Municipal Bank, the Riga Chamber of Commerce Bank and the Riga Bank of Commerce, were founded and managed by Riga Germans. The banks, by granting credit to local entrepreneurs and by investing their resources directly in industrial enterprises, helped to funnel Riga German capital into heavy industry.[38] The clearest evidence of the important role played by local capital lies in the fact that of the forty-eight major joint-stock industrial corporations based in Riga by 1913, twenty-eight were controlled by domestic, chiefly Riga German, interests.[39]

A not inconsiderable number of Riga's machine building and metallurgical plants were established and financed by the local German community without substantial outside involvement. This was true for the Mantel Machine Building Corporation, the Motor Corporation, Pirwitz & Company, the Pohle Machine Corporation, Rosenkranz & Company, the Sirius Corporation and the Stella Corporation, all of which manufactured machinery and industrial equipment; the Aetna Corporation and Starr & Company, both producers of wire and nails; the Atlas Corporation, Komet, the Riga Rolling Mill and the Riga Steel Corporation, all producing tools and cast iron goods; the shipyards of Lange & Son and the Bolderaa Machine Factory; Ressort, which manufactured springs for railroad cars; and Leutner & Company, a maker of bicycles and, after 1900, of automobiles.[40] Riga German participation in the chemical industry was also quite extensive. In some cases small chemical factories established by local merchants long before the industrial boom prospered and grew into major manufacturers. The most noteworthy examples of this development were the soap and candle manufacturing firms of H. A. Brieger and C. Kirstein; the J.C. Koch varnish factory; G. Thalheim, a petroleum refinery; the Vulkan match factory; and J.W. Mündel, which manufactured rubber goods. Still other chemical firms were established by Riga German entrepreneurs as industrialization provided new market opportunities and fresh sources of raw materials. Among the major chemical producers financed by local Germans were Fockenhof, Agthe, Frey & Company, founded in 1899; the Ruhtenberg Company, established in 1889 by the tobacco merchant and industrialist A.G. Ruhtenberg*; the Russo-Baltic Lacquer Factory, owned by W. Hjort; and the Mühlgraben Chemical Corporation, established in 1892 by engineer Max Höflinger as the first producer of super-phosphate fertilizers in the Russian Empire.[41]

Foreign presence in a given firm did not, of course, preclude significant Riga German involvement in it as well. It was not uncommon for local German investors and entrepreneurs, often working in conjunction with the Riga banks, to share control of companies with foreign interests; and in many firms there was a tendency for foreign participation to decrease with the passage of time. The Russo-Baltic Wagon

---

*Ruhtenberg also owned a cigar-making factory.

Corporation, for example, was originally financed entirely with *Reich*-German capital; but in 1894 Russo-Baltic stock was sold on the Riga exchange with the result that by the turn of the century the bulk of its share capital was held by investors in Riga—among them several prominent German merchants and the Riga Bank of Commerce—and St. Petersburg.[42] A similar process unfolded in the Phoenix Corporation, a rival manufacturer of railroad rolling stock founded in 1894 with capital supplied by *Reich*-German investors, St. Petersburg banks and Riga German interests, chief among them the Riga Bank of Commerce. By 1900 the amount of Phoenix stock in *Reich*-German hands fell from its original figure of thirty per cent to eighteen.[43]

A major feature of the Riga German contribution to industrialization was the provision of technical and managerial expertise. This was made possible largely by the Baltic Polytechnical Institute, which produced thousands of trained engineers, accountants, business administrators, architects and applied scientists. The institute was highly regarded throughout the empire, and its graduates included many Russians, Poles, Jews, Latvians and Estonians; but Germans from Riga and elsewhere in the Baltic provinces were always a large element in the student body, German graduates of the institute were very prominent in local industry, commerce and banking. In some establishments, these men totally dominated the technical and managerial staff. Among the twenty-one senior technical employees of the French-controlled rubberware manufacturer Provodnik at the turn of the century, fifteen were German alumni of the Baltic Polytechnical Institute.[44] Such a high degree of involvement by local people in the technical side of industry was uncommon in Russian cities.

The moneyed, educated upper layers of Riga German society unquestionably benefited from the growth and transformation of their city's economy. The same can be said for the great majority of the German lower middle class. Few Germans belonged to the poorer classes; but many of them did engage in skilled artisan work. Census statistics show that the Riga artisan class in 1867 was 64.4 per cent German, 16.8 per cent Russian and 7.1 per cent Latvian, while other nationalities together comprised 11.7 per cent. By 1881 the Germans ("customary language") were still in the majority with 52.5 per cent, whereas Russians accounted for 12.4 per cent, Latvians for 16.6 per cent, Jews for 15.9 per cent and others for 2.6 per cent.[46] What is more, nearly all master craftsmen were Germans, while non-German artisans tended to be concentrated in less lucrative, and often less skilled, trades.

Evidence concerning the fate of the artisan class during the industrialization of the late nineteenth century is lamentably scarce. Only the 1881 census gives a breakdown of the artisan class by trade. The survey of local trade and handicraft production taken by the city statistical commission in 1884 is useful in some ways, but is too close chronologically to the 1881 census to be of any help in gauging the long-term impact of industrialization and demographic change on the artisans. Guild membership lists are available, but as fewer and fewer artisans joined the guild after the repeal of the *Zunftzwang* they do not tell the whole story.

TABLE 2

GERMAN GRADUATES OF THE BALTIC POLYTECHNICAL INSTITUTE, 1865-1900

This table is based on a survey of the careers of 440 men who graduated from the Baltic Polytechnical Institute during the period 1865-1900. This group includes all graduates in fields other than agronomy who can be identified as ethnic Germans by means of their membership in any one of the three German fraternities. Since many German students did not join fraternities, this group excludes many German graduates, whose numbers were well in excess of 440.

Occupation	Geographical Distribution			
	In Riga	Elsewhere in the Baltic	Elsewhere in the Russian Empire	Abroad
Wood Processing Industry	13	7	8	4
Machine Fabrication/ Metallury	40	9	41	9
Glass, Porcelain and Chinaware Industry	1	1	2	1
Textile Industry	7	4	15	3
Food Processing Industry	6	7	16	2
Cement and Brick Industry	5	2	11	0
Chemical Industry	23	4	25	3
Tobacco Processing Industry	1	0	0	0
Petroleum Industry	0	0	3	0
Electro-Technical Industry	1	0	4	1
Railroads	41	19	33	3
Construction	24	11	9	7
Mining	0	0	0	2
Education/Journalism	19	9	13	2
Municipal Government	26	6	2	0
Civil Service/Military	6	7	13	0
Banking	20	7	8	0
Commerce	36	6	31	4
Other	5	6	30	13
Total[45]	284	105	264	54

In spite of this paucity of evidence, it is possible to assess the impact of social and economic change on the German artisans in general terms. That the impact was in part a negative one is undeniable. The members of the artisan guild, an almost exclusively German group which represented the more affluent segment of the local artisan class, had been able for centuries to rest secure in their undisputed control of nearly all skilled crafts in Riga. The 1866 repeal of the *Zunftzwang* forced the German artisans to compete with an influx of new craftsmen, many of them Latvians from rural villages, who were content to charge lower prices for their services than the guild would have permitted, and who, like the Latvian shopkeepers, could find a ready clientèle among the city's growing Latvian population. The growth of factories capable of manufacturing certain goods cheaply and in great quantity could be ruinous for artisans dependent on traditional manufacturing techniques. Blacksmiths, locksmiths, tanners, potters and some others were particularly hard hit in this way. Still other crafts were rendered obsolete by technological progress. Rope-makers, for example, fell on hard times when steamships replaced sailing vessels. After 1879 not a single new master rope-maker applied for admission to the artisan guild.[47]

For most Riga German artisans, however, industrialization and urbanization were economically beneficial. The demand for many varieties of skilled labour and craftsmanship increased. This was most certainly true for the construction trades. The tripling of the city's population within the space of three decades generated a construction boom in housing, and industrial development necessitated considerable factory construction and renovation. The total number of buildings in Riga jumped from 5,808 in 1864 to 22,330 by 1900.[48] The employment situation for masons, painters, carpenters, glaziers and plumbers was consequently quite good. Urban population growth also worked to the advantage of those artisans who provided goods and services which industry could not supply, or which, if factory-made, were of a quality unacceptable to consumers who could afford luxury items. Bakers, barbers, butchers, confectioners and chimney-sweeps had little to fear from industrializaiton and everything to gain from the wider local market. For others like hatters, cobblers, glovers, jewellers, carriage-makers and cabinet-makers, the growing market for luxuries was highly lucrative. German artisans in particular profited from the luxury trade. Their shops were better equipped, as a rule, to produce high quality wares, and guild membership, for which many German artisans continued to opt long after the end of the *Zunftzwang,* was considered a hallmark of excellence. Even for those artisans who were faced with direct factory competition, the picture was not entirely bleak. Factories hired considerable numbers of artisans as skilled workmen and fore-men. In 1884 the Russo-Baltic Wagon Corporation alone employed 132 *zünftig* artisans, mostly blacksmiths and tool-makers.[49] Some master craftsmen even managed to expand their shops into small factories. Master blacksmith G. Ostwald established an iron foundry employing forty-five workers in 1888, master carpenters J.H. Lucht and C. Steinert both owned and managed sawmills, and master glover A. Wunsch successfully transformed his shop into a glove factory.[50]

The Riga German minority, with relatively few exceptions, benefited from the industrialization of their city. This circumstance played a decisive role in shaping the German reaction to the imperial govern-ment's policies. Industrialization and its attendant commercial boom were possible for Riga only because the city was a Russian port. Riga and its immediate surrounding area possessed very little in the way of natural resources which could supply the needs of industry or serve as commercial commodities. The city was viable as a commercial and industrial centre only because of the availability of raw materials from the Russian interior. Riga German merchants exported Russian timber, flax and agricultural produce; and Riga industry was based on the processing of Russian raw materials for export and of import commodi-ties for sale on the Russian market. It was hardly a coincidence that the industrialization of Riga began in earnest only with the construction of a railroad network linking the city to its Russian hinterland.

The late nineteenth century also witnessed a growing financial inter-dependence between Riga German and Russian banks and industry. Russian capital, much of it supplied by the St. Petersburg banks, played a significant role in Riga industry during the 1890's and 1900's. Russian investment figured prominently in the Union Corporation, Lange & Son, the Phoenix Corporation, the Russo-Baltic Wagon Corporation, the Hübner Manufacturing Corporation (cotton textiles), the Hart-mann Oil Refinery, K.C. Schmidt (cement, petroleum products) and Provodnik.[51] The Riga banks, controlled by local German interests, began to invest heavily in European Russia and Russian Poland at about the same time. All three Riga banks were important share holders in joint-stock St. Petersburg banks; and the Riga Bank of Commerce invested large sums in the Russian machine building and metallurgical industry.[52]

Russian industrialization was in large part stimulated and sponsored by the imperial government. Accordingly, that government pursued policies which directly encouraged the development of industry in Riga. The progressive raising of import duties during the 1880's, culminating in the almost prohibitive tariff of 1891, fostered the growth of heavy industry in Riga, as foreign manufacturers began to establish affiliates within the Russian Empire rather than be driven from the market. More direct government assistance came in the form of subsidies, loans and even occasional suspension of import duties on plant machinery.[53] Government contracts could be lucrative sources of income for Riga industry. In 1897–1898 alone, for example, the Russo-Baltic Wagon Corporation supplied more than five thousand railroad cars to the state-owned railroad system; and the shipyard of Lange & Son was a frequent recipient of Admiralty contracts for warships.[54] Paradoxically, the same government whose Russification programmes so discomfited the Riga Germans followed economic policies which were materially beneficial to that minority.

The Riga Germans were very much aware of their dependency on Russian markets and raw materials, and, notwithstanding the aggravation caused by Russification and by violations of the *Rechtsstaat*, were appreciative of the imperial government's commitment to industrialization. In 1900, for example, the *Rigaer Tageblatt** published a lengthy article glowing with praise for Finance Minister Sergei Witte's industrial development strategy, citing his protectionist trade policies and his efforts to stabilize the ruble as particularly laudable achievements.[55] An industrial exhibition held in 1901 in conjunction with Riga's seven hundredth anniversary jubilee provided an occasion for Riga Germans to profess publicly their support for government economic policy. In a speech on the opening day of the exhibit, Karl Lovis, a professor at the Baltic Polytechnic Institute and a founder and director of the machine fabrication firm of Felser & Company, emphasized that Riga owed its prosperity to its attachment to the empire, for, "Riga and its surrounding area form the natural western border of the Russian Empire on the Baltic."[56] In its coverage of the exhibition, the *Rigasche Rundschau* placed a particular stress on the role of the Russian government in promoting the city's industrial and commercial growth:

> The development of a country's industry is unquestionably dependent upon measures and laws enacted by the government. This is something which recent history has fully confirmed. One has only to think of the systematically enacted protective tariff system, the trade treaties, the currency reform, the laws facilitating the formation of joint-stock corporations . . . and a whole series of other, lesser government measures.[57]

In light of the prevailing economic conditions, it was unlikely that any form of German nationalism that encouraged anti-government

---

*In 1882 the *Neue Zeitung für Stadt und Land* had become the *Rigaer Tageblatt*.

politics in the name of national solidarity, let alone separatism or disloyalty to the empire, would have much of a constituency in Riga. There was certainly no need for the great majority of Riga Germans to retreat into a defensive national shell, as some of the literati advocated. On the contrary, the strengthening of the economic bonds between the Riga German community and the Russian interior served to reinforce traditional German loyalty to the empire. The only important segment of Riga German society whose material position deteriorated during this period comprised the literati, and it was precisely to this group that a variety of German nationalism finally did appeal. Literati campaigns in defense first of constitutional tradition and later of national interests did not evoke much response from the remainder of the Riga German community, and this led to a sense of isolation and frustration among the literati. Julius Eckardt captured this feeling when he wrote in his memoirs that, "The most important new railroads led toward the east—the awakening Baltic industry found its markets in the east— from the east came throngs of new men, who sought employment and profit in the developing borderland. Our export trade was always oriented toward the procurement of Polish and west Russian raw materials. Now the transport of goods from Riga into the empire began to play a leading role and to create hundreds of new bonds between the Baltic and the Russian business world. We live in a time of constantly increasing dominance of material interests, which enfeebles the feeling for life's ideals."[58] Eckardt, of course, was not a German nationalist. By "life's ideals" he meant defence of legal and constitutional principles; but his disdain for the political side effects of industrialization was shared by the nationalists of a later generation. It is noteworthy that, while the *Rigaer Tageblatt* and the *Rigasche Rundschau/Zeitung für Stadt und Land* frequently published articles proudly describing the march of material progress in Riga, the nationalist *Düna-Zeitung* was very restrained in its coverage of the subject.

In short, the transformation of the Riga economy which marked the late nineteenth century had significant political connotations for the local German minority. The material advantage reaped from industrialization by nearly all levels of Riga German society does much to explain their rejection of political nationalism.

Chapter 6

FROM CONFRONTATION TO COMPROMISE
1890–1905

The social changes attendant upon industrialization had important effects upon nationality relationships within Riga. Municipal elections continued to serve as the principal forum for political rivalry among the major national groups, although a municipal reform implemented by the imperial government in all Baltic and Russian cities in 1892 severely restricted the franchise.* The special provision allowing literati to vote in the Baltic cities was dropped, Jews were entirely disenfranchised, and, although the three-class electoral system was abandoned, the property qualification for the franchise was raised considerably. Three elections were held under the terms of the 1892 reform statute before the Revolution of 1905—in 1893, 1897 and 1901. As in earlier elections, conservative and avowedly anti-nationalist election committees representing the interests of the German elite nominated candidates to compete with slates offered by nationalist Latvian and Russian committees.

At first glance it might appear that Latvian chances of victory were better than they had been during the 1880's. The Latvian middle class did grow in size, wealth and political sophistication with the passage of time; but the Latvians were still faced with virtually insurmountable handicaps. By the beginning of the 1890's the Latvian national movement had begun to fragment, as a serious split developed between the established leadership in the Latvian Union and a group of younger left-wing activists known collectively as the "new current". The latter, much influenced by *Reich*-German Social Democracy, accused the Latvian Union of ignoring the interests of the Latvian working class in favour of more upwardly mobile Latvians.[1] Adherents of the "new current" played a role in a violent general strike in Riga during the spring of 1899; and after the turn of the century they began to form coherent political organizations. In 1902 a radical group broke away from the Latvian Union to form the rival Riga Latvian Association,

*See below, pp.94–5.

which blended nationalism with socialism after the manner of the Polish PPS; and in 1904 a clandestine congress held in Riga witnessed the establishment of the Latvian Social Democratic Workers' Party, a Marxist organization which represented itself as proletarian internationalist, rejecting nationalism as bourgeois.[2]

The Latvian Union was able to retain the upper hand in the Latvian election committees, whose chief goal of proportional national representation in the duma remained unchanged; but the challenge from the left did divide Latvian strength and divert somewhat the attention of the leadership from the contest against the Germans. Even more importantly, the new restrictions on the franchise accrued to the benefit of the wealthier Germans, while costing the Latvians votes. As before, the conservative German committees were able to elect all of their chosen candidates to the duma.[3]

The Russian national party in Riga, at least during the 1890's, also maintained its accustomed approach to municipal elections. The campaigns of 1893 and 1897 saw the usual formation of Russian-Latvian alliances for the purpose of gaining national representation in the duma. The local Russian nationalists, moreover, had a long-standing connection to those circles in the imperial government most disposed to fear and suspect the Riga Germans as a disloyal, subversive element. To cite one evidence of this, the local nationalist newspaper, *Rizhskii vestnik,* was subsidized by the central government.[4] The aim of the Russian nationalists in Riga was not, consequently, to serve their own local interests only, but also to act as defenders of what they perceived to be imperial interests against a traitorous minority. An 1891 *Rizhskii vestnik* editorial exhorted Riga's Russians to be on their guard against the "absurd dreams of separatism" harboured by the German comunity;[5] and in 1900 the Russian newspaper argued, in much the same way as Governor Zinoviev ten years earlier, that the interests of state security demanded restrictions on German participation in local government.[6]

In 1901, however, a striking realignment of political forces took place. As in the past, the Latvian election committee nominated a slate of candidates pledged to act as Latvian national representatives; but the Latvian-Russian alliance collapsed. The Russian election committee executed a complete about-face and cast its lot with the conservative Germans. Under the terms of the new alliance, the conservative slate included ten candidates selected by its Russian ally. The pact with the Germans attracted broad support within the Russian community, and even the normally anti-German *Rizhskii vestnik* endorsed the combined slate without reservation.[7]

There were a number of compelling reasons behind this radical and sudden shift in Russian political orientation. The alliance with the Latvians had been troubled for more than a decade. From the very inception of the Latvian nationalist movement its leaders had looked to the imperial government and to Russian nationalists both in Riga and in St. Petersburg and Moscow for help in their struggle against the Germans. Russian and Latvian nationalists shared the desire to weaken the German position in Riga. The ultimate goal of the Russian nationalists, however, was the Russification of the region, not the replacement of the German elite with Latvians. The Latvian nationalists made useful temporary allies, but their programme was not something that their Russian counterparts could take seriously. The Russian national party had even less respect for the idea of Latvian nationhood than did the local Germans. The *Rizhskii vestnik* scoffed at Latvian pretensions to cultural independence, labeling them "dreams" in an 1891 editorial, and ten years later cautioning Latvian nationalists that they would have to accept the inevitable "fusion" of the Latvian population with the Russians.[8] As the Latvians came to realize the true nature of Russian nationalist intentions, and as it began to dawn upon them that government Russification programmes were just as harmful to Latvian cultural aspirations as they were to the Germans, an ever widening gap yawned between the Latvian and Russian nationalist camps in Riga.

To ideological incompatibility must be added a belated Russian recognition that alliances with the Latvians had little chance of success. A pact with the wealthier Germans was eminently more pragmatic. It also appears that the Russian-German alliance was at least in part produced by a gradual shift in the imperial government's attitude toward the Baltic Germans, a change which first began to make itself felt in the mid-1890's. The imperial government, aware of the urgent need for economic modernization but fearful of the social disruption which that process was bound to cause, had begun to realize its community of interests with the conservative Germans, who were natural allies in any effort to maintain social stability and public order.* The growth of the radical "new current", on the other hand, cast doubts on the wisdom of continued government co-operation with the Latvians. The ties between the imperial government and the Riga Russian leadership were such that this broad policy change found one of its chief manifestations in the formation of a Russian-German electoral alliance destined to endure until the outbreak of the First World War.

The German approach to municipal politics was, of course, closely

---

*See below, pp. 93–104.

related to their perception of the nationality question, and this perception had begun to alter. Social, demographic and economic change forced growing numbers of Germans to re-evaluate their time-honoured assumptions concerning nationality relationships. The emergence of a self-consciously Latvian middle class clearly contravened the German image of the Latvians as a group of lower social classes rather than a genuine nationality. At the same time, the attacks on the Germans themselves as a national group by the imperial government as well as by local Russian and Latvian nationalists could only serve to make the Germans more conscious of their own national identity. A few Germans did turn to a form of German nationalism during this period; but mainstream German public opinion still did not share the nationalists' appraisal of the Germans and Latvians as fully separate, competitive national groups or their advocacy of national solidarity as a political panacea. The picture which emerges from the commentary of the German press and from the behaviour of the German political leadership is one that bespeaks confusion and uncertainty over the nationality question. The nationalism exhibited by the *Düna-Zeitung* found no echo in either the *Rigaer Tageblatt* or the *Rigasche Rundschau,* both of which had difficulty reconciling new realities with long-established beliefs and values.

A *Rigasche Rundschau* editorial pronounced in 1902 that, "By 'nation' we understand the natural community of men who possess a consciousness of community because they have been forged into a unified entity by habitation of a common geographical region, common ancestry, customs and language."[9] This is a very standard definition of nationality to which few genuine nationalists, German, Latvian or Russian, would have objected. Indeed it differs very little from the definition offered by the Latvian nationalist newspaper *Baltijas vestnesis* in 1887, which declared that, "by 'nation' is signified the community of men whose spiritual characteristics, customs, traditions and especially language is the same, and who have inherited from their forefathers the spiritual wealth which attests to the uniqueness of the community."[10] The *Rigasche Rundschau* also cautioned Germans against cultural snobbery *vis-a-vis* the Latvians, contending that, "We must cease to entertain the foolish notion that the educated Latvian is by definition a raw *parvenu* and that his language is an inferior idiom."[11] It would appear that the *Rigasche Rundschau* had come to recognize language and ethnicity as determinants of nationality, and that it was prepared to accept the Latvians as a distinct and separate nation which should be respected as such by the German community.

The *Rigasche Rundschau,* however, was far from consistent in its appraisal of the nationality question. Old ways of thinking die hard. In spite of its apparent recognition of Latvian nationhood, it persisted in labeling the Latvian national movement as a social, rather than a genuinely national, phenomenon. A 1902 article flatly stated that the troubled relationship between Latvians and Germans in Riga was a confrontation between different social classes rather than a national rivalry:

> We have often repeated and stressed on the most different of occasions that now, just as twenty years ago, the relations between our German population and the 'Latvians' is essentially and fundamentally social and not national.[12]

Characteristic of the *Rigasche Rundschau's* uncertain and often contradictory approach to the nationality question was an analysis of the differences between the Baltic Germans and their Latvian neighbours printed in the summer of 1902: "One says so easily that nationality leaves its special imprint upon people, that it is the decisive way to differentiate among them. This would be a conclusive argument if the Latvian national character were really at variance with that of the Baltic Germans. But the Baltic German is no longer the same as the *Reich-German* . . . Over the centuries the Baltic air and soil, as well as Baltic history, have made him what he is. The same factors have shaped the Latvian national character. Many Germans have become Latvians and many Lativans have become Germans . . . Baltic Germans become accustomed to life in Germany with difficulty, because they have been raised on the same soil which has given the Latvians their national character."[13] This passage, for all its vague and tortuous language, is illustrative of the quandary in which many Germans found themselves regarding nationality. The *Rigasche Rundschau* was willing in theory to concede that Germans and Latvians co-existed in Riga as two distinct nationalities, but it found it impossible to translate this theory into either a recognition of the Latvian national movement as anything other than an attempt to incite social unrest among the urban lower classes or a complete acceptance of language and ethnicity as the primary determinants of collective identity.

The *Rigaer Tageblatt* was equally vexed by the city's changing national complexion. Its assessment of linguistic and ethnic nationality did not differ substantially from that presented by the rival *Rigasche Rundschau:*

> Although an individual does not speak the German language with his family or in his everyday life, he still might often refer to himself as German and be recognized as such by others only because his parents were German. Just as often, an individual who constantly speaks German at home and in his

everyday life will refer to himself as Latvian and be perceived by others as such . . . Here the family tree has no meaning in determining nationality. Nationality is not inherited but self-acquired.[14]

In other words, Germans and Latvians represented nationalities which were separate but interchangeable according to personal choice and social circumstances. This argument was an attempt to reconcile the earlier German concept of a supranational Baltic community within which language was a mark of social class with the nationalist contention that Latvians and Germans existed as two fully distinct nationalities.

Although the German perception of the nationality question began, albeit hesitantly, to move away from the old certainties, the Germans persisted in their conscious rejection of nationality as a political principle and continued to view the electoral contests against the Latvians and their sometime Russian allies as a struggle between the ruling classes and the lower social orders rather than as a competition among the Germans, Latvians and Russians as national groups. German political behaviour was still inspired by a social conservatism that opposed the admission of lower class representatives to the municipal duma. Hence their conservative election committees strove, as before, to maintain governmental "continuity"—that is, to secure control of the duma for the wealthy, largely German upper classes. As the *Rigasche Rundschau* argued in its endorsement of the 1901 conservative slate, "Continuity can only suffer from the sudden mass influx of new elements," because, "The aspirations of the lower social elements to gain political power would mean a democratization of governmental principles for which conditions here are still far from ripe."[15]

To the German political leadership the Latvian national party was merely a collection of radical firebrands who stood for the interests of the broad masses. In its *post-mortem* analysis of the 1901 election, the *Rigasche Rundschau* described Latvian demands for national representation in the duma as nothing more than the advocacy of "an admission to political power of those layers of society which up until the present have been denied it."[16] The Germans believed the Latvian nationalists to be guilty of consciously using a fraudulent national ideology to cloak what was actually a form of social radicalism. Perhaps not surprisingly, the Germans were utterly incapable of distinguishing between the socially moderate Latvian Union, which represented the Latvian middle class, and the genuinely radical politicians associated with the "new current". This confusion led to a serious miscalculation, which sheds further light on the German attitude toward political nationalism. Blinded by the misconception that all Latvian nationalism was merely disguised social radicalism, the German leaders actually found the "new current" radicals more palatable than their middle class rivals in the Latvian Union. The reason for this astounding judgement lay in the frequent criticism leveled by the radicals at the Latvian Union for its excessive interest in "nationalist trivia."[17] In the eyes of the radicals this just diverted attention from the material plight of the working class; but strict censorship prevented the radicals from articulating their views openly, and the Germans were deceived into thinking that the radical attack on the moderate Latvian preoccupation with national issues was somehow an attack on the "radicalism" of the Latvian Union. Accordingly, among the Latvians included on the conservative slates in the 1893, 1897 and 1901 elections were several representatives of the "new current."[18]

For their own part, the conservative leaders were careful to deny any national purpose. Questions of nationality, said the *Rigasche Rundschau,* were not the business of municipal government: "Aside from the subsidies granted to the three national theatres, we know of no aspect of municipal government in which the special interests of Germans, Latvians, Russians, Poles, etc. can be identified. The institutions of municipal administration are a-national and the educational system is Russian."[19] Thus in municipal elections, "a grouping of voters by nationality is not right, because the decisive factor should be common interests and requirements."[20] The conservative election committees echoed this sentiment, never tiring of insisting that their candidates "represent only the interests of the city, and not those of any territorial, religious or national group."[21]

The nationalist *Düna-Zeitung,* of course, argued in favour of German national solidarity as an electoral strategy; but its efforts to politicize the nationality question were sternly rebuffed by the rest of the German-language press and by the German political leadership. Both the *Rigasche Rundschau* and the *Rigaer Tageblatt* chastised the *Düna-Zeitung* for adopting what they felt to be the unhealthy attitude of the Latvians;[22] and the *Baltische Monatschrift* printed a point-by-point rebuttal of Seraphim's proposals for a nationalist electoral programme.[23]

The behaviour of the German elite which governed Riga was consistent with its anti-nationalist rhetoric. The conservative election committees continued to nominate some non-German candidates, claiming that ideological compatibility, rather than nationality, was the only criterion for candidacy. It is impossible to be absolutely certain of the nationality of every conservative candidate after 1893, but among the ninety-six elected in that year were at least two Latvians and four Russians. The 1897 slate included a minimum of three Latvians and three Russians; and the combined Russian-German slate of 1901 numbered among its successful candidates at least ten Latvians, eight Russians and one Pole.[24] Viewed from the German perspective, the electoral alliance with the Russians was not so much a pact between two nationalities directed against a third as an effort at co-operation within the upper layer of local society to defeat the "radical" Latvians. There had, after all, always been a small admixture of wealthy Russians in the predominantly German social elite.

In the duma, the Germans claimed their continued willingness to subsidize Russian and Latvian cultural life as proof of their determination to govern in the interest of all, and not as representatives only of the German population. This policy was also serviceable as a device for securing the co-operation and allegiance of the more affluent and presumably more conservative portion of Latvian and Russian society. Whatever the reason, the German-controlled duma was relatively generous in this regard. The annual subsidies granted to the Latvian and Russian theatres since the mid-1880's were substantially increased during the 1890's and 1900's; and in 1897 the duma voted unanimously to build a Russian theatre at a cost to the city of nearly 350,000 rubles.[25] The Latvians were beneficiaries of an 1899 grant of city land on which to build a trade school and an ethnographical museum; and the 1903 city budget provided a subsidy for a second Latvian theatre.[26]

The Riga Germans' dogged adherence to the essentials of their traditional approach to the nationality question is rooted in the manner in which they adapted to social change. The German concept of nationality as a subsidiary function of social class was the product of a social structure wherein the upper classes were largely German and the indigenous lower classes Latvian. The social and economic changes which characterized the late nineteenth century operated in such a way as to preserve to a significant degree the old relationships between nationality and social class. The German community retained its elite status. In pre-industrial Riga they had been merchants, artisans and professional people. In industrialized Riga they comprised a new elite which included entrepreneurs, technicians, business executives, bankers, skilled workers and factory foremen as well as those merchants, artisans and literati who managed to adapt to the new environment while remaining in more traditional occupations. The Latvian community of the pre-industrial era had been exclusively lower class. By the opening years of the twentieth century this was no longer the case. Because upwardly mobile Latvians no longer necessarily Germanized, Riga's Latvian community included a small but highly visible layer of industrialists, merchants and professional people; but the overwhelming majority of Latvians were still lower class. Latvian peasants who migrated to Riga during the late nineteenth century were neither moneyed nor educated enough to be anything other than factory workers, or at best shopkeepers and clerks. The development of Latvian middle and upper classes was a lengthy, gradual process which was still in a relatively early stage at the turn of the century. There is also little evidence of change in the social structure of the local Russian community. Apart from a few merchants, industrialists, professional people and crown civil servants, the Russian community was essentially lower class.

The old pattern of de-nationalization as an accompaniment to social mobility is also still discernible during this period, although it was certainly not as common as it had once been. The Latvian national movement did exert a certain restraint upon the de-nationalization of upwardly mobile Latvians. The better educated and more affluent segment of Latvian society saw retention of their native national identity to be an increasingly viable and appealing option. Most of the Latvian middle class came to regard Germanization as old-fashioned at best, treasonable at worst. Yet not all Latvians felt this way. As late as 1901 the Latvian press still attributed the poor showing made by the Latvian election committee slate in that year's contest to the tendency of some propertied Latvians to identify so strongly with the Germans that they cast their ballots for conservative German candidates.[27] The evidence from the German side is more striking. The German community did not, on the whole, disapprove of the de-nationalization of downwardly mobile Germans. They accepted it as a matter of course. Many German *Kleinbürger*, finding themselves in an increasingly Latvian milieu as the influx of peasants from the countryside swelled, simply became Latvians.[28] School Russification also played an important part in strengthening the tendency of downwardly mobile Germans to Latvianize. Sent to Russian schools and surrounded by Latvian-speaking peers, many *Kleinbürger* children came to identify themselves as Latvians.[29] An excellent example of the de-nationalization process is provided by the fate of artisans who migrated to Riga from the small German settlement of Hirschenhof in rural Livland. Not possessing the skills of their urban German counterparts, the Hirschenhof migrants normally remained *unzünftig* and often sank to the level of semi-skilled labourers. Nearly all of them Latvianized after prolonged residence in Riga.[30] Gustav Bocke, a Rhineland German who taught during this period at the Baltic Polytechnical Institute, has supplied in his memoirs what is perhaps the best characterization of the de-nationalization phenomenon. Bocke was amazed to discover that, "If a German worker married a Latvian girl, the remnants of German nationality which he still preserved from his parents' home, from school, or from military service would disappear like snow in March; and the children would speak only Latvian."[31]

In the final analysis, the Germans' reluctance to part with their time-honoured perception of nationality is understandable, because that perception still by and large corresponded with the relationship of nationality to social class in turn-of-the-century Riga. In spite of the growth of Latvian national consciousness, the pressure exerted by Russian nationalism and the development of an embryonic nationalism within certain local German circles, the concept of nationality as a function of social class was still a viable one in Riga. The emergence of self-consciously Latvian upper and middle classes did force the Germans to reassess their argument that the Latvians were a group of lower social classes rather than a nation; but the uncertain and hesitant manner in which the Germans arrived at this conclusion was indicative of the fact that national and class affiliations still did largely coincide.

In light of the prevailing relationship between nationality and social class, the German view of the Latvian national movement as one led by social radicals was, however misconceived, logical. Most Germans saw their own nationality as a function of their class, and it seemed obvious to them that politicians operating in the name of a nationality which was chiefly lower class were in reality champions of the lower strata of urban society against the traditional ruling classes. For the Germans themselves, a politicization of the nationalty question had little attraction. They were still mainly upper and middle class, and a concerted, open defense of class interest was eminently more appealing and sensible to them than political organization on the basis of linguistic nationality.

By the beginning of the 1890's, relations between the Riga German community and the imperial government had been strained for more than two decades. The dominant political ideology within the German community was a rigid conservatism which sought to defend every vestige of the estates system against administrative reform and, after 1885, Russification. This conservatism was not, however, destined to remain unopposed for long. As early as 1880 both the *Rigasche Zeitung* and the *Zeitung für Stadt und Land* began to question the wisdom of sustained defense of the estates sytem. Openly taking issue with the leadership of the estates and the executive board of the duma, the *Rigasche Zeitung* counselled acceptance of the new laws and institutions: "In the long run a double administration is untenable. Events show that the transitional period will be as short as possible, and it is unquestionable that the future belongs to the new institutions rather than to the magistracy."[32] The best course would be to work for as quick a transfer of power to the new institutions as could be effected. Continued resistance, on the other hand, the newspaper labelled "quixotic."[33] When *Baltische Monatschirft* editor Friedrich Bienemann called for blind resistance to all change, the *Rigasche Zeitung* accused him of being, "so embittered that he has forgotten the reality within which we must work."[34]

In a similar vein, the *Zeitung für Stadt und Land* contended that, "Although the new laws were not at first greeted sympathetically here . . . people should have the political wisdom to be realistic and to say to themselves that everything does not depend on the letter of these laws alone, but rather on the spirit in which they are enforced by sensible, patriotic men with good intentions."[35] The *Zeitung für Stadt und Land* repeated its plea for the acceptance of the imperial government's reforms in a later issue which hailed the introduction of justices of the peace as a progressive measure: "We can greet this new law in a joyful spirit and state with conviction that it will have a salutary influence on our judicial system."[36]

A handful of duma members agreed that rigid conservatism was unproductive and self-defeating, because, in the words of City Secretary Eugen Alt, "We do not possess the strength to maintain two separate municipal governments. We must, therefore, concentrate as much of our governmental responsibility as possible in the new institutions and thereby win over . . . those who have contributed their talents to the estates system."[37]

The leaders of both the estates and the duma, however, remained committed to unbending resistance to the new system and defense of what remained of the old. They were fully supported in this by the *Rigaer Tageblatt* and the *Baltische Monatschrift*. Indeed, as the 1880's wore on the tendency toward rigidity was strengthened by the challenges of Russification.

A more conciliatory spirit did begin to pervade relations between the Riga German community and the imperial government during the middle of the 1890's. The background of this improvement was complex. A major factor was the belated realization by the German leadership that the new administrative and legal forms did not jeopardize the political and social position of the traditional ruling classes in Riga. Events showed that the new institutions were just as effective as the estates system in barring the urban lower classes from participation in the government. Conservative German election committees had won every election from 1878 to 1890 handily, insuring that the duma remained under the control of the same individuals who had dominated the estates system. The revised municipal statute of 1892 placed the city administration even more securely in the hands of the German upper classes. The 1877 statute had enfranchised all urban property owners, whereas after 1892 only those who owned city real estate valued in excess of 1,500 rubles enjoyed the right to vote in municipal elections. The size of the electorate fell from approximately 6,000 in 1890 to 2,291 in 1893.[38]

Gradually the Riga Germans came to understand and appreciate the socially conservative nature of the imperial government's administrative reforms. An 1898 *Rigasche Rundschau* editorial bemoaned the dangerous "democratization" of municipal government in western Europe, pointing out that in cities like Hamburg, Berlin and Paris the masses were able to elect socialists and "fanatical radicals" to positions of civic responsibility. In the Russian Empire, on the other hand, the government had been wise enough to prevent this: "We are fortunate that the relatively aristocratic municipal governmental system makes it possible to entrust city government to men who are not subject to the influence or pressure exerted by the broad masses."[39]

While the post-1877 municipal administrative system gradually proved itself as a defender of upper class interests, the old estates system became so debilitated that its preservation ceased to be a viable basis for political action. The magistracy was abolished in 1889, and the two guilds suffered from dwindling membership as well as the progressive loss of public authority. The artisan guild had been in general decline since the repeal of the *Zunftzwang* in 1866; and a new generation of commercial and industrial entrepreneurs saw little reason to pay initiation fees and membership dues to a merchant guild whose political and administrative powers were in the last stages of eclipse.

TABLE 3

THE DECLINE OF GUILD MEMBERSHIP, 1850–1889[40]

| | Number of New Members | |
	Artisan Guild	Merchant Guild
1850–54	229	203
1855–59	178	222
1860–64	178	199
1865–69	107	102
1870–74	86	74
1875–79	90	76
1880–84	96	44
1885–89	107	64

The membership of the municipal duma gradually came to include fewer men who were tied to the old system by a career in local public service that antedated the 1877 reform. A new generation of industrialists and technocrats began to replace the literati and merchants as the dominant element in municipal government. The proportion of literati in the duma declined steadily from 26.4 per cent in 1878 to 12.5 per cent in 1897; and the proportion of duma members who belonged to one of the estates fell from 79.2 per cent in 1878 to 43 per cent in 1901.[41] If the literati and estates officials represented the segment of the Riga German community most estranged from the central authorities, those involved in industrial development comprised a group who were being drawn ever more closely to Russia and who were the direct beneficiaries of the imperial government's economic policies. The proportion of duma members who participated in industrialization as entrepreneurs, financiers or company directors rose from 27.8 per cent in 1878 to 37.5 per cent in 1897; and the percentage who pursued technical careers increased from a mere 1.4 in 1878 to 17.5 in 1901.[42]

The shift in the occupational background of duma members and its effect upon relations between the municipal administration and the imperial government reveals itself most clearly in the differences among the four men elected by the duma to the mayoralty during the period 1878–1905. Riga's first two mayors, Robert Büngner (1878–1885) and August von Oettingen (1886–1889), held office when relations with the central authorities were at their lowest ebb. Both men were ultimately dismissed from office or forced to resign for resisting state policy. Büngner and von Oettingen had both spent years in public service under the estates system, and it is understandable that they would do their utmost to defend it. As a lawyer and *Rechtsgelehrte* magistrate, Büngner had participated in the ill-fated municipal reform movement of the 1860's, and at the time of his mayoralty he was also a burgomaster in the estates system. As a Baltic noble, von Oettingen had never been involved in the urban estates system, but he had had a distinguished career in the Livland diet, which elected him marshal of the provincial nobility from 1857 to 1862. He had also served as provincial governor from 1862 to 1868, a time when the imperial government was giving open encouragement to the attempts of Baltic German liberals to reform local government on the basis of the estates system.

The two succeeding mayors, Ludwig Kerkovius (1890–1901) and George Armitstead (1901–1912), were men of a very different stamp. Although he came from a long-established patrician family and had served in the magistracy since 1874, Kerkovius was not tied to the past.

A timber merchant who had acquired part ownership of the large sawmill "John Hammer", he was typical of those among the old elite who successfully adapted to Riga's changing social and economic environment. Armitstead had very little connection with the estates system. The grandson of a British immigrant, he held an engineering degree from the Baltic Polytechnical Institute. After working in railroad construction in the Russian interior during the early 1870's, he returned to his native Riga to become part owner of a factory that produced super-phosphate fertilizers; and by the time of his mayoralty he had also been appointed director of the Baltic Cellulose Corporation.[43]

Under the guidance of Kerkovius and Armitstead, the Riga municipal administration became more amenable to compromise and co-operation with the imperial government than had been the case earlier. As vice-mayor from 1878 to 1890, Kerkovius had had to resume the daily business of municipal government after the departures of Büngner and von Oettingen. After his election to the mayoral office he clearly realized the fruitlesness of continued resistance to the imperial government and strove instead to achieve a *modus vivendi* with it. On his death in 1904, the *Rigasche Rundschau* noted that, "When Kerkovius took office it was above all important that he find a ground for practical, if not ideological, agreement with the then governor Zinoviev in order to protect municipal self-government from bogging down in legal controversies and conflicts over administrative competence. The most difficult task which he faced was to reach this goal while earning and maintaining the trust of both sides. He was successful because he always kept only attainable goals in sight and perceived the *salus publica* to lie in the preservation only of that which was preservable."[44] Armitstead continued Kerkovius' policy of co-operation with the central authorities. A technocrat, he was not interested in legal altercations. A contemporary assessment of him declared him to be an, "Enemy of all doctrine and of ideological phrase-making, who always deals with realities, with things that are practically attainable."[45]

An important factor in the improvement of relations between the German-controlled Riga duma and the imperial government, then, was the social and economic transformation of the Riga German community from a traditional urban elite with a vested interest in the estates system into a new elite of industrialists, financiers and technocrats whose material interests were best served through co-operation with the imperial government.

The Germans continued to find some features of the new judicial and administrative institutions objectionable. They particularly disliked the added powers granted by the 1892 municipal statute to the provincial governor *vis-a-vis* the duma. The 1877 statute had permitted the governor to overturn duma decisions if he judged them to be illegal; but after 1892 he was able to veto legislation passed by the duma if he felt that it "did not correspond to the general state interest or was injurious to public welfare."[46] This virtually gave the governor a blank cheque. The German leadership also complained that the municipal government was not granted adequate sources of revenue, especially in view of the fact that it was required to subsidize a number of crown agencies in the city. At the turn of the century support for crown agencies accounted for twelve per cent of the city's annual expenditure.[47] The municipal government's only recourse was to borrow heavily from commercial banks, thus creating a huge public debt.

In spite of these criticisms, which were common to city governments throughout the empire, the Riga Germans slowly came to the conclusion that the new institutions did provide better civic services than had the estates system. One of the principal motivations behind the indigenous reform movement of the 1860's had, after all, been the realization that there were inadequacies in the estates system that rendered it all but incapable of providing effective government for a rapidly growing city.

The new judicial and police institutions were often singled out for praise. In his 1901 survey of the city administration Nikolai Carlberg, chief of the municipal statistical commission and a duma member after 1890, lauded the reformed judicial system for freeing the municipality from court expenditures.[48] As early as 1887 the Chamber of Commerce petitioned the Ministry of Finance for the establishment in Riga of commercial courts like those in operation in the cities of European Russia, claiming that the estates courts were simply ineffective.[49] By the 1890's the new police institutions introduced in 1888 also found a positive reception. In 1894 the *Rigasche Rundschau* declared that, "In the main the police reform is viewed in this region as one which corresponds to our needs."[50] Three years later the *Rigaer Tageblatt* agreed, arguing that the estates system was an anachronism: "It is the task of the state to wield judicial and administrative authority. Justice and administration should not be placed in the hands of individual estates. The judicial reform . . . brought necessary change to the Baltic region. The judicial and police authorities in the countryside and the magistracies in the cities disappeared to make place for institutions controlled by the state."[51]

By the same token, the institutions of municipal administration gained German favour because they provided the city with effective day-to-day government. A history of Riga industry published in 1910 by the Riga Technical Association, a local organization for professional engineers and architects, claimed that the municipal reforms played an important role in creating the framework for Riga's modernization.[52] Carlberg's survey emphasized that the new institutions had demonstrated their worth through practical achievements like the improvement of the water and gas supply, the extension of the sewer system, the electrification of the trolleys, street paving and the construction of the Russian theatre, a municipal slaughterhouse and a badly needed Dvina bridge.[53] In a similar vein, the *Rigaer Tageblatt* took the occasion of the 1901 jubilee to proclaim that the municipal administrative system had "proved its value" by bettering the quality of civic services.[54]

The softening of German resistance to the new institutions of local administration notwithstanding, the Russification programme which accompanied the various reforms remained as a nagging grievance. The enforced use of Russian as the sole language of local government was at least an inconvenience; and German parents were faced with the unenviable choice of sending their children to a Russian school, placing them in an illegal German educational circle in Riga, or if they could bear the cost, sending them abroad for an education. The effects of Russification in shaping the Riga German response to the policies of the imperial government should not, however, be overestimated. Most of the secondary literature exaggerates the negative impact of Russification on the German minority in the Baltic provinces.[55]

The school Russification programmes were not always effectively or thoroughly applied. It was no easy task to enforce the use of Russian in classrooms where German teachers taught German and Latvian pupils. In May, 1892 the curator of the Riga school district was forced to admit that the 1889 Russification of boys' private schools was not working because in many of the schools the faculty and administrative staff were themselves not conversant in Russian.[56] A year later he complained that the unsanctioned use of German and Latvian in classrooms was hindering the government's efforts at Russification. In consequence, "The pupils' answers in their written and oral final examinations, the findings of the school inspectors and my own knowledge of the nature of instruction dispensed in the schools all unfortunately lead me to the conclusion that the results for which we had hoped since the introduction of the Russian language in the majority of the schools in the Riga district have not been satisfactorily realized. Many pupils who have taken every subject, with the exception of religious instruction, in Russian for two or three years have an unsatisfactory command of that language."[57] The schools were in fact able to effect a degree of informal circumvention of the Russification programme. Even more revealing is the situation which prevailed at the Baltic Polytechnical Institute after

Russification was formally begun there in 1896. Many of the German professors, irreplaceable but unable to lecture in Russian, were permitted to teach in German; and Wolfgang Wachtsmuth, a local German who studied chemistry there at the turn of the century, claims in his memoirs to have taken his final state examinations in German as late as 1902.[58]

The effects of administrative Russification were also mixed. Russian may have been the only permissible language of debate in the municipal duma after 1889, but that did not alter the basic fact that nearly all of the duma members were German. Making the best of the inconvenience imposed by Russification, the duma often did its real business in informal "private sessions" where German was used as the language of debate. The official, Russian-language sessions were not infrequently reduced to a mere formality. Even the nationalist *Rizhskii vestnik* had to admit in 1894 that the Russification of the duma had had "no particular significance."[59] The Russification of the courts, police and civil service was a more onerous burden from the German perspective, but on the whole the German community seems to have been able to adjust to this situation as well. Either they learned Russian or managed somehow to circumvent the law. Most municipal employees during this period were German;[60] and many Germans still held crown civil service positions. Some of these people had little, if any, command of the Russian language. As late as 1901, the *Iuridicheskaia gazeta* complained that, "The Baltic region is still full of individuals who hold public and civil service positions and yet do not understand the Russian language."[61]

Russification did pose a serious problem for many of the literati, but it is evident that for the bulk of the German population it was more of a nuisance factor than a serious material threat. School Russification was not always effective and administrative Russification was in many ways superficial. However objectionable the Riga Germans found it, Russification did not and, of itself, could not change the fundamental fact that the German community retained its dominant social, economic and political position in Riga. What is more, the Russification programmes did not create enough real difficulty to function as a barrier to a gradual *rapprochement* with the imperial government.

The imperial government, for its part, also began to move in the direction of *rapprochement*. The force which had motivated government policy since 1881, in the non-Russian borderlands and in the Russian interior alike, was the stern conservatism of Alexander III and his leading advisors. The tsar devoted much of his energy and attention to the defense of autocratic government, social stability and public order against those who sought, either through violent or peaceful means, to change and disrupt them. Thus his reign witnessed the strengthening of the political police, the tightening of censorship laws, the reduction of university autonomy, the introduction of rural land captains as well as appointed, rather than elected, justices of the peace, the reduction of peasant representation in the zemstvos and the implementation of the conservative municipal statute of 1892. The Russification programmes carried out in the borderlands must be viewed in this context. They were a function of the government's social and political conservatism. The tsar and his advisors desired the transformation of the empire into a Russian nation-state because they believed that this would strengthen the autocratic principle. As Pobedonostsev argued, "The power of the state is based solely on the unity of consciousness between the people and the state;"[62] and the men who governed Russia were convinced that reverence for autocracy was a Russian national trait.

Imperial policy toward the Germans in Riga during the 1880's was a direct product of this mentality; but by the beginning of the next decade the government began to re-examine its presuppositions about the Riga Germans and ultimately to change its policies toward them. Those among the tsar's counselors who had been most ready to denounce the Riga Germans as traitors and to recommend Russification and religious persecution as remedies had departed from the scene. Katkov died in 1887, and Count Tolstoi followed him to the grave in 1889. Pobedonostsev continued to serve as Chief Procurator of the Holy Synod until his death in 1905, but his influence with Alexander III, and after 1894 with Nicholas II, declined steadily.

Pobedonostsev's eclipse was partly due to ill health and the infirmities of advancing age. Another factor was directly related to his policies in the Baltic provinces. This was his celebrated confrontation with Hermann Dalton, a German Reformed pastor in St. Petersburg. In 1889 Dalton, a man with connections in the imperial court, published a scathing attack on Pobedonostsev for his sponsorship of religious persecution in the Baltic provinces. Dalton's outcry drew foreign attention to the religious conflict in the Baltic provinces. The Evangelical Alliance, an organization embracing Protestant churches throughout Europe and America, expressed public outrage and appealed to the tsar to intervene against the persecution of the Baltic Lutheran church. Pobedonostsev's handling of the affair was inept. He responded to Dalton with a hysterical accusation to the effect that Dalton and the Evangelical Alliance were partners in a German, Protestant, Roman Catholic and Jewish plot against Russia. This only made Pobedonostsev look foolish, even in the eyes of the tsar. What is more, it was a blow to Russia's international prestige. The Chief Procurator's influence with the tsar consequently suffered a blow from which it never recovered.[63] Alexander III died in 1894, but Podebonostsev had never been close to Nicholas II, and his decline continued until his influence outside the Holy Synod itself was virtually nil.[64]

The last years of Alexander III's reign also witnessed a subtle shift in the government's general goals and outlook. The atmosphere of fear and suspicion that enveloped the government in the wake of Alexander II's assassination had by this time begun to lift. The decade following the assassination had seen the weakening and fragmentation of the revolutionary movement, partly due to internal problems and partly to the government's repressive policies. The tsar himself came to feel that the time for sole concentration on negative, defensive policies had passed, and that it was perhaps safe to devote more of his attention to creative, positive measures.[65] As Pobedonostsev's stock fell, that of Count Sergei Witte rose. As Minister of Finance from 1892 to 1903, Witte played an important part in setting the general tone of government policy. He was a conservative, a firm supporter of the theory that autocracy was the best form of government for Russia; but he believed just as wholeheartedly in the need for material progress. The surge of industrial development and railroad construction that characterized the 1890's was largely the product of Witte's ambitious economic policies. Witte considered himself a Russian nationalist; but he was not a proponent of Russification. His memoirs are scattered with references to the folly of policies which only served to alienate members of minority groups whose wealth and talent were needed in the drive for industrialization.[66] Witte specifically denounced the Russification programmes in the Baltic provinces, because, "They reflected nationalist views, and were implemented not to protect the dignity, interests and national individuality of the local Russians, but rather to oppress the native people, whose interests were not taken into account."[67]

Witte's tolerance for minority groups did not bring about any real change of heart on Alexander III's part. Nicholas II shared most of his father's prejudices. So too did many of Witte's colleagues. Nonetheless the realization did dawn even on those in the government who mistrusted the minority population that in Riga and elsewhere in the Baltic provinces the Germans were a bastion of social conservatism and support for the autocracy. A thorough extirpation of the German element there would have brought social revolution in its train, a prospect made all the more frightening from a conservative point of view by the development of a Latvian radical movement in the 1890's. In Riga, moreover, the Germans functioned as agents of much needed modernization. The conservative nationalist *Moskovskie vedomosti* captured the new spirit when it declared in 1903 that, "We Russians should behave toward our Baltic Germans with trust and sympathy and have both the will and the desire to support them if not their language and nationality. We must through them support the element in that region which has always been conservative, politically responsible and possessed of the conviction that Russia's strength lies in the maintenance of the monarchical principle, the element which has given Russia more than a few loyal servants and statesmen."[68]

The imperial government did not, of course, abandon or reverse its Russification programme in Riga. The progressive Russification of the school system continued without abatement; and most of the measures taken against the Baltic Lutheran church remained in force. All of this notwithstanding, there is ample evidence that the government did indeed seek a *modus vivendi* with the Riga German community during the 1890's and early 1900's. The first hint of this came with the 1892 revised municipal statute, a conservative reform designed to assure that municipal governments would remain in the hands of the urban upper classes. The effect of the new statute in Riga, of course, was to guarantee continued German control of the duma. Had the primary object of the imperial government been to weaken the German element in Riga, the revised statute could have been altered in such a way as to loosen its grip on the municipal administration. The imperial government was certainly capable of this. The 1892 statute specifically deprived Jews of the franchise; and the rebellious Poles were never granted institutions of municipal self-government. In the name of social conservatism, however, the statute was implemented in Riga in essentially the same form and manner as in the cities of European Russia.

The imperial government's chief agent in Riga, Governor Mikhail A. Zinoviev, began to reappraise his initial suspicions concerning the local Germans in the early 1890's. During the late 1880's he had distinguished himself as an energetic advocate of Russification; but after several years' tenure in his position he was insightful enough to recognize that the imperial government had a basic community of interests with the Germans as a conservative elite. One of the long-cherished goals of Russian nationalists had been the replacement of the Baltic diets with Russian zemstvos. Charged with the task of investigating the manner in which this might best be achieved, Zinoviev produced a report which defended the diets as the best possible guarantors of "order and welfare" in the Baltic provinces. Local government, in order to be effective, must reflect, "the character, customs and cultural needs of the population and the internal and external history of the region."[69] The diets fitted these requirements. To replace them with zemstvos would be folly, because "such violent treatment of the historically developed life of this province would unquestionably be ruinous for its economic well-being and consequently for the interests of the empire as a whole."[70] Zinoviev had completely reversed his earlier position on the indigenous forms of local self-government in the Baltic provinces.

Zinoviev's defense of the diets had no direct bearing on the Germans in Riga, but it was symptomatic of the mellowing of his attitude toward the Germans in general. After 1890 he began to demonstrate a much more co-operative spirit in dealing with the municipal administration, a change in behaviour which earned him a certain popularity among the Germans. When he died in office in 1895 even the nationalist *Düna-Zeitung* was moved to write that, "Mikhail Alexandrovich Zinoviev came to our land as a stranger. Like so many of his countrymen, he did not react sympathetically to our land's historically developed individuality. Entrusted with a mission that was by definition antagonistic to our nature and being, he found himself involved in a sharp conflict . . . What he should be remembered for is how, as time passed, Mikhail Alexandrovich Zinoviev drew ever nearer to the land whose chief official he was and how he came more and more to identify himself with its interests . . . The nearer he drew the more objective his views and the more mature his understanding of Livland's needs became."[71]

Relations between the Riga municipal administration and subsequent governors were relatively untroubled. Zinoviev's immediate successor, Vladimir Surovtsov, suffered from medical problems which prevented him from playing an active role in local politics. Mikhail Pashkov, who held the post from 1901 to 1905, was not an energetic civil servant and was given to long sojourns away from Riga. There was no return to the acrimonious relationship which had existed between the municipal administration and the provincial governors during the 1880's.

The imperial government did make some concrete concessions to the Riga Germans. The only subject taught in German in the city schools was Protestant religious instruction; and an imperial rescript of 10 June 1902 increased the number of hours devoted to it. This was hardly a reversal of school Russification, but it would have been unthinkable in the 1880's. In any event, several hundred German parents submitted a formal address expressing gratitude to the tsar for this measure.[72]

The most significant manifestation of the imperial government's new-found willingness to co-operate with the Riga Germans concerned the application of the Russian artisan craft statute in Riga. One of the major bones of contention between the Riga municipal administration and the imperial authorities during the 1880's had been the transfer of jurisdiction over artisan crafts from the magistracy to the new institutions of municipal government. This controversy remained unsettled in the mid-1890's, because duma jurisdiction in this area was predicated upon the existence of administrative machinery provided by the Russian artisan craft statute, which had never been implemented in Riga. The abolition of the magistracy in 1889 made solution of the problem much more pressing. With the magistracy gone and the duma unable to exercise jurisdiction over craft production, Riga's artisan guild was in a particularly difficult situation. It had relied on the magistracy to determine the legality of decisions passed by the bench of elders and to act as an appellate instance in the adjudication of disputes within the guild. The German leadership was quite willing to transfer jurisdiction in this area to the duma, but it did wish to preserve the traditional legal framework of artisan craft practice, without which the continued existence of the artisan guild was problematic. During the 1880's the central authorities had been extremely unco-operative, not to say unreasonable, in this matter; but in 1892 the imperial government approved a duma proposal that transfered jurisdiction to the duma while maintaining the traditional craft laws and guaranteeing the continued existence of the artisan guild. Governor Zinoviev had played an important part in reaching this compromise, and the local press was quite exuberant in its praise of the governor and the municipal administration: "New life from ruins! Our centuries-old craft practices remain unshaken. The provincial government and the municipal duma are the builders who have assembled the scattered bricks of the Riga craft laws and rebuilt them with the mortar of co-operation. It is good when the government and the organs of local self-government work together to support the existing strengths of the community."[73]

The imperial government also relented somewhat in its policies toward the Baltic Lutheran Church. The campaign to convert Latvians to Orthodoxy received less and less emphasis; and in 1894 Nicholas II amnestied nearly two hundred Baltic German pastors who had been arraigned on criminal charges for ministering to Latvian and Estonian reconverts.

By the beginning of the twentieth century, the imperial government had made an effort at reconciliation with the Riga Germans. Russification was not withdrawn, but the central authorities ceased harassing the German leadership, made some concrete concessions to the German population and encouraged the Russian political leaders within Riga to move into an electoral alliance with the Germans against the Latvians. This re-orientation of government policy toward the Riga Germans progressed haltingly and unevenly. Acts of leniency often closely preceded or followed upon measures aimed at Russification. Given the degree of mistrust and suspicion with which many imperial officials had apprehended the Baltic Germans for more than a generation, this is hardly surprising. The imperial government never relinquished the hope that one day the Riga Germans could be totally assimilated into the Russian mainstream; and the tendency to suspect them of at least potential disloyalty could not but persist in a period when relations between Russia and Germany were poor. Nonetheless, the appeal of supporting a conservative local social elite had begun to outweigh or at least to balance these other considerations.

Chapter 7

EPILOGUE: THE PASSING OF AN AGE

On the eve of the 1905 Revolution the Riga Germans stood out as an example of a minority group which remained steadfastly loyal to the multi-national Russian Empire and, save for a handful of literati, rejected political nationalism. The decisive factor in the Riga German approach to the complex nationality question ultimately proved to be the social and economic environment in which they lived. As agents of industrialization they retained their elite social status, while the bulk of the city's growing Latvian population remained lower class. This circumstance ensured the continued viability of the traditional German belief that linguistic nationality was a subsidiary function of social class. It also led the Germans to view Latvian nationalism as a false front for social radicalism. In German eyes, the proper response to the Latvian movement was defence of class privilege, not counter-nationalism.

Relations between the Riga Germans and the imperial government were troubled for much of the period from 1855 to 1905. After initially encouraging a local German reform movement, the government of Alexander II reversed itself and strove to implement reforms in Riga which would render the city administratively uniform with its counterparts in European Russia. The Riga Germans, frustrated at the rejection of their own reform programme, fearful that the imperial government was undermining the Baltic *Rechtsstaat* and believing the reforms to be too "democratic", did everything in their power to resist government policy by legal means. This was a conflict between a reform-minded central government and local ruling classes which were jealous of their long-established social and political privileges. In another, equally important sense, it was a conflict between bearers of a *Rechtsstaat* tradition and a government which did not recognize the supremacy of the written law. It was not seen by either side as a struggle between a Russian government and a German minority over the rights of national minorities *per se*. Government policy underwent a major transformation in the 1880's. Fearing that the Germans were subversive and convinced that the best guarantee of social and political stability was the creation of a nationally and religiously uniform empire, Alexander III presided over a programme of systematic Russification and religious persecution in the Baltic provinces and other minority areas. Some Riga Germans, particularly literati whose livelihoods were directly threatened by Russification, were attracted to a form of political nationalism. Most of the secondary literature implies that the majority of Riga Germans followed the literati on the road to organized nationalism, but this was simply not the case. Social and economic realities worked against the development of German nationalism and instead strengthened German loyalty to the Russian Empire. The Germans were a conservative social elite, and in the final analysis the imperial government placed a higher priority on the maintenance of a conservative social and political *status quo* than on Russification for its own sake. If the government had dislodged the Germans from their position of dominance in local society, it would have removed the group most committed to the preservation of stability and order. Consequently, the Russification programmes were superficial in many respects, and by the 1890's the central authorities had begun to make a few concessions to the Germans. Russification never presented enough of a material threat to the Germans to create an atmosphere in which they would feel the need to defend themselves by recourse to political nationalism. What is more, the Riga Germans based their elite social status on their role as entrepreneurs, business executives, financiers and technicians in an industrial complex which depended on Russian markets and raw materials and which directly profited from government encourgement of heavy industry. This economic bond could only reinforce German attachment to the Russian Empire and certainly discouraged feelings of alienation, let alone separatism or disloyalty.

The equilibrium of political and social forces that characterized the late nineteenth century in Riga dissolved in the Revolution of 1905. The twentieth century had opened on a disturbing note in the Russian Empire. An industrial slump brought unemployment and wage reductions to thousands of urban workers, whose political and economic grievances were vented in a wave of illegal strikes. In the overpopulated and impoverished countryside a series of poor harvests drove desperate peasants to sporadic outbursts of violence. Social and economic malaise served in turn as a spur to the activity of a wide array of political forces ranged against the autocracy. Nowhere were conditions more explosive than in the Baltic provinces. The plight of the Latvian and Estonian peasantry was particularly severe,[1] and the Baltic urban working class suffered badly from a slump whose effects were especially pronounced in the machine building and metallurgical industries. More than five thousand Riga factory labourers were turned out of work between 1901 and 1905.[2]

Hoping in part to distract public attention from domestic woes, the inept government of Nicholas II provoked a war with Japan which broke out at the close of January, 1904. This proved to be a grave miscalculation. As the Japanese administered one humiliating defeat after another to their blundering Russian adversaries, popular opposition to the war and anger at the government responsible for it mounted. On Sunday, 9 January 1905, troops opened fire on a workers' demonstration in front of the Winter Palace in St. Petersburg. With this act public outrage at government policy boiled over. The empire erupted in a turmoil of strikes, demonstrations and bloody riots. When reports of the "Bloody Sunday" incident reached Riga, a joint committee of Latvian, Russian and Jewish socialists called for a general strike. The strike petered out after a couple of weeks, but Riga, like most major Russian cities, was troubled by intermittent strikes and demonstrations, some of them violent, throughout the spring and summer. The revolutionary movement was galvanized by the Imperial Manifesto of 27 October, promising civil liberties for all Russian subjects and a popularly elected national legislature. The October Manifesto fell far short of satisfying the regime's more radical opponents, who paralyzed the empire's major urban centres with a national general strike. In Riga the Latvian left demanded the establishment of a democratic republic, a constituent assembly elected by "four-tail" (equal, direct, universal and secret) suffrage, the abolition of large-scale private property and substantial concessions to the national minorities.[3] From late October through early December, conditions in Riga were violent and chaotic. In the words of a local German commentator, it was unsafe "to venture out onto the streets without a revolver."[4] The imperial government succeeded in reasserting its authority in the city by the middle of December; but in the meantime unrest had spread to the Baltic countryside, where peasant riots continued until order was restored by military force in February, 1906.

The Revolution of 1905 affected German-Latvian relations profoundly. The Germans were stunned by the suddenness and violence of the revolutionary events. Scores of them were killed, and millions of rubles in damage was done to German property.[5] It seemed that the fury of the Latvians knew no bounds. The shock felt by Germans throughout the Baltic provinces was mirrored in "The Latvian Psychosis", an article submitted in 1906 to the *Reich*-German periodical *Die Zukunft* by a Baltic German noble who signed himself with the pseudonym "Meinhard von Segeberg." The author, like so many of his compatriots, was at an utter loss to explain what he termed the "severe mass psychosis" that underlay Latvian behaviour. How, he asked, could the Germans continue to live with the Latvians after their display of violence?[6] Equally disturbing from the German standpoint was the hostile attitude assumed by the Latvian urban middle class. At first some of the Germans had hoped to make common cause with this group in defense of order and property,[7] but the nationalistic Latvians, however anxious they were about the spread of violence, could not bring themselves to deal with the Germans. The Revolution seemed a heaven-sent opportunity to be rid of German dominance once and for all. Throughout 1905 the Latvian nationalist press maintained that the German elite was only receiving its just deserts. The liberal and moderately conservative middle class Latvian parties that sprang up after the October Manifesto expressed no desire whatsoever to co-operate with the Germans. They demanded an autonomous Latvia in which the old elite would have no place. German behaviour also helped to destroy the possibility of future collaboration. The Germans, particularly the rural nobility, eagerly assisted the savage "pacification" of the Baltic provinces by Russian military units during the winter of 1905–1906. Hundreds of Latvians, many of them innocent of any serious crime, were either hanged on the order of field court martials or simply shot without the benefit of any trial whatsoever. In Latvian eyes, this made the Germans the henchmen of brutal repression with whom no compromise could ever be arranged.

The Revolution also forced the Germans to reassess their relationship with the autocracy. Their staunch loyalty to the regime had at least in part been rooted in their conviction that it was the best guarantor of their own elite status; but in 1905 the imperial authorities proved incapable of protecting their German clients from Latvian wrath. German accounts of 1905 speak of betrayal, of the abandonment by the imperial government of its most loyal subjects in their hour of need. Russian military formations did restore order in 1906 with a vengeance but their troops had been absent at the height of the revolt, so that for the first time the Riga Germans were exposed to the weakness of the Russian autocracy. In the aftermath of the Revolution, when the Germans sought causes and explanations for this misfortune, preferably ones which avoided discussion of their possible culpability, the Russian government made an easy scapegoat. Baltic German analyses of the events of 1905–1906 repeatedly point an accusing finger at Russification for creating an anti-German mentality among the Latvians and for destroying the respect for law and order among the lower classes which the old German system had allegedly once instilled in them.

The Revolution of 1905 destroyed many of the old certainties for the Riga Germans, compelling them to readjust their perception of themselves, of their Latvian neighbours and of the imperial government. Many of the Germans still hoped for a return to an era of mutual trust and support between themselves and the regime. Government help against the Latvians had been belated, but it had come in the end; and the Revolution had certainly demonstrated the unquestioning loyalty and reliability of the German population. The October Manifesto was especially encouraging in this light. It seemed to promise a Russian *Rechtsstaat* in which the rights of minority citizens would be respected. Perhaps all the wrongs of Russification would be undone. As early as April, 1905, Lutheran sensibilities were assuaged by a decree permitting conversion from Orthodoxy to other religions; and two months later the Committee of Ministers denounced school Russification in minority areas. Immediately following the promulgation of the October Manifesto the Riga Germans, in collaboration with representatives of the Baltic nobility, made use of the newly granted freedom of assembly to establish the Baltic Constitutional Party, whose programme called for a constitution, the re-introduction of minority languages in schools and local administration and greater autonomy for municipal and provincial organs of self-government. Characteristically, the new party rejected political nationalism and strove to represent itself as a supra-national advocate of Baltic regional interests.[8] The early history of the Baltic Constitutional Party reflects a certain current of optimism that surfaced at the time. Although none of the party's candidates won election to the first two State Dumas, the restricted franchise introduced for elections to the third State Duma in 1907 brought victory to seven representatives of the Baltic Constitutional Party. As Duma deputies they affiliated themselves with the pro-government Russian Octobrist Party, and for a few years collaborated closely with the cabinet headed by Prime Minister Peter A. Stolypin.

The course of municipal politics was not altered by the Revolution. The franchise for city elections was still governed by the municipal statute of 1892, and German economic strength was more than sufficient to ensure the overwhelming victory of conservative German candidates in the elections of 1905, 1909 and 1913.[9] The electoral alliance between the Germans and the propertied Russians remained in force throughout the period from 1905 to 1914. Indeed, the threat posed to order and property by the events of 1905–1906 stengthened the bonds between the German and Russian upper classes. A noteworthy sign of this was the admission after 1905 of Russians to exclusive German social clubs whose doors had once been closed to them.[10] The all-important economic ties linking the Riga Germans to the Russian Empire continued to be an influential factor in shaping relations with the imperial government. By 1908 Riga industry had fully recovered from the turn-of-the-century depression and entered a boom period marked by particular prosperity in the chemical and rubberware industries and in the local shipyards, beneficiaries of Admiralty contracts assigned to recoup the horrendous losses incurred by the fleet in the war with Japan.[11]

These encouraging signs notwithstanding, the relationship between the Riga German community and the imperial government deteriorated after 1905. A return to the mutually supportive and harmonious relations of the past was not possible. By encouraging Russian nationalism the government sought to attract popular sympathy to its programmes and to bind together the disparate and competing parties in the State Duma, where Stolypin was able to assemble a pro-government majority composed of the Octobrists and various right-wing factions. The only thing which the right and the Octobrists had in common was their Russian nationalism. This was reflected in the passage of a series of Russifying measures, the most significant of which was the 1910 attack on Finnish autonomy. The German deputies were compelled to break with the Octobrists over the issue of Finland, and German hopes for further concessions from the government proved groundless. School Russification was eased by an April, 1906 law allowing the establishment of non-Russian private schools and the use of languages other than Russian in the first two elementary grades of public schools. But this was only a half-measure. Russification remained in force as a nagging source of grievance and a reminder of the government's lack of regard for a loyal minority.

Another, less traditional, form of German response to the post-revolutionary political atmosphere was a turn to nationalism. This proceeded logically from the Revolution itself. The Germans had been attacked by the Latvians both as a social elite and a nationality. The hostile behavior and surprising organized strength of the Latvian middle class had finally brought home to the Germans the idea that the Latvians were indeed a nation in their own right. Recognition of this was a necessary prerequisite for the development of German national consciousness. The imperial government's inability to protect the German elite in a crisis also played a role, creating in the Germans a sense of vulnerability and isolation. If the government could not guarantee their security, they would have to band together in self-defense. National solidarity now appeared to be in the material interest of a much broader segment of the German community than had been the case before 1905. During the Revolution the Germans set up informal militia units *(Selbstschutz)* when it became apparent that the authorities were helpless in the face of mounting violence; but nationalist Germans felt the need for a more broadly-based organization that could serve their interests in a variety of ways in the long run. The October Manifesto removed all barriers to the legal establishment of a German nationalist organization, and in May, 1906 the German Union in Livland was born.

The German Union was a direct outgrowth of the Euphony Club, which was absorbed into the new organization. The goals and programmes of the German Union were essentially the same as those of the Euphony Club: "The unification, preservation and strengthening of the cultural, spiritual and economic position of the entire German population."[12] The difference lay in the scale of operations. The Euphony Club had had few members, minimial public support and limited financial resources. By 1908 the German Union boasted 24,141 members, more than 15,000 of whom lived in Riga.[13] Its annual expenditures were many times those of its tiny predecessor. The Union's educational programmes were its most conspicuous success. It financed a wide variety of German-language schools in Riga and throughout Livland province and contributed to the maintenance of a German teachers' college in Mitau. The Union was also much more outward looking than the Euphony Club, whose activities did not extend beyond Riga itself. It co-operated closely with sister German Unions in Kurland and Estland and made an attempt, albeit unsuccessful, to co-ordinate its programmes with German nationalist organizations in other parts of the Russian Empire.[14] The three Baltic German Unions did have ties with the German *Reich*. Groups in Germany like the Pan-German League gave financial and organizational support to their Baltic brethren;[15] and there is solid evidence of Pan-German inclinations in certain Baltic German quarters. A leading proponent of this school was Baron Eduard von Stackelberg-Sutlem, who wrote of the need for emphasis on, "the idea of the supra-state 'national' community, which gives us Balts, Bohemian Germans, German colonists in Russia and others who have emigrated or been cut off [from Germany] the right to call ourselves Germans."[16] An occasional note of interest in a racial, Social Darwinist approach to nationalism also began to surface. In 1905 the *Baltische Monatschrift* published a favourable review of Friedrich Lange's *Reines Deutschtum (Pure Germandom)*, which used the theories of Gobineau and similar lights to claim an inborn German racial superiority.[17] Even more striking is a speech delivered by local nationalist T. von Berent to the Livland German Union in March, 1907. Maintaining that the Baltic Germans stood "on a higher cultural plane than the rest of the empire," von Berent spoke of the struggle against other, lesser nations for which the Germans must gird themselves to win their "place in the sun."[18]

Pan-German sentiment and sympathy for racial theories of nationalism remained, however, the exception rather than the rule in the German Union. Like the nationalists of the early 1900's, the Union stressed local, Baltic German, rather than Pan-German, feeling. Seraphim, reviewing Julius Eckardt's memoirs for the *Baltische Monatschrift* in 1911, praised Eckardt as a Baltic patriot who never forgot his homeland and stressed the "inner antithesis of Baltic to *Reich*-German life."[19] The great majority of Union members did not feel a sense of common identity with the *Reich*-Germans and were uncomfortable about their organization's links to the *Reich*.[20] Baltic German nationalists remained with few exceptions, in Seraphim's words, "loyal and true to the tsar and the Russian Empire."[21]

The turn to nationalism was not a complete or satisfying solution to the problems of the day for a large segment of the German population in Riga. Although there was a rush of enthusiasm for nationalist activity in the years immediately following the revolution, interest in it began to fade among the mercantile and industrial elite and among the artisans. Throughout the brief life span of the German Union its leaders and most active participants were literati and nobles, the former because of the continuing shortage of professional opportunities and the latter in response to the rural violence of 1905–1906. Most urban Germans were not entirely comfortable with the idea of national solidarity. Class differences were so deeply felt within the urban community that they impeded the growth of national consciousness. Attempts to mix merchants and artisans at social functions in the name of national solidarity invariably brought discomfort and embarrassment. Questions like the propriety of artisan women extending their hands to be kissed by upper class gentlemen could assume crisis proportions at these gatherings.[22] Many Germans continued to de-nationalize with downward social mobility, a phenomenon that frequently elicited criticism from the nationalist leadership.[23] Other Germans, particularly members of the business community and the civil service, shied away from involvement with the Union because they did not think its activities befitted patriotic Russian subjects. Many of those who joined the Union did so more out of fear than conviction; and their commitment to the nationalist cause remained half-hearted at best. The Union's leaders were very much aware of this problem, and seemingly never tired of berating the rank and file membership for their "unchivalrous and suicidal" indifference.[24] The most eloquent testimony to this is the sharp drop in Union membership to sixteen thousand in 1914—a loss of one-third since the high point of 1908.[25]

A sense of malaise and of unresolved tension pervaded the German mood, especially after 1910, when it had become apparent that neither nationalism nor renewed co-operation with the imperial government was satisfactory. Politically, the Germans were cast adrift. The old ways were irretrievable and a new political synthesis seemed unattainable.

The situation remained such until the summer of 1914 brought the World War and the eventual occupation of Riga by the Imperial German army; but for the Riga Germans the changes ushered in by war and subsequent revolution did not bring succour. Their world was destroyed forever. Riga emerged from the ruins of the tsarist empire as capital of an independent Latvian republic, where the Germans lived on as a dwindling, powerless minority, mistrusted by their Latvian rulers and with their economic strength gradually overshadowed by that of the triumphant Latvian bourgeoisie. The ultimate fate of the Riga German community does not, however, obscure the fact that before 1905 they provided an instructive illustration of the way in which the social and economic environment can function as a decisive factor in questions of nationality.

APPENDIX I

A SURVEY OF MAJOR INDUSTRIAL ENTERPRISES IN RIGA AT THE BEGINNING OF THE TWENTIETH CENTURY

I. The Metallurgical, Machine-Building and Tool Industry

Firm: AETNA CORP.
Date Founded: 1897
Number of Workers: 500
Products: Wire, nails, steel pens

A joint-stock company established by a group of Riga German merchants and Baltic nobles. Its shareholders were virtually all members of the local German community.

Firm: ATLAS CORP.
Date Founded: 1899
Number of Workers: 280
Products: Tools, cast iron wares

A joint-stock company whose founders and chief shareholders were Riga Germans and Baltic nobles.

Firm: BING AND COMPANY
Date Founded: 1894
Number of Workers: 100
Products: Needles

Owner E. Bing was a Riga resident with Reich-German *citizenship.*

Firm: BIRMAN TINPLATE FACTORY*
Date Founded: 1885
Number of Workers: 200
Products: Tinplated wares

---

*Further detail concerning ownership is unavailable.

117

Firm: BOLDERAA MACHINE FACTORY
Date Founded: 1866
Number of Workers: 200
Products: Ships, Marine equipment

Established and owned by a group of Riga German merchants.

Firm: BUSCH BROS. METALWARE FACTORY*
Date Founded: 1900
Number of Workers: 200
Products: Hardware

Firm: ERBE SAW AND FILE CORP.
Date Founded: 1887
Number of Workers: 400
Products: Tools

Founded by local German entrepreneur Otto Erbe with substantial investment from Germany. In 1898 it became a joint-stock company. Although a significant portion of the shares were held by Reich-German investors, the majority were in local hands.

Firm: FELSER AND COMPANY
Date Founded: 1873
Number of Workers: 905
Products: Diesel motors, steam engines, turbines, agricultural machinery, equipment for sawmills, and distilleries

Founded by British engineer William Weir and two Riga Germans—engineer Karl Felser and Karl Lovis, a professor at the Baltic Polytechnical Institute. In 1891 it became a joint-stock company, and by the twentieth century a substantial proportion of its share capital was held by Reich-German investors, although Riga Germans also played an important role. The controlling interest, however, was held by the Vavel'berg banking house in St. Petersburg.

Firm: KLEIN BROS.
Date Founded: 1896
Number of Workers: 227
Products: Machine components for blast furnaces, steelworks and rolling mills

A joint-stock affiliate of the Klein firm in Dahlbruch, Germany. Its share capital was 100 per cent Reich-German.

---

*Further detail concerning ownership is unavailable.

Firm: KOMET
Date Founded: ?
Number of Workers: ?
Products: Files

Owned by the Riga German entrepreneur Eugen Grundmann.

Firm: LANGE AND SON
Date Founded: 1869
Number of Workers: 1,500
Products: Ships and marine machinery

Established by two Riga Germans—engineer A. Lange and master anchorsmith J. Skuje. In 1899 it became a joint-stock company whose largest shareholder was the St. Petersburg International Bank of Commerce.

Firm: LEUTNER AND COMPANY
Date Founded: 1886
Number of Workers: 130
Products: Bicycles, automobiles

Established by the Riga German entrepreneur Alexander Leutner. In 1897 it became a limited liability company with its stocks distributed among Leutner and a group of Riga Germans that included two merchants and three professors at the Baltic Polytechnical Institute.

Firm: MANTEL MACHINE-BUILDING CORP.
Date Founded: 1879
Number of Workers: 636
Products: Turbines, pumps, and cranes

Established by the Riga German R.H. Mantel, who was a docent at the Baltic Polytechnical Institute. Mantel went into partnership with a local German named Karl Lorch in 1886 and with merchant guild elder Karl Beck in 1890. In 1898 the firm became a joint-stock company. Although about 6 per cent of the share capital was held by Reich-German *interests, the vast majority of shareholders were Riga Germans.*

Firm: MOTOR CORP.
Date Founded: 1895
Number of Workers: ?
Products: Transmissions

Established as a joint-stock company by Riga German engineer Richard Kablitz. Its share capital at the turn of the century was 92 per cent domestic and 8 per cent Reich-German.

Firm: OSTWALD IRON FOUNDRY
Date Founded: 1888
Number of Workers: 45
Products: Cast iron goods

Owned and established by the master blacksmith G. Ostwald, a local German.

Firm: PESSIS IRON FOUNDRY
Date Founded: 1901
Number of Workers: 100
Products: Cast iron household goods and machine parts

Established and owned by the Latvian engineer A. Pessis.

Firm: PHOENIX CORP.
Date Founded: 1894
Number of Workers: 2,800
Products: Railroad rolling stock

A joint-stock company among whose major shareholders numbered St. Petersburg banks, the most important of which was the St. Petersburg International Bank of Commerce. A significant proportion of shares was also held by the Riga Bank of Commerce, while foreign, chiefly Reich-German, *investors held 18 per cent of the share capital by 1900.*

Firm: PIRWITZ AND COMPANY
Date Founded: 1876
Number of Workers: 300
Products: Turbines, machinery for sawmills

Established and owned by the Riga German engineer Gustav Pirwitz.

Firm: POHLE MACHINE CORP.
Date Founded: 1870
Number of Workers: 700
Products: Parts for railroad locomotives, railroad signal equipment and machinery for sawmills

Established by Richard Pohle, a Prussian immigrant, and Riga ironmaster J. Weitmann. It became a joint-stock company in 1897. All of its share capital was held by Riga interests.

Firm: RESSORT
Date Founded: 1894
Number of Workers: 150
Products: Springs for railroad cars

Established and owned by the Riga German entrepreneur A. Tietjans.

Firm: RIGA KNIFE FACTORY
Date Founded: 1887
Number of Workers: 250
Products: Knives

Established by the Riga German entrepreneur E. Maussner, part of whose founding capital was Reich-German.

Firm: RIGA LOCK CORP.
Date Founded: 1886
Number of Workers: 700
Products: Locks

A joint-stock affiliate of the Reich-German *lock manufacturing firm of Herminghaus and Voorman. Its share capital was 100 per cent* Reich-German.

Firm: RIGA ROLLING MILL
Date Founded: 1899
Number of Workers: ?
Products: Rails

Established as a joint-stock company by the Riga German engineer B. v. Schubert. All of the shareholders were Riga merchants and Baltic nobles.

Firm: RIGA STEEL CORP.
Date Founded: 1898
Number of Workers: ?
Products: Various steel products for industrial use

Established as a joint-stock company by a group of Riga German merchants and Baltic nobles under the organizational leadership of merchant V. Smolian. All of its share capital was held by Riga interests.

Firm: RIGA WIRE INDUSTRY
Date Founded: 1873
Number of Workers: 650
Products: Wire, nails

Established as an affiliate of the Westphalian Wire Industry in Hamm, Germany. Its share capital was 100 per cent Reich-German.

Firm: ROSENKRANZ AND COMPANY
Date Founded: 1852
Number of Workers: ?
Products: Industrial machinery

Established by the Riga German engineer P.H. Rosenkranz. By the beginning of the twentieth century the firm was still owned by the Rosenkranz family.

Firm: RUSSIAN STEEL PEN CORP.
Date Founded: 1895
Number of Workers: 300
Products: Steel pens

Established as a joint-stock company. Its share capital was held partly by Riga German and partly by Russian interests, although the directorate was entirely made up of Riga Germans.

Firm: RUSSO-BALTIC FILE FACTORY
Date Founded: ?
Number of Workers: ?
Products: Files

The ownership was split between the Riga German merchant Ferdinand Meyer, a Reich-*German investor named E. Bergmann, and the British firm of Thomas Firth and Sons, which also had major sums invested in the Riga textile industry.*

Firm: RUSSO-BALTIC WAGON CORP.
Date Founded: 1874
Number of Workers: 3,800
Products: Railroad rolling stock

Established as an affiliate of Van den Zypen and Charlier in Cologne-Deutz, Germany. Until 1894, when its stocks were sold on the local market, its share capital was 100 per cent Reich-German. *After 1894 this situation changed radically, and by the onset of the twentieth century the bulk of the capital was held by Riga and St. Petersburg investors. Among the chief Riga shareholders were the Riga Bank of Commerce, local German merchants F. Meyer, K. Amelung and Chr. Schroeder, and the Riga Jewish entrepreneur Schaje Berlin.*

Firm: SALAMANDER IRON FOUNDRY
Date Founded: 1899
Number of Workers: ?
Products: Cast iron and steel goods for industrial use

Established by a group of Riga Germans, but bought from them in the early years of the twentieth century by the British firm of Thomas Firth and Sons.

Firm: SIRIUS CORP.
Date Founded: 1901
Number of Workers: 75
Products: Machine parts

Established as a joint-stock company by a group of Riga German and Jewish merchants and Baltic nobles. Most of its share capital was held by local investors.

Firm: SÖNNECKEN SAW AND FILE FACTORY
Date Founded: 1879
Number of Workers: 100
Products: Tools

Established by Gustav Sönnecken with the support of a substantial Reich-German *capital investment. By the opening of the twentieth century it was still controlled by the Sönnecken family.*

Firm: STARR AND COMPANY
Date Founded: 1870
Number of Workers: 500
Products: Wire and nails

Established by a group of Riga German entrepreneurs. In 1900 it became a joint-stock company whose share capital was entirely local.

Firm: STELLA CORP.
Date Founded: 1899
Number of Workers: ?
Products: Machinery for sawmills

A joint-stock company founded by a group of Riga German merchants and Baltic nobles. Its share capital was provided by local investors.

Firm: STRAUCH AND KRUMING MACHINE FACTORY
Date Founded: 1895
Number of Workers: ?
Products: Ships and marine machinery

One of the founders, Alexander Strauch, was alderman of the Riga merchant guild.

II. The Textile Industry

Firm: BALTIC LINEN MANUFACTURING CORP.
Date Founded: 1860
Number of Workers: 420
Products: Linen textiles

Established as a joint-stock company by a group of Riga German merchants. The directorate of the company at the turn of the century was still Riga German, but by that time the share capital was two-thirds Reich-German.

Firm: HARTWIG AND COMPANY
Date Founded: 1884
Number of Workers: 350
Products: Linen textiles

Established by a local German entrepreneur. The details of the firms ownership by 1900, however, are not available.

Firm: HOLM AND COMPANY
Date Founded: 1837
Number of Workers: 400
Products: Woollen textiles

Established by a Riga German merchant named G.J. Tank and acquired by the Riga German firm of Holm and Company in 1861. In 1900 it became a joint-stock company with half of its share capital held by Riga investors and half by Reich-German investors.

Firm: ILGEZEEM WOLLENWARE CORP.
Date Founded: 1881
Number of Workers: 400
Products: Woollen textiles

A joint-stock company with 100 per cent British share capital.

Firm: RIGA COTTON MANUFACTURING CORP. IN STRASDENHOF
Date Founded: 1840s
Number of Workers: 602
Products: Cotton textiles

Originally established by the Riga German entrepreneur T. Pychlau. In 1890 it was bought by a British investment group and became a joint-stock company with a share capital that was 67 per cent British, 28 per cent Reich-German, and 5 per cent local.

Firm: RIGA COTTON SPINNING CORP.
Date Founded: 1878
Number of Workers: 400
Products: Cotton textiles

Established in 1878 by the Riga firm of Sporket and Krüpe, it was taken over in 1881 by the Riga German entrepreneur W. Eickert. In 1897 it was reorganized as a joint-stock company by a group of Riga German merchants and industrialists. Information with regard to the distribution of the firm's share capital is not available.

Firm: SASSENHOF COTTON SPINNING AND WEAVING CORP.
Date Founded: 1895
Number of Workers: 929
Products: Cotton textiles

A joint-stock company controlled by British interests.

Firm: TEXTIL
Date Founded: 1897
Number of Workers: 850
Products: Woollen textiles

A joint-stock company founded jointly by Riga German entrepreneurs and British investors. By the twentieth century its share capital was 64 per cent British, 32 per cent local, and 4 per cent Reich-German.

Firm: VOGELSANG
Date Founded: 1859
Number of Workers: 150
Products: Ribbon and lace

Established by the Riga German firm of Brandenburg, taken over by the Riga German entrepreneur J. Vogelsang in 1878.

III. The Wood and Paper Products Industry

Firm: BERLIN SAWMILL
Date Founded: 1820
Number of Workers: 450
Products: Wood products

Established and owned by the Riga German Wöhrmann family until the early 1880s, when it was taken over by the local Jewish entrepreneur Schaje Berlin.

Firm: BEYER AND VANAG
Date Founded: ?
Number of Workers: ?
Products: Wood products

A sawmill. The nationality of its owners, both local residents, cannot be determined.

Firm: BREDESEN AND COMPANY
Date Founded: late 1870s
Number of Workers: ?
Products: Wood products

A sawmill. Owned and established by the Riga German wood export merchant Otto Bredesen.

Firm: BRONIKOWSKY SAWMILL
Date Founded: early 1880s
Number of Workers: ?
Products: Wood products

Established and owned by Donat Bronikowsky, a Riga Pole.

Firm: BRUHNS AND COMPANY
Date Founded: 1884
Number of Workers: ?
Products: Paper

Established and owned by the Riga German merchant Eduard Bruhns.

Firm: DOMBROWSKIS SAWMILL
Date Founded: 1869
Number of Workers: ?
Products: Wood products

Established by the Riga Latvian merchant Jacob Dombrowskis and by 1900 still owned by the Dombrowskis family.

Firm: DRÜHL SAWMILL
Date Founded: 1870s
Number of Workers: ?
Products: Wood products

Established and owned by the Riga German wood export merchant Carl W. Drühl.

Firm: FIALKOWSKY SAWMILL
Date Founded: 1870s
Number of Workers: ?
Products: Wood products

Established and owned by a local wood merchant whose nationality cannot be determined.

Firm: JOHN HAMMER SAWMILL
Date Founded: 1863
Number of Workers: ?
Products: Wood products

Established by the British entrepreneur John Hammer. By the turn of the century the firm was owned by the Hammer family and by former Riga mayor Ludwig Kerkovius.

Firm: HINDIN SAWMILL
Date Founded: 1890s
Number of Workers: ?
Products: Wood products

Owned by the local Jewish entrepreneur S.J. Hindin.

Firm: HÖPFE SAWMILL
Date Founded: 1870s
Number of Workers: ?
Products: Wood products

Established and owned by the Riga German wood merchant Friedrich W. Höpfe.

Firm: ILGEZEEM STEAM SAWMILL
Date Founded: 1873
Number of Workers: 400
Products: Wood products

Established by the Riga German merchant G. Lomani, it became a joint-stock company in 1895. The exact distribution of share capital is unavailable.

Firm: KLEINBERG SAWMILL
Date Founded: 1870s
Number of Workers: ?
Products: Wood products

Established by the Riga German wood merchant Woldemar Kleinberg, and by the twentieth century still owned by the Kleinberg family.

Firm: LUCHT SAWMILL
Date Founded: early 1870s
Number of Workers: ?
Products: Wood products

Established and owned by Riga German master carpenter J.H. Lucht.

Firm: MAIMIN AND DUBROWSKY
Date Founded: 1890s
Number of Workers: ?
Products: Wood products

A sawmill. Owned and established by two Riga Jewish entrepreneurs.

Firm: MAKSIMOV SAWMILL
Date Founded: 1890s
Number of Workers: ?
Products: Wood products

Owned and established by the local Russian merchant D. Maksimov.

Firm: MERCURY CORP.
Date Founded: 1890s
Number of Workers: 400
Products: Wooden kegs

A joint-stock company established and controlled by a group of Riga German entrepreneurs.

Firm: MICHELSOHN SAWMILL
Date Founded: late 1880s
Number of Workers: ?
Products: Wood products

Owned and established by the local Jewish merchant C. Michelsohn.

Firm: PERFECT CORP.
Date Founded: late 1890s
Number of Workers: 300
Products: Wood products

A sawmill. A joint-stock company established and controlled by a group of Riga German merchants.

Firm: PYCHLAU SAWMILL
Date Founded: 1865
Number of Workers: 417
Products: Wood products

Founded by the Riga German merchant A. Wulff, bought by another local German merchant, T. Pychlau, in the 1880s, and finally acquired in the 1890s by the Riga German entrepreneur W.O. von Sengbusch.

Firm: RIGA PAPER CORP.
Date Founded: 1858
Number of Workers: 672
Products: Paper

Established as a joint-stock company by a group of Riga German merchants. By the twentieth century nearly all of its share capital was held by local investors.

Firm: ROEDER AND KNOPP
Date Founded: 1872
Number of Workers: 126
Products: Paper

Founded and owned by the Riga German merchants C.L.F. Roeder and Gustav Knopp.

Firm: SATURN
Date Founded: 1890s
Number of Workers: ?
Products: Wood products

A sawmill. Owned by a group of Riga German merchants.

Firm: SCHAPIRO SAWMILL
Date Founded: early 1880s
Number of Workers: ?
Products: Wood products

Established and owned by the Riga Jewish merchant P. Schapiro.

Firm: SCHEPELER SAWMILL
Date Founded: 1880s
Number of Workers: ?
Products: Wood products

Established and owned by A. Schepeler, a local German merchant.

Firm: C. STEINERT
Date Founded: 1867
Number of Workers: 102
Products: Wood products

A sawmill. Established by the Riga German master carpenter Chr. Steinert and still owned by the Steinert family by the turn of the century.

Firm: WELZER SAWMILL
Date Founded: early 1880s
Number of Workers: ?
Products: Wood products

Owned and established by the Riga German merchant Friedrich Ludwig Welzer.

IV.   The Chemical and Rubber Goods Industry

Firm: BALTIC CELLULOSE CORP.
Date Founded: 1896
Number of Workers: 212
Products: Cellulose

Established as a joint-stock company by a group of Riga German merchants. Its share capital was two-thirds domestic, one-sixth Reich-German and one-sixth British.

Firm: H.A. BRIEGER
Date Founded: 1849
Number of Workers: 90
Products: Candles, soap, perfumes

Established by the Riga German merchant H.A. Brieger and still owned by the Brieger family at the turn of the century.

Firm: ESTANOVICH BROS.
Date Founded: 1885
Number of Workers: ?
Products: Industrial chemicals

Established and owned by the local Russian entrepreneurs Alexander and Viacheslav Estanovich.

Firm: FOCKENHOF, AGTHE, FREY AND COMPANY
Date Founded: 1899
Number of Workers: 100
Products: Industrial chemicals, principally sulphur

Established by the Riga German merchant W. Agthe and the local German chemist L. Frey.

Firm: GLOVER CHEMICAL CORP.
Date Founded: 1899
Number of Workers: 200
Products: Industrial chemicals

A joint-stock company with most of its share capital in the hands of Swedish investors, although local and Reich-*German capital did play a role.*

Firm: HARTMANN CORP.
Date Founded: 1859
Number of Workers: 231
Products: Petroleum products, dyes, varnish

Established by a group of Riga German merchants. It became a joint-stock company in 1896. Most share capital was in the hands of Russian banks by the twentieth century.

Firm: C. KIRSTEIN
Date Founded: 1860
Number of Workers: ?
Products: Candles, soap

Established by the Riga German merchant Carl Gustav Kirstein and still owned by the Kirstein family at the turn of the century.

Firm: S.P. KLIMOV
Date Founded: 1885
Number of Workers: 250
Products: Petroleum products, oil cloth

Established and owned by the Riga Russian merchant S.P. Klimov.

Firm: J.C. KOCH
Date Founded: 1842
Number of Workers: ?
Products: Varnish

Established by Riga merchant guild elder J.C. Koch and still owned by the Koch family at the turn of the century.

Firm: S. MEISEL AND SONS
Date Founded: 1898
Number of Workers: ?
Products: Analine dyes

Owned by the Riga Jewish industrialist Moritz Meisel.

Firm: F. MÜHLEN
Date Founded: 1880
Number of Workers: 110
Products: Perfume, soap

An affiliate of a firm in Cologne, Germany.

Firm: MÜHLGRABEN CHEMICAL CORP.
Date Founded: 1892
Number of Workers: 350
Products: Super-phosphate fertilizers

Established by the Riga German engineer Max Höflinger as the first producer of super-phosphates in the Russian Empire. In 1900 it became joint-stock corporation with most of the shares held by local investors.

Firm: J.W. MÜNDEL
Date Founded: 1864
Number of Workers: ?
Products: Rubber goods, galoshes

Established by the Riga German entrepreneur J.W. Mündel and still owned by the Mündel family at the turn of the century.

Firm: OELRICH AND COMPANY*
Date Founded: 1874
Number of Workers: 250
Products: Petroleum products

Firm: PROVODNIK
Date Founded: 1888
Number of Workers: 2,767
Products: Rubber goods, galoshes, linoleum

A joint-stock company whose share capital was 60 per cent French and 40 percent domestic. Although the board of directors included some Riga Germans, there was proportionately little Riga German investment in the firm.

Firm: RIGA BONE MILL
Date Founded: 1870
Number of Workers: ?
Products: Bonemeal and super-phosphate fertilizers

Established by the British entrepreneur R. Thomson, but bought in 1885 by George Armitstead, a Riga German financier and engineer who served as mayor of Riga from 1901 to 1912.

---

*Further detail concerning ownership is unavailable.

Firm: A.G. RUHTENBERG
Date Founded: 1889
Number of Workers: ?
Products: Industrial chemicals

Established and owned by the Riga German tobacco entrepreneur A.G. Ruhtenberg.

Firm: RUSSIA CO.*
Date Founded: 1896
Number of Workers: ?
Products: Rubber goods

Firm: RUSSIAN ANALINE DYE FACTORY
Date Founded: 1890s
Number of Workers: ?
Products: Analine dyes

Owned by two Riga Latvians, Arthur Weinberg and Leo Gans.

Firm: RUSSIAN-RHENISH LEAD PAINT FACTORY*
Date Founded: 1890s
Number of Workers: ?
Products: Paint

Firm: RUSSO-BALTIC LACQUER FACTORY
Date Founded: 1890s
Number of Workers: ?
Products: Lacquer

Owned by the Riga German merchant W. Hjort.

Firm: KARL CHR. SCHMIDT CORP.
Date Founded: 1853
Number of Workers: 965
Products: Petroleum products, cement

Established by the Riga German merchant K.C. Schmidt. In 1876 it was reorganized as a joint-stock company. The largest shareholders were the Schmidt family and several Moscow firms.

---

*Further detail concerning ownership is unavailable.

Firm: G. THALHEIM
Date Founded: 1869
Number of Workers: ?
Products: Petroleum products

Established by the Riga German merchant G. Thalheim and still owned by the Thalheim family by the twentieth century.

Firm: TRAMPEDOCH AND COMPANY
Date Founded: 1885
Number of Workers: 120
Products: Industrial chemicals

Since 1897 a joint-stock company. Further details are not available.

Firm: VULKAN
Date Founded: 1873
Number of Workers: 70
Products: Matches

Established by the Riga German merchant A. Hirschmann.

V. The Glass, China, Porcelain and Tile Industry

Firm: BALTIC GLASS FACTORY
Date Founded: 1896
Number of Workers: 350
Products: Glassware

Owned by the Riga German chemicals entrepreneur Max Höflinger.

Firm: J.C. JESSEN
Date Founded: 1886
Number of Workers: 500
Products: Porecelain

Established and owned by the Riga German merchant J.C. Jessen.

Firm: KERKOVIUS AND COMPANY
Date Founded: 1890s
Number of Workers: ?
Products: Glassware

Established and owned by three Riga German merchants—W. Kerkovius, Robert and Woldemar Fränkel.

Firm: KUZNETSOV
Date Founded: 1843
Number of Workers: 1,966
Products: Porcelain and glassware

Established by the Riga Russian Old Believer merchant M.S. Kuznetsov and still owned by the Kuznetsov family at the turn of the century.

Firm: E.F. VOLKMANN
Date Founded: before 1883
Number of Workers: ?
Products: Glassware

Owned by the Riga German merchant Eugen Volkmann.

Firm: J.C. ZELM
Date Founded: 1870s
Number of Workers: ?
Products: Tiles, plaster

Established by the Riga German merchant J.C. Zelm and at the turn of the century owned by his son, J.F. Zelm.

VI.   The Leather Goods Industry

Firm: AMERICAN-BALTIC LEATHERWORKS
Date Founded: 1899
Number of Workers: ?
Products: Various leather goods

Owned by the Riga German merchant F.R. Laurentz.

Firm: C. BRIEGER
Date Founded: before 1865
Number of Workers: ?
Products: Various leather goods

Established by the Riga German merchant Eduard Brieger and still owned by the Brieger family at the turn of the century.

Firm: S.I. DOLGOV
Date Founded: 1812
Number of Workers: ?
Products: Various leather goods

Still owned by the Dolgovs, a local Russian family, at the turn of the century.

Firm: H. KIELSTEIN
Date Founded: 1878
Number of Workers: 52
Products: Various leather goods

Established by the Riga German merchant H. Kielstein and at the turn of the century owned by his son, G.H. Kielstein.

Firm: E. KNIGGE
Date Founded: 1840
Number of Workers: ?
Products: Leather gloves

Owned by the Riga German merchant Eduard Knigge.

Firm: JULIUS PRÜFFERT AND CO.
Date Founded: 1870s
Number of Workers: approx. 50
Products: Various leather goods

Established and owned by the Riga German leather merchant Julius Prüffert and still owned by the Prüffert family by the turn of the century.

Firm: A. WUNSCH
Date Founded: 1890s
Number of Workers: ?
Products: Leather gloves

Owned by the Riga German master glover A. Wunsch.

Firm: L. ZEITEMANN
Date Founded: 1870s
Number of Workers: ?
Products: Various leather goods

Established and owned by the Riga German merchant Louis Zeitemann.

VII. The Food Processing Industry

Firm: E. ARNAL
Date Founded: 1865
Number of Workers: less than 25
Products: Carbonated beverages

Established and owned by the Riga German merchant Emil Arnal.

Firm: G.G. BERGBOHM
Date Founded: late 1870s
Number of Workers: ?
Products: Alcoholic spirits

Established and owned by the Riga German merchant Georg Gottlieb Bergbohm.

Firm: G.A. BERTELS
Date Founded: 1864
Number of Workers: less than 25
Products: Alcoholic spirits, vinegar

Established and owned by the Riga German merchant Georg A. Bertels.

Firm: CLASSEN AND COMPANY
Date Founded: late 1870s
Number of Workers: ?
Products: Beer

Established and owned by the Riga German merchant Richard Classen.

Firm: A. GRÜNUPP
Date Founded: early 1870s
Number of Workers: less than 25
Products: Beer

Established and owned by the Latvian merchant A. Grünupp.

Firm: B.E. HEINRICH
Date Founded: 1871
Number of Workers: less than 25
Products: Candy, syrups

Established and owned by the German immigrant B.E. Heinrich.

Firm: ILGEZEEM BREWERY
Date Founded: 1863
Number of Workers: ?
Products: Beer

Established as a joint-stock company by a group of Riga German merchants, including magistrates G.D. Hernmarck, A. Faltin and A. Kriegsmann. By the turn of the century its capital was still 100 per cent local.

Firm: C.G. KUNTZENDORFF
Date Founded: 1796
Number of Workers: 50
Products: Beer

Established by the Riga German merchant C.G. Kuntzendorff and still owned by the Kuntzendorff family by the turn of the century.

Firm: M.H. KYMMEL
Date Founded: 1888
Number of Workers:
Products: Starches

Established and owned by the Riga German merchant Mathias Kymmel.

Firm: P.R. KYMMEL
Date Founded: 1815
Number of Workers: 50–100
Products: Beer

Established by the Riga German merchant P.R. Kymmel and still owned by the Kymmel family by the turn of the century.

Firm: LIETZ AND GRUNDMANN
Date Founded: late 1870s
Number of Workers: ?
Products: Syrup

Owned by the Riga German entrepreneurs Karl Christoph Lietz and Wilhelm Grundmann.

Firm: LIVONIA CORP.
Date Founded: 1899
Number of Workers: 100
Products: Beer

Established as a joint-stock company by a group of Riga German entrepreneurs. Its share capital was all held by local investors.

Firm: C. LOVIS
Date Founded: 1810
Number of Workers: ?
Products: Beer

Established by the Riga German merchant Christoph Lovis and still owned by the Lovis family at the turn of the century.

Firm: T. RIEGERT
Date Founded: before 1870
Number of Workers: 150
Products: Candy

Established by the Riga German confectioner T. Riegert and still owned by the Riegert family at the turn of the century.

Firm: H.P. SCHWABE
Date Founded: 1854
Number of Workers: ?
Products: Alcoholic spirits

Established by the Riga German merchant H.P. Schwabe and by the twentieth century owned by another Riga German named Emil Schmidt.

Firm: L.A. SCHWEINFURTH
Date Founded: 1864
Number of Workers: 50–100
Products: Carbonated beverages

Established by the Riga German merchant L.A. Schweinfurth and still owned by the Schweinfurth family at the turn of the century.

Firm: STARR AND COMPANY
Date Founded: 1868
Number of Workers: 150–200
Products: Chicory

Established and owned by the Riga German merchant Karl A. Weiss.

Firm: CHR. K.C. STRITZKY
Date Founded: 1869
Number of Workers: 150
Products: Beer

Established and owned by the Riga German merchant Chr. K.C. Stritzky.

Firm: TANNHÄUSER BREWERY
Date Founded: early 1870s
Number of Workers: ?
Products: Beer

Established by the Riga German merchant E.A. Puls and still owned by the Puls family at the turn of the century.

Firm: WALDSCHLÖSSCHEN BREWERY
Date Founded: 1863
Number of Workers: 170
Products: Beer

Established by the Riga German commercial firm of Dauder & Co., but by the turn of the century owned by the Riga German entrepreneur A. Bungner.

Firm: A.A. WOLFFSCHMIDT
Date Founded: 1863
Number of Workers: 211
Products: Alcoholic spirits

Established by the Riga German merchant A.A. Wolffschmidt. In 1898 it became a joint-stock company. All of the share capital was held by local investors.

VIII.   The Tobacco Processing Industry

Firm: A. BERGWITZ
Date Founded: 1875
Number of Workers: 150–200
Products: Tobacco

Established by a group of Riga German merchants as Gley & Co. In 1878 it was taken over by the Riga German entrepreneur Friedrich August Bergwitz.

Firm: I.V. GUSEV
Date Founded: 1852
Number of Workers: 120
Products: Tobacco

Established by the local Russian merchant Ivan V. Gusev and still owned by the Gusev family by the turn of the century.

Firm: F. KROSS
Date Founded: before 1860
Number of Workers: 150–200
Products: Tobacco

Established by the Riga German firm of Mey Bros., acquired by the Riga German merchant Ferdinand Kross in the late 1860s, and taken over by another Riga German merchant, Wilhelm Hellwig, in the late 1880s.

Firm: A.S. MAIKAPAR
Date Founded: 1887
Number of Workers: 235
Products: Tobacco

Established and owned by the Riga Jewish entrepreneur Abram Samailov Maikapar.

Firm: MÜNDEL AND COMPANY
Date Founded: 1849
Number of Workers: 500
Products: Tobacco

Established and owned by the Riga German merchant J.W. Mündel and still owned by the Mündel family at the turn of the century.

Firm: POPOV BROS.
Date Founded: 1883
Number of Workers: 45
Products: Tobacco

Established by two Riga Russian merchants and still owned by the Popov family at the turn of the century.

Firm: A.G. RUHTENBERG
Date Founded: 1839
Number of Workers: 700
Products: Tobacco

Established by the Riga German firm of Koffsky and Kuchczynski, it was acquired by another Riga German, A.G. Ruhtenberg in 1864. By the turn of the century it was still owned by the Ruhtenberg family.

Firm: LEO WISSOR
Date Founded: 1860
Number of Workers: 250
Products: Tobacco

Established by the Riga German merchant Leo Wissor, the firm was acquired in 1872 by another Riga German merchant named Ludwig Elias Bujanhoff.

IX. Miscellaneous Industries

Firm: C.W. HESSE
Date Founded: 1875
Number of Workers: 600
Products: Corks, zinc and nickel coated goods

Established and owned by the Riga German industrialist Carl Woldemar Hesse.

Firm: KRIEGSMANN CORP.
Date Founded: before 1865
Number of Workers: 930
Products: Cork, linings for railroad refrigerator cars

Established by the Riga German merchant and magistrate A. Kriegsmann, the firm became a joint-stock company in 1895. Its share capital, although one-sixth domestic, was controlled by Swedish investors.

Firm: SELLIER AND BELLOT
Date Founded: 1883
Number of Workers: 46
Products: Percussion caps and cartridges

Established as an affiliate of the Prague firm of the same name.

Firm: SENGBUSCH AND COMPANY
Date Founded: 1870s
Number of Workers: 600
Products: Cork

Established and owned by the Riga German entrepreneurs K.G. and W.O. Sengbusch.

Firm: UNION CORP.
Date Founded: 1885
Number of Workers: 653
Products: Electric generators, engines for electric streetcars

Established by Heinrich Dettmann, a local optician who held Reich-German citizenship. In 1898 it became a joint-stock affiliate of the Reich-German firm Siemens. Its share capital was 62.6 per cent Reich-German, 30.8 per cent in the hands of Moscow and St. Petersburg banks (principally the St. Petersburg International Bank of Commerce), and 6.6 per cent local.

APPENDIX II

BIOGRAPHICAL SKETCHES OF THE MEMBERS OF THE RIGA MUNICIPAL DUMA, 1878-1905[1]

Member: Alt, Eugen
Period of Duma Service: 1878-1900
Nationality: German
Estate Membership:* Mag.

A lawyer: Served as an official of the Magistracy from 1868 to 1872. In 1873 he became a Rechtsgelehrte *magistrate.*

Member: Armitstead, George[2]
Period of Duma Service: 1901-1905
Nationality: German
Estate Membership: —

From 1869 to 1871 worked in railroad construction in inner Russia; 1872-1875 owned and directed a brickworks in Kurland; after 1880 a co-owner of the "Riga Bone-Meal Factory," a firm which produced bone-meal and later super-phosphate fertilizers; 1892-1894 a director of the "Dünaburg-Vitebsk Railroad Corporation"; 1896-1901 a director of the "Baltic Cellulose Corporation" in Riga. Served as Riga Mayor, 1901-1912.

Member: Augsburg, Alexander C.
Period of Duma Service: 1890-1905
Nationality: German
Estate Membership: M-elder

A local merchant. Owned a passenger steamship line.

---

*The abbreviations used for the estates are: M-ald. = Merchant Guild Alderman; M-elder = Merchant Guild Elder; M = Merchant Guild member; A-ald. = Artisan Guild Alderman; A-elder = Artisan Guild Elder; A = Artisan Guild member; C. Burg. = Chief Burgomaster; Burg. = Burgomaster; Mag. = Magistrate.

Member: Ballod, Andreas
Period of Duma Service: 1886–1893, 1897–1905
Nationality: Latvian
Estate Membership: —

A wood merchant of the first guild.

Member: Barclay de Tolly, Eugen
Period of Duma Service: 1878–1893
Nationality: German
Estate Membership: Mag.

A lawyer and Rechtsgelehrte *magistrate; on board of the "Riga-Mitau Railroad Corporations" during the 1880's and early 1890's.*

Member: Bartsch, Johann H.
Period of Duma Service: 1878–1890
Nationality: German
Estate Membership: A

A master mason who expanded his shop into a construction firm of the first guild.

Member: Baum, Robert
Period of Duma Service: 1890–1905
Nationality: German
Estate Membership: Mag.

A lawyer; served as an official for the magistracy and became a Rechtsgelehrte *magistrate in 1886.*

Member: Baumann, Johann Fr.
Period of Duma Service: 1882–1886
Nationality: Latvian
Estate Membership: —

An architect.

Member: Beck, Robert
Period of Duma Service: 1878–1882
Nationality: German
Estate Membership: Burg.

A local merchant and member of the magistracy; owner of the small cotton textile factory "R.H. Beck," which folded in the 1880s.

Member: Becker, Bernhard
Period of Duma Service: 1878–1886
Nationality: German
Estate Membership: —

Technical Director of the "Riga Dünaburg Railroad Corporation."

Member: Berg, Christoph
Period of Duma Service: 1886–1893
Nationality: Latvian
Estate Membership: —

A second guild hardware merchant.

Member: Bergengrün, Carl
Period of Duma Service: 1878–1886
Nationality: German
Estate Membership: Mag.

A local merchant; owner of a first guild shipping firm; director of the "Riga Sawmill Corporatjon in Muckenholm."

Member: Bergmann, Adolph
Period of Duma Service: 1890–1893, 1901–1905
Nationality: German
Estate Membership: M

A physician.

Member: Bergmann, Carl Julius
Period of Duma Service: 1890–1901
Nationality: German
Estate Membership: A

A master locksmith whose shop was registered in the second guild.

Member: Berkholz, August
Period of Duma Service: 1878–1893
Nationality: German
Estate Membership: Burg.

A lawyer and Rechtsgelehrte *magistrate.*

Member: Bernhardt, G.F.
Period of Duma Service: 1882–1886
Nationality: German
Estate Membership: A

A master cabinet-maker.

Member: Bierich, Robert
Period of Duma Service: 1882–1893
Nationality: German
Estate Membership: M

A local merchant who owned a first guild shipping firm and who was on the board of directors of the Riga Bank of Commerce and of the Riga Municipal Discount Bank.

Member: Blumenbach, Alexander v.
Period of Duma Service: 1890–1901
Nationality: German
Estate Membership: —

A lawyer; served as legal official for the magistracy 1852–1868; in the provincial civil service 1868–1872; after 1872 an upper echelon administrator for the "Dünaburg-Vitebsk Railroad Corporation."

Member: Bochmann, E. v.
Period of Duma Service: 1897–1901
Nationality: German
Estate Membership: M

A physician; after 1874 director of Riga General Hospital.

Member: Boehm, Johann F.P.
Period of Duma Service: 1893–1901
Nationality: German
Estate Membership: M

Co-owner of the porcelain and tile factory "Zelm and Boehm."

Member: Bokhanov, Andrei
Period of Duma Service: 1901–1905
Nationality: Russian
Estate Membership: —

Adequate information lacking.

Member: Bornhaupt, Conrad
Period of Duma Service: 1878–1905
Nationality: German
Estate Membership: M

A lawyer; an official in the provincial court system, 1866–1889; in the early 1890s a director of the "Riga-Mitau Railroad Corporation"; a founding member of the German nationalist "Euphony Club."

Member: Bötticher, Emil v.
Period of Duma Service: 1878–1905
Nationality: German
Estate Membership: Burg.

A lawyer.

Member: Braun, Peter Robert
Period of Duma Service: 1886–1905
Nationality: German
Estate Membership: M-elder

Owner of a first guild shipping firm; a director of the Riga Chamber of Commerce Bank.

Member: Brieger, H.A.
Period of Duma Service: 1878–1882
Nationality: German
Estate Membership: M

Owner of the soap and candle factory "H.A. Brieger."

Member: Brunstermann, Friedrich
Period of Duma Service: 1878–1905
Nationality: German
Estate Membership: A-ald.

Alderman of the artisan guild.

Member: Brückmann, E.A.
Period of Duma Service: 1886–1890
Nationality: German
Estate Membership: M

A restaurant owner and wine merchant of the second guild.

Member: Brutzer, Gregor
Period of Duma Service: 1878–1882
Nationality: German
Estate Membership: M

A physician; founder and director of a local institution for the mentally ill.

Member: Buchardt, Theodor
Period of Duma Service: 1897–1905
Nationality: German
Estate Membership: M

A pharmacist; owner of a pharmacy.

Member: Buhse, F.
Period of Duma Service: 1882–1890
Nationality: German
Estate Membership: M

A natural scientist with a doctoral degree from Dorpat University; owned a landed estate near Riga.

Member: Büngner, Robert[3]
Period of Duma Service: 1878–1885
Nationality: German
Estate Membership: Burg.

A lawyer; served as Riga mayor from 1878 until his dismissal in 1885.

Member: Burchard, Julius
Period of Duma Service: 1878–1905
Nationality: German
Estate Membership: M

A merchant of the first guild.

Member: Busch, Alfred Theodor
Period of Duma Service: 1886–1905
Nationality: German
Estate Membership: M-elder

A pharmacist; owner of first guild wholesale drug firm; founding member of the German nationalist "Euphony Club."

Member: Butte, A.H.
Period of Duma Service: 1897–1901
Nationality: German
Estate Membership: —

A director of the "Poderaa" cement factory.

Member: Carlberg, Nikolai
Period of Duma Service: 1890–1893, 1897–1905
Nationality: German
Estate Membership: —

Employed 1883–1889 in the provincial civil service; after 1889 chief of the Riga Statistical Commission; chief editor of the Baltische Monatschrift *for a few months during 1890; a founding member of the German nationalist "Euphony Club."*

Member: Classen, W.
Period of Duma Service: 1878–1882
Nationality: German
Estate Membership: A

A master chimney-sweep.

Member: Deubner, Karl
Period of Duma Service: 1878–1886
Nationality: German
Estate Membership: M-elder

A merchant; director of the "Riga Steamship Corporation"; a director of the Riga Chamber of Commerce Bank.

Member: Dolgov, A.O.
Period of Duma Service: 1886–1897
Nationality: Russian
Estate Membership: —

A second guild leather merchant.

Member: Dolgov, S.I.
Period of Duma Service: 1897–1905
Nationality: Russian
Estate Membership:

Owner of the leather goods factory "S.I. Dolgov."

Member: Dorster, Theodor
Period of Duma Service: 1886–1905
Nationality: German
Estate Membership: A-elder

A master barber.

Member: Einberg, J.
Period of Duma Service: 1882–1886
Nationality: Latvian
Estate Membership: —

A lawyer.

Member: Erhardt, Jacob
Period of Duma Service: 1886–1905
Nationality: German
Estate Membership: M-elder

A merchant; director of "Baltic Linen Mfg. Corporation"; director of "Provodnik"; director of "Mühlgraben Chemical Corporation."

Member: Estanovich, A.
Period of Duma Service: 1890–1905
Nationality: Russian
Estate Membership: M

Part owner of the "Estanovich Bros." chemical factory.

Member: Fahrbach, Georg
Period of Duma Service: 1878–1890
Nationality: German
Estate Membership: M

A first guild merchant; agent for the "Moscow Fire Insurance Corporation"; director of the "Ilgezeem Brewery Corporation."

Member: Feldt, Wilhelm
Period of Duma Service: 1878–1882
Nationality: German
Estate Membership: M-elder

A merchant.

Member: Fränkel, Karl Robert
Period of Duma Service: 1890–1897
Nationality: German
Estate Membership: —

A first guild merchant.

Member: Freiland, L.
Period of Duma Service: 1890–1893
Nationality: German
Estate Membership: A-elder

A master butcher.

Member: Freytag von Loringhoven, Alfred Baron
Period of Duma Service: 1901–1905
Nationality: German
Estate Membership: —

A Baltic noble; provincial judge before 1889.

Member: Frobeen, Heinrich
Period of Duma Service: 1901–1905
Nationality: German
Estate Membership: M

An accountant.

Member: Gablenz, Heinrich
Period of Duma Service: 1886–1890
Nationality: German
Estate Membership: A

A master wainwright.

Member: Grade, Eduard
Period of Duma Service: 1878–1886
Nationality: German
Estate Membership: —

Wood merchant; owner of the sawmill "J.A. Schmidt & Co."; President of the Riga Municipal Discount Bank.

Member: Grossberg, M.
Period of Duma Service: 1901–1905
Nationality: Latvian
Estate Membership: —

Adequate biographical detail lacking.

Member: Grosswald, Friedrich
Period of Duma Service: 1901–1905
Nationality: Latvian
Estate Membership: —

A lawyer; Chairman of the Riga Latvian Union.

Member: Grünupp, Andrei
Period of Duma Service: 1890–1893, 1897–1905
Nationality: Latvian
Estate Membership: —

Owned a brewery.

Member: Haffelberg, Christoph
Period of Duma Service: 1901–1905
Nationality: German
Estate Membership: A

A master bookbinder.

Member: Haffner, Gustav
Period of Duma Service: 1893–1905
Nationality: German
Estate Membership: —

A lawyer; municipal civil servant in revenue department and in city poor-house administration since 1882.

Member: Hagen, Julius
Period of Duma Service: 1893–1901
Nationality: German
Estate Membership: —

An architect; 1875–1891 consultant for the provincial government; 1887–1905 docent at the Baltic Polytechnical Institute.

Member: Harmsen, W.
Period of Duma Service: 1882–1901
Nationality: German
Estate Membership: A

A master painter.

Member: Hartmann, Karl Georg
Period of Duma Service: 1893–1897
Nationality: German
Estate Membership: M-elder

A second guild merchant who traded in lamps and kerosene.

Member: Hartmann, Karl J.F.
Period of Duma Service: 1890–1905
Nationality: German
Estate Membership: M-elder

A merchant; director of the machine fabrication firm "R. Pohle"; a director of the woollen textile firm "Holm & Co."

Member: Hartmann, Wilhelm
Period of Duma Service: 1878–1882
Nationality: German
Estate Membership: M-elder

Owner of the "Hartmann" petroleum refinery.

Member: Hausmann, Constantin
Period of Duma Service: 1886–1893
Nationality: German
Estate Membership: —

A lawyer; employed as an official for the magistracy, 1867–1889.

Member: Heede, Martin
Period of Duma Service: 1878–1882
Nationality: German
Estate Membership: A-elder

A master bookbinder.

Member: Heimann, Alexander v.
Period of Duma Service: 1886–1893
Nationality: German
Estate Membership: —

An administrative executive with the Riga Bank of Commerce; President of the "Riga-Mitau Railroad Corp."

Member: Hellmann, H.
Period of Duma Service: 1890–1893
Nationality: German
Estate Membership: —

Teacher at the City Real School, 1879–1887; director of the City Real School after 1887.

Member: Helmsing, C.A.
Period of Duma Service: 1886–1890
Nationality: German
Estate Membership: —

Part-owner of a shipping firm; part-owner of the "Hartmann" oil refinery; a deputy director of both the Riga Chamber of Commerce Bank and the Riga Bank of Commerce.

Member: Hesse, C.W.
Period of Duma Service: 1890–1905
Nationality: German
Estate Membership: —

Owner of the cork factory "C.W. Hesse."

Member: Hillner, Alfred
Period of Duma Service: 1878–1890
Nationality: German
Estate Membership: M

A pastor; founding member of the "Euphony Club."

Member: Höflinger, Eugen
Period of Duma Service: 1890–1901
Nationality: German
Estate Membership: —

A first guild merchant who traded in lamps and kerosene; a deputy director of the Riga Chamber of Commerce Bank.

Member: Hollander, Eduard
Period of Duma Service: 1878–1890
Nationality: German
Estate Membership: C. Burg

A lawyer.

Member: Holst, Karl
Period of Duma Service: 1878–1882
Nationality: German
Estate Membership: M

A lawyer; official in the provincial court system.

Member: Hopfc, F.W.
Period of Duma Service: 1878–1886
Nationality: German
Estate Membership: A

A master carpenter; owner of a sawmill.

Member: Jansen, K.F.
Period of Duma Service: 1893–1905
Nationality: German
Estate Membership: M-elder

A first guild wine merchant.

Member: Jaksch, Oskar
Period of Duma Service: 1878–1905
Nationality: German
Estate Membership: M-elder

A first guild merchant who traded in clocks, jewellery, fine chinaware.

Member: Jauch, Carl
Period of Duma Service: 1901–1905
Nationality: German
Estate Membership: A

A master baker.

Member: Juon, Wilhelm Adolf
Period of Duma Service: 1890–1905
Nationality: German
Estate Membership: M-elder

Part owner of a first guild textile wholesale firm.

Member: Jürgens, Eduard
Period of Duma Service: 1893–1905
Nationality: German
Estate Membership: M

A chemist; director of the chemical firm "G. Thalheim."

Member: Kählbrandt, A.
Period of Duma Service: 1882–1893
Nationality: German
Estate Membership: M

A lawyer; official in the provincial court system, 1862–1889; a director of the Riga Municipal Discount Bank.

Member: Kallmeyer, Moritz
Period of Duma Service: 1878–1882
Nationality: Jewish
Estate Membership: —

A first guild merchant.

Member: Kamarin, N.P.
Period of Duma Service: 1890–1897
Nationality: Russian
Estate Membership: —

A first guild merchant.

Member: Kamarin, P.G.
Period of Duma Service: 1882–1886
Nationality: Russian
Estate Membership: M

A first guild merchant and father of the above.

Member: Kennert, August
Period of Duma Service: 1878–1882
Nationality: German
Estate Membership: —

A merchant.

Member: Kerkovius, Georg
Period of Duma Service: 1893–1905
Nationality: German
Estate Membership: —

An engineer; 1874, active in railroad construction in Russia and in the construction of the port of Libau; 1875–1879 active in the construction and technical direction of the Riga-Tuckum and Riga-Bolderaa railroad lines; 1880–1885 head engineer for the on-going Riga port reconstruction project; 1886–1891 head engineer for construction of Riga-Pskov railroad line; 1892–1897 owner of a small Riga string manufacturing firm; after 1901 chairman of the board of directors of the "Baltic Cellulose Corporation."

Member: Kerkovius, Ludwig
Period of Duma Service: 1878–1905
Nationality: German
Estate Membership: Mag.

A merchant; part owner of the "John Hammer" sawmill; served as Riga vice-mayor from 1878 to 1890 and as mayor from 1890 to 1901.

Member: Kerkovius, Rudolf
Period of Duma Service: 1878–1893
Nationality: German
Estate Membership: —

A merchant; owner of a first guild import-export firm; a deputy director of the Riga Chamber of Commerce Bank.

Member: Khrustalev, Averian D.
Period of Duma Service: 1878–1890
Nationality: Russian
Estate Membership: M

A second guild tobacco merchant.

Member: Kieseritzky, N.
Period of Duma Service: 1893–1901
Nationality: German
Estate Membership: M

A pharmacist; owner of a pharmacy.

Member: Kirstein, Johann Karl
Period of Duma Service: 1878–1882
Nationality: German
Estate Membership: M

Owner of a soap and candle factory.

Member: Klein, E. v.
Period of Duma Service: 1878–1882
Nationality: German
Estate Membership: M

A lawyer; official in the provincial judicial system.

Member: Kleingarn, Heinrich
Period of Duma Service: 1878–1882
Nationality: German
Estate Membership: M

A merchant.

Member: Klingenberg, Gustav
Period of Duma Service: 1893–1905
Nationality: German
Estate Membership: A

A master locksmith.

Member: Klot, N. v.
Period of Duma Service: 1893–1905
Nationality: German
Estate Membership: —

A lawyer.

Member: Knieriem, August
Period of Duma Service: 1878–1890
Nationality: German
Estate Membership: Mag.

A lawyer; official in the magistracy court system until becoming a Rechtsgelehrte *magistrate in 1881.*

Member: Knigge, H.E.
Period of Duma Service: 1886–1897
Nationality: German
Estate Membership: A

A master glover; owner of a leather goods factory.

Member: Koch, J.C.
Period of Duma Service: 1878–1882
Nationality: German
Estate Membership: M-elder

Owner of the varnish factory "J.C. Koch."

Member: Kohzer, R.
Period of Duma Service: 1886–1897
Nationality: ?
Estate Membership: —

A carriage maker.

Member: Kornilov, A.G.
Period of Duma Service: 1886–1890
Nationality: Russian
Estate Membership: —

Adequate biographical detail lacking.

Member: Korolev, M.S.
Period of Duma Service: 1886–1890
Nationality: Russian
Estate Membership: —

Adequate biographical detail lacking.

Member: Kosikovskii, K.V.
Period of Duma Service: 1890–1893
Nationality: Russian
Estate Membership: —

Adequate biographical detail lacking.

Member: Kressler, W.A.
Period of Duma Service: 1901–1905
Nationality: German
Estate Membership: —

A landscape gardener.

Member: Kreyenberg, W.C.
Period of Duma Service: 1878–1882
Nationality: German
Estate Membership: A

A master rope-maker.

Member: Kröger, H.A.
Period of Duma Service: 1882–1890
Nationality: German
Estate Membership: M-elder

Part owner of the "Hartmann" oil refinery; a director of the "Riga Sawmill Corporation in Muckenholm"; a director of the "Ilgezeem Woollenware Corporation."

Member: Kundt, J.G.
Period of Duma Service: 1878–1882
Nationality: German
Estate Membership: A

A master clockmaker.

Member: Kymmel, C.R.
Period of Duma Service: 1893–1905
Nationality: German
Estate Membership: —

Owner of the "P.R. Kymmel" brewery.

Member: Laerum, Henrik
Period of Duma Service: 1893–1901
Nationality: German
Estate Membership: M

Owner of a first guild shipping firm; a director of the Riga Municipal Discount Bank.

Member: Lange, Woldemar
Period of Duma Service: 1897–1901
Nationality: German
Estate Membership: M-elder

A director of the furniture factory "Perfect, Inc."; part owner of a sawmill.

Member: Lashkov, Ivan
Period of Duma Service: 1901–1905
Nationality: Russian
Estate Membership: —

A tobacco merchant.

Member: Laurentz, Friedrich R.
Period of Duma Service: 1893–1901
Nationality: German
Estate Membership: —

Owner of a shipping company; part owner of the paper factory "Bruhns & Company"; a director of the "Meteor" brush factory; owner of the "American-Baltic Leatherworks" factory; a deputy director of the Riga Municipal Discount Bank.

Member: Leepin, Reinhold
Period of Duma Service: 1901–1905
Nationality: Latvian
Estate Membership: —

A physician.

Member: Lehmann, Emil
Period of Duma Service: 1893–1905
Nationality: German
Estate Membership: —

*An engineer; held technical position in a Moscow factory, 1869–1870;
1870–1872 employed by the "Riga-Mitau Railroad Corp."; 1872–1873
employed by the "Riga-Dünaburg Railroad Corp."; 1873–1881 employed first
in construction and then in technical administration of the "Riga-Dünaburg
Railroad Corp."; 1895–1899 head of technical bureau of a Riga engineering
consultant firm; after 1899 owner of a consultant firm.*

Member: Lieven, Victor
Period of Duma Service: 1901–1905
Nationality: German
Estate Membership: —

*A chemist with a doctorate from Dorpat University; director of a cement
factory near Riga; probably a Baltic noble.*

Member: Lieventhal, K.A.
Period of Duma Service: 1882–1893
Nationality: Latvian
Estate Membership: —

*A physician; docent at the Baltic Polytechnical Institute, of which he eventually
became Vice-Director.*

Member: Lifschitz, Leib
Period of Duma Service: 1882–1890
Nationality: Jewish
Estate Membership: —

A first guild tobacco merchant.

Member: Lomani, Gordian Karl
Period of Duma Service: 1886–1897
Nationality: German
Estate Membership: M

Owner of a sawmill.

Member: Lorch, Friedrich E.
Period of Duma Service: 1893–1901
Nationality: German
Estate Membership: M

A first guild merchant.

Member: Lösevitz, Gustav
Period of Duma Service: 1882–1886
Nationality: German
Estate Membership: Mag.

A first guild merchant.

Member: Lovis, Karl
Period of Duma Service: 1882–1886
Nationality: German
Estate Membership: —

A professor of enginnering at the Baltic Polytechnical Institute; co-founder of the machine fabrication firm "Felser & Co."; co-founder of the metallurgical firm "Sirius Corp."

Member: Lucht, J.H.
Period of Duma Service: 1878–1886
Nationality: German
Estate Membership: A

A master carpenter and sawmill owner.

Member: Lübeck, Moritz
Period of Duma Service: 1882–1886
Nationality: German
Estate Membership: M

A first guild timber merchant.

Member: Lucas, E.U.
Period of Duma Service: 1886–1893
Nationality: German
Estate Membership: A

A master mason whose shop was registered in the second guild.

Member: Luntz, W. Jankelowitsch
Period of Duma Service: 1890–1893
Nationality: Jewish
Estate Membership: —

A first guild merchant.

Member: Lyra, Richard
Period of Duma Service: 1893–1897
Nationality: German
Estate Membership: —

A first guild timber merchant; a director of the Riga Municipal Discount Bank.

Member: Makarov, K.G.
Period of Duma Service: 1890–1893
Nationality: Russian
Estate Membership: —

Owner of a noodle factory.

Member: Maksimov, Nikolai
Period of Duma Service: 1901–1905
Nationality: Russian
Estate Membership: —

Owner of a sawmill; a director of the Russian Mutual Credit Union.

Member: Mansfeldt, J.W.
Period of Duma Service: 1897–1901
Nationality: German
Estate Membership: M

A second guild furniture and carpet merchant.

Member: Medne, Peter
Period of Duma Service: 1882–1901
Nationality: German
Estate Membership: A

A master carpenter and construction contractor whose firm was registered in the second guild.

Member: Mentzendorff, A.
Period of Duma Service: 1878–1882
Nationality: German
Estate Membership: M-elder

A first guild wine and tobacco merchant.

Member: Merkuleev, N.D.
Period of Duma Service: 1882–1893, 1901–1905
Nationality: Russian
Estate Membership: —

A second guild tea merchant.

Member: Mertens, O.
Period of Duma Service: 1890–1897
Nationality: German
Estate Membership: —

A lawyer; administrative official for the "Riga-Dünaburg Railroad Corp."

Member: Meyer, Josef
Period of Duma Service: 1878–1893
Nationality: German
Estate Membership: M

A first guild grain merchant.

Member: Mihlit, D.
Period of Duma Service: 1901–1905
Nationality: Latvian
Estate Membership: —

A second guild tobacco merchant; tavern owner.

Member: Minus, H.D.W.
Period of Duma Service: 1878–1882
Nationality: German
Estate Membership: M

A merchant.

Member: Minuth, A.A.
Period of Duma Service: 1878–1886
Nationality: German
Estate Membership: A-ald.

A master locksmith; owner of a safe-making factory.

Member: Minuth, W.
Period of Duma Service: 1886–1890
Nationality: German
Estate Membership: A

A master coppersmith.

Member: Molien, Gustav[4]
Period of Duma Service: 1878–1879
Nationality: German
Estate Membership: M-ald.

A merchant; a director of the Riga Bank of Commerce.

Member: Mitschke, J.
Period of Duma Service: 1886–1897
Nationality: German
Estate Membership: M

A second guild hardware merchant.

Member: Moritz, Erwin
Period of Duma Service: 1878–1882
Nationality: German
Estate Membership: M

A lawyer.

Member: Moritz, Erwin
Period of Duma Service: 1890–1905
Nationality: Latvian
Estate Membership: —

A cab driver.

Member: Müller, Karl C.
Period of Duma Service: 1893–1901
Nationality: German
Estate Membership: —

An engineer; 1873–1874 employed by an engineering consultant firm; 1877–1879 employed by the "Riga-Dünaburg Railroad Corp."; 1879–1880 employed by the "Dünaburg-Vitebsk Railroad Corp."; 1881–1882 employed by a firm of architects; 1882–1886 employed by the machine fabrication firm "Rosenkranz & Co."; after 1886 empoyed by the city of Riga in the office of the municipal engineer.

Member: Mündel, A.J.K.
Period of Duma Service: 1893–1905
Nationality: German
Estate Membership: M-elder

Owner of the tobacco factory "Mündel & Co." and of the rubber goods factory "J.W. Mündel."

Member: Niedermeier, Anton
Period of Duma Service: 1893–1905
Nationality: German
Estate Membership: A

A master miller; owner of a steam flour mill.

Member: Nikoronov, M.A.
Period of Duma Service: 1901–1905
Nationality: Russian
Estate Membership: —

A tax inspector.

Member: Nipp, Heinrich
Period of Duma Service: 1878–1882
Nationality: German
Estate Membership: M-elder

Owner of a first guild shipping firm; a director of the "Riga-Bolderaa Railroad Corp."

Member: Oettingen, August v.[5]
Period of Duma Service: 1878–1889
Nationality: German
Estate Membership: —

A Baltic noble; 1857–1862 marshal of the Livland nobility; 1862–1868 governor of Livland province; 1886–1889 mayor of Riga.

Member: Oettingen, Max v.[6]
Period of Duma Service: 1882–1889
Nationality: German
Estate Membership: —

A Baltic noble; a lawyer; one of the authors of Russisch-Baltische *Blätter.*

Member: Offenberg, Peter Baron
Period of Duma Service: 1890–1897
Nationality: German
Estate Membership: —

A Baltic noble.

Member: Ostwald, G.W.
Period of Duma Service: 1878–1882
Nationality: German
Estate Membership: A-elder

A master cooper; owner of a factory that made carbonated beverages.

Member: Pabst, August
Period of Duma Service: 1890–1905
Nationality: German
Estate Membership: —

An engineer; a director of the "Riga Steamship Corp."

Member: Pander, J.C.
Period of Duma Service: 1886–1897
Nationality: German
Estate Membership: —

A technical employee of the "Riga-Mitau Railroad Corp."

Member: Pannewitz, M.G.
Period of Duma Service: 1897–1905
Nationality: German
Estate Membership: M-elder

Owner of a shipping firm.

Member: Peterson, Rudolf
Period of Duma Service: 1893–1901
Nationality: ?
Estate Membership: —

Asst. Director of the Livland governor's chancery.

Member: Pickardt, Carl v.
Period of Duma Service: 1890–1897
Nationality: German
Estate Membership: Mag.

A lawyer; served as Riga vice-mayor, 1890–1897.

Member: Pimenov, V.P.
Period of Duma Service: 1882–1886
Nationality: Russian
Estate Membership: —

A merchant.

Member: Pirang, Nikolai
Period of Duma Service: 1901–1905
Nationality: ?
Estate Membership: —

An engineer employed by the "Popov Bros." tobacco firm.

Member: Plates, Ernst Arnold
Period of Duma Service: 1893–1905
Nationality: German
Estate Membership: M

Held a doctorate from Heidelberg University in political economy; owner of a print shop; editor of the Latvian newspaper Mahjas Weesis.

Member: Plawneek, N.
Period of Duma Service: 1878–1882
Nationality: Latvian
Estate Membership: —

An official in the "Latvian trades."

Member: Plawneek, N.B.
Period of Duma Service: 1897–1905
Nationality: Latvian
Estate Membership: M

A merchant.

Member: Pychlau, Reinhold
Period of Duma Service: 1878–1882
Nationality: German
Estate Membership: M

A part owner of a cotton textile factory.

Member: Radsing, Peter
Period of Duma Service: 1901–1905
Nationality: Latvian
Estate Membership: A

A master mason; owner of a first guild construction firm.

Member: Rauthe, C.A.
Period of Duma Service: 1886–1890
Nationality: German
Estate Membership: A

A master carpenter.

Member: Rebinin, Fedor
Period of Duma Service: 1878–1886
Nationality: Russian
Estate Membership: —

A merchant; on the executive committee of the Russian nationalist "Bee" society; a director of the Russian Mutual Credit Union.

Member: Redlich, Alexander
Period of Duma Service: 1897–1905
Nationality: German
Estate Membership: —

A hardware merchant.

Member: Reimers, W.H.M.
Period of Duma Service: 1897–1905
Nationality: German
Estate Membership: —

A jeweller.

Member: Reymer, A.G.
Period of Duma Service: 1890–1901
Nationality: German
Estate Membership: —

Owner of a restaurant.

Member: Richter, Theodor v.
Period of Duma Service: 1886–1890
Nationality: German
Estate Membership: —

A lawyer; until 1889 an official in the provincial judicial system.

Member: Röpenack, Nikolai
Period of Duma Service: 1901–1905
Nationality: German
Estate Membership: Mag.

A lawyer.

Member: Ruetz, P.
Period of Duma Service: 1890–1905
Nationality: German
Estate Membership: M-elder

A agent for the "Russia" insurance company; a director of the Riga Municipal Discount Bank; a director of the "Ilgezeem Sawmill Corp."

Member: Sawitzky, Johann Alexander
Period of Duma Service: 1893–1905
Nationality: German (?)
Estate Membership: —

Adequate biographical data lacking.

Member: Schalit, Leib M.
Period of Duma Service: 1890–1893
Nationality: Jewish
Estate Membership: —

A first guild timber merchant.

Member: Scheuber, Georg
Period of Duma Service: 1882–1886
Nationality: German
Estate Membership: M

A second guild merchant.

Member: Scheubner, Otto v.
Period of Duma Service: 1882–1890
Nationality: German
Estate Membership: —

Part owner of the textile factory "Holm & Co."; vice-chairman of the "Riga-Mitau Railroad Corp."

Member: Schleicher, Robert
Period of Duma Service: 1886–1897
Nationality: German
Estate Membership: —

Owner of a glove factory.

Member: Schmidt, Carl Alphons
Period of Duma Service: 1893–1905
Nationality: German
Estate Membership: —

Director of the oil refinery and cement factory "C. Chr. Schmidt & Sons."

Member: Schmidt, Carl Christoph
Period of Duma Service: 1882–1886
Nationality: German
Estate Membership: M

Founder and director of the oil refinery and cement factory "C. Chr. Schmidt & Sons."

Member: Schmidt, Carl Martin
Period of Duma Service: 1890–1901
Nationality: German
Estate Membership: A

A master locksmith whose shop was registered in the second guild.

Member: Schneidemann, Adolph
Period of Duma Service: 1878–1882
Nationality: German
Estate Membership: —

Owner of a woollen textile factory and of a steam flour mill.

Member: Schröder, G.W.
Period of Duma Service: 1890–1901
Nationality: German
Estate Membership: —

A first guild timber merchant.

Member: Schubert, Bernhard v.
Period of Duma Service: 1893–1905
Nationality: German
Estate Membership: —

An engineer; a director of the "Riga Rolling Mill, Inc."; a director of the "Riga-Dünaburg Railroad Corp."

Member: Schultz, C.F.
Period of Duma Service: 1878–1882
Nationality: German
Estate Membership: M

Owner of a first guild shipping firm.

Member: Schultz, Robert
Period of Duma Service: 1886–1890
Nationality: German
Estate Membership: —

A second guild hardware merchant.

Member: Schwartz, J.C.
Period of Duma Service: 1878–1890
Nationality: German
Estate Membership: Mag.

A lawyer.

Member: Schwartz, Paul A.
Period of Duma Service: 1893–1897
Nationality: German
Estate Membership: M-elder

On the board of directors of the Riga Chamber of Commerce Bank, "Provodnik," "Salamander" and "M.H. Kymmel."

Member: Schwarzbort, D.
Period of Duma Service: 1882–1893
Nationality: Jewish
Estate Membership: —

A first guild sugar merchant.

Member: Schwenn, J.C.
Period of Duma Service: 1882–1886
Nationality: German
Estate Membership: A

A master coppersmith.

Member: Schweder, Gotthard
Period of Duma Service: 1878–1890
Nationality: German
Estate Membership: —

Director of the City Gymnasium

Member: Sehl, J.H.
Period of Duma Service: 1886–1890
Nationality: Latvian
Estate Membership: —

A fisherman.

Member: Sellmer, Adolph
Period of Duma Service: 1878–1882
Nationality: German
Estate Membership: M-elder

A first guild merchant.

Member: Sengbusch, O. v.
Period of Duma Service: 1886–1893
Nationality: German
Estate Membership: —

A first guild merchant; owner of a sawmill; a director of the "Baltic Fire Insurance Corp."

Member: Seuberlich, R. Wilhelm
Period of Duma Service: 1893–1901
Nationality: German
Estate Membership: —

A first guild merchant.

Member: Shelukhin, P.T.
Period of Duma Service: 1878–1882
Nationality: Russian
Estate Membership: M

A first guild merchant; an accountant for the Russian Mutual Credit Union.

Member: Shutov, I.A.
Period of Duma Service: 1878–1882
Nationality: Russian
Estate Membership: M

A second guild merchant.

Member: Shutov, S.I.
Period of Duma Service: 1901–1905
Nationality: Russian
Estate Membership: —

A lawyer.

Member: Skribanowitz, T.
Period of Duma Service: 1897–1901
Nationality: ?
Estate Membership: —

A clothing merchant.

Member: Smolian, Viktor
Period of Duma Service: 1893–1905
Nationality: German
Estate Membership: —

Part owner of the banking house of "Miriam & Smolian"; a director of the "Riga Steelworks Corp."; a director of the keg factory "Mercury, Inc."

Member: Sperling, Woldemar Georg
Period of Duma Service: 1893–1901
Nationality: ?
Estate Membership: —

A first guild merchant.

Member: Stahl, A.K.
Period of Duma Service: 1901–1905
Nationality: German
Estate Membership: A

A master bookbinder.

Member: Stapprani, P.F.
Period of Duma Service: 1897–1905
Nationality: German
Estate Membership: —

An engineer; technical director of the "Riga-Mitau Railroad Corp."

Member: Stein, H. v.
Period of Duma Service: 1878-1890
Nationality: German
Estate Membership: —

A director of the "Riga-Dünaburg Railroad Corp."; secretary of the Riga Chamber of Commerce; administrative secretary of the Baltic Polytechnical Institute.

Member: Steinert, C.D.
Period of Duma Service: 1890-1905
Nationality: German
Estate Membership: A

A master carpenter; owner of a sawmill.

Member: Stieda, Hermann
Period of Duma Service: 1878-1905
Nationality: German
Estate Membership: M-elder

A first guild merchant; a deputy director of the Riga Chamber of Commerce Bank; a founding member of the nationalist "Euphony Club."

Member: Strandmann, Arvid v.
Period of Duma Service: 1897-1901
Nationality: German
Estate Membership: —

A Baltic noble; a lawyer educated at Dorpat University; a director of the metallurgical firm "Sirius"; a founding member of the nationalist "Euphony Club."

Member: Strauch, A.
Period of Duma Service: 1878-1897
Nationality: Latvian
Estate Membership: —

An official of the "Latvian trades."

Member: Strauch, A. Jr.
Period of Duma Service: 1901-1905
Nationality: Latvian
Estate Membership: —

Owner of a sawmill.

Member: Strauss, G.A.
Period of Duma Service: 1882–1886
Nationality: German
Estate Membership: A

A master cobbler.

Member: Taube, C.W.
Period of Duma Service: 1878–1886
Nationality: German
Estate Membership: M-elder

A first guild merchant; a director of the Riga Municipal Discount Bank.

Member: Taube, W.J.
Period of Duma Service: 1882–1886
Nationality: German
Estate Membership: A-ald.

A master needle-maker.

Member: Thonagel, Julius
Period of Duma Service: 1893–1897
Nationality: ?
Estate Membership: —

A lawyer.

Member: Tiemer, H.
Period of Duma Service: 1878–1890
Nationality: German
Estate Membership: Mag.

Owner of a first guild shipping firm.

Member: Tiling, Theodor
Period of Duma Service: 1886–1890
Nationality: German
Estate Membership: —

A physician.

Member: Tiugin, Aleksandr
Period of Duma Service: 1893–1901
Nationality: Russian
Estate Membership: —

A wine merchant.

Member: Tode, E.
Period of Duma Service: 1878–1882
Nationality: German
Estate Membership: M

A first guild wine merchant.

Member: Tode, R.
Period of Duma Service: 1893–1905
Nationality: German
Estate Membership: —

A wine merchant; owner of the carbonated beverage factory "G.A. Schwein-furth"; director of the Riga Municipal Discount Bank.

Member: Treu, E.
Period of Duma Service: 1890–1893
Nationality: ?
Estate Membership: —

A tavern owner.

Member: Treyer, J.M.
Period of Duma Service: 1893–1905
Nationality: German
Estate Membership: M-elder

Owner of a sawmill.

Member: Tunzelmann, Max
Period of Duma Service: 1878–1893
Nationality: German
Estate Membership: M

A lawyer.

Member: Vajen, Wilhelm
Period of Duma Service: 1886–1890
Nationality: German
Estate Membership: M

A first guild merchant.

Member: Vogelsang, J.
Period of Duma Service: 1897–1901
Nationality: German
Estate Membership: —

Owner of a ribbon and lace factory; a director of the "Riga Cotton Spinning Corp."

Member: Wandeberg, J.G.
Period of Duma Service: 1878–1882
Nationality: German
Estate Membership: A

A master instrument maker.

Member: Wäber, Alexander
Period of Duma Service: 1886–1890
Nationality: German
Estate Membership: —

Although he was an ethnic German, Wäber was one of the leaders of the Latvian nationalist movement in Riga as a journalist and as a member of the Riga Latvian Union.

Member: Wegner, Wilhelm
Period of Duma Service: 1901–1905
Nationality: German
Estate Membership: M

A merchant.

Member: Weiss, C.A.
Period of Duma Service: 1882–1886
Nationality: German
Estate Membership: M

Part owner of the wire and nail factory "Starr & Co."

Member: Weiss, Otto
Period of Duma Service: 1878–1886
Nationality: German
Estate Membership: A

A master hatter.

Member: Wengel, Wilhelm
Period of Duma Service: 1897–1901
Nationality: German
Estate Membership: A

A master saddle maker.

Member: Werner, F.
Period of Duma Service: 1886–1897
Nationality: German
Estate Membership: A

A master carpenter.

Member: Wihksne, Simon
Period of Duma Service: 1901–1905
Nationality: Latvian
Estate Membership: A

A master carpenter; owner of a second guild construction firm.

Member: Wilm, Robert
Period of Duma Service: 1878–1886
Nationality: German
Estate Membership: Mag.

A lawyer.

Member: Wirkau, Arnold Emil
Period of Duma Service: 1893–1897
Nationality: German
Estate Membership: M

A first guild coal merchant.

Member: Wolfschmidt, A.
Period of Duma Service: 1886–1905
Nationality: German
Estate Membership: M-elder

Owner of the "A. Wolfschmidt" distillery; a director of the machine fabrication firm "Aetna"; a director of the "Ilgezeem Sawmill Corp."

Member: Wyganowsky, Floryan v.
Period of Duma Service: 1901–1905
Nationality: Polish
Estate Membership: —

An engineer; owned a consulting firm in Riga.

Member: Zander, C.
Period of Duma Service: 1882–1901
Nationality: German
Estate Membership: M-ald.

A first guild merchant; on the boards of the Riga Chamber of Commerce Bank, the "Baltic Fire Insurance Corp.," and the "Riga-Tuckum Railroad Corp."

Member: Zirkwitz, Rudolf Heinrich
Period of Duma Service: 1893–1905
Nationality: German
Estate Membership: —

An architect.

Member: Zwingmann, Eugen V.
Period of Duma Service: 1893–1905
Nationality: German
Estate Membership: —

A lawyer; justice of the peace; official in the magistracy courts, 1868–1889; head of the district post office.

APPENDIX III

THE ORGANIZERS OF THE GERMAN NATIONALIST EUPHONY CLUB: BIOGRAPHICAL SKETCHES

Bornhaupt, Conrad
A lawyer; official in the provincial judicial system, 1866–1889; a director of the Riga-Mitau Railroad Corp. in the early 1890s; served in the municipal duma, 1878–1905

Bruiningk, Hermann v.
A lawyer; archivist and secretary of the Livland provincial diet.

Busch, Theodor
A pharmacist; elder in the merchant guild; owned first guild drug wholesaling firm; served in the municipal duma, 1886–1905.

Carlberg, Nikolai
In the provincial civil service, 1883–1889; after 1889 chief of the Riga Statistical Commission; chief editor of the *Baltische Monatschrift* for a few months during 1890; served in the municipal duma, 1890–1893, 1897–1905.

Friesendorff, Ernst
Taught Greek at the Riga City Gymnasium, 1873–1879; in St. Petersburg as director of a German-language school, 1880–1899; director of a commercial school run by the Riga Chamber of Commerce, 1900–1907.

Gernet, Bruno v.
A Riga municipal civil servant.

Girgensohn, Karl
A teacher at the Riga City Girls' School.

Hillner, Alfred
A Lutheran pastor; served in the municipal duma, 1878–1890.

Hollander, Bernhard
Teacher at the Riga City Real School, 1883–1908; in 1891 forced by Russification to switch from teaching history to teaching religion; also a docent at the Baltic Polytechnical Institute, 1886–1898.

Kählbrandt, Emil
A Lutheran pastor.

Keller, Karl
A Lutheran pastor.

179

Löffler, Hermann
  Teacher at the Riga City Girls' School, 1884–1889; after 1889 taught German at the Riga City Gymnasium.
Neumann, A.
  Teacher of German language at the Riga City Gymnasium.
Oettingen, Arved v.
  A Livland noble.
Redlich, Franz
  An accountant.
Rieder, Woldemar v.
  A physician.
Schabert, Oskar
  A Lutheran pastor; taught religion at the Riga City Gymnasium.
Schröder, Christoph
  A physician.
Sivers, Max v.
  A Baltic noble.
Stieda, Hermann
  A merchant; alderman of the merchant guild; deputy director of the Riga Chamber of Commerce Bank; served in the municipal duma, 1878–1905.
Strandmann, Arvid v.
  A lawyer and a Baltic noble; director of the Sirius Corporation; served in the municipal duma, 1897–1901.
Tobien, Alexander v.
  A provincial civil servant.
Transehe-Roseneck, Astaf v.
  A Baltic noble.
Walter, Karl
  Teacher at the Riga City Real School.
Wittram, Alfred
  An official in the municipal court system until the demise of the magistracy in 1889; after 1889 had a private legal practice.

APPENDIX IV

THE BALTIC GOVERNORS-GENERAL AND THE GOVERNOR OF LIVLAND PROVINCE DURING THE LATE NINETEENTH CENTURY

Baltic Governors-General

1848–1861	Alexander Suvorov
1861–1864	Wilhelm von Lieven
1864–1866	Peter Shuvalov
1866	Eduard Baranov
1866–1870	Peter Albedinskii
1870–1876	Peter Bagration

In 1876 the office of Governor-General in the Baltic provinces was abolished by order of Tsar Alexander II.

Governors of Livland Province

1847–1862	Magnus von Essen
1862–1868	August von Oettingen
1868–1871	F. von Lysander
1872–1874	Michael von Wrangell
1874–1882	Alexander Uexküll-Güldenbrandt
1883–1885	Ivan Shevich
1885–1895	Mikhail N. Zinoviev
1895–1900	Vladimir Surovtsov
1901–1905	Mikhail Pashkov

NOTES

Abbreviations

BA. SaR.   Baltische Archivfilme. Stadtarchiv Riga
BM   *Baltische Monatschrift*
DZ   *Düna-Zeitung*
FRSR-1883   *Firmenregister der Stadt Riga 1883*
NZSL   *Neue Zeitung für Stadt und Land*
PFGR-1891   *Perechen' firm g. Rigi na 1891 god*
PSZ   *Polnoe sobranie zakonov Rossiiskoi Imperii*
RA   *Rigascher Almanach*
RAB   *Rigasches Adress-Buch*
RR   *Rigasche Rundschau*
RS   *Rigasche Stadtblätter*
RT   *Rigaer Tageblatt*
RV   *Rizhskii vestnik*
ZSL   *Zeitung für Stadt und Land*

Chapter 1

1. Nationality was determined in the census by "customary language" (übliche Sprache) rather than by mother tongue. F. Jung-Stilling, *Riga in Den Jahren 1866-1870. Ein Beitrag zur Städte-Statistik* (Riga, 1873), p. 37.

2. BA. SaR.: "Bürgerverzeichniss, 1800-1899; W. Lenz, *Die Entwicklung Rigas zur Grosstadt* (Kitzingen am Main, 1954), p. 21; *RS,* 1862, No. 31, pp. 280–281.

3. There were roughly eight hundred literati in Riga during this period. The nature of the census materials precludes a more exact figure. Jung-Stilling, pp. 13–14.

4. Ibid., p. 30.

5. Workers accounted for 35.1 per cent of the Latvian labour force, and those engaged in "personal service" for 36.8 per cent. Many of the Latvians at the very bottom of the social spectrum were recent migrants from the country-side. The results of the 1858 (tenth) revision showed that ten per cent of the

actual Riga population were peasants still officially resident in rural communities. Ibid., p. 29; B.I. Vilks, *Formirovanie promyshlennogo proletariata v Latvii vo vtoroi polovine XIX v.* (Riga, 1957), p. 40.

6. The "Latvian trades" included longshoremen, weavers, hempbinders, fishermen, beer and salt carters, cab drivers, bird-catchers and the people employed by the city port authority to supervise the weighing and quality control of export and import goods.

7. J.G. Kohl, *Die deutsch-russischen Ostseeprovinzen* (Dresden, 1841), I, 414.

8. Jung-Stilling, *Riga in den Jahren 1866-1870*, pp. 30–31, 38.

9. The guild membership lists reveal that 625 of the 2,566 persons who joined the guild between 1800 and 1864 had unmistakeably Russian names. Ba. Sa R: Bürgerverzeichniss, 1800–1889; H.J. Böthführ, *Die Rigasche Rathslinie von 1226 bis 1876* (Riga, 1877), pp. 297–307.

10. According to the census, 19.1 per cent of the civilian Russian labour force were engaged in commerce, 19.8 per cent were non-certified artisans and 57.5 per cent were workers. Jung-Stilling, pp. 30–31; P.G. Ryndziunskii, *Gorodskoe grazhdanstvo doreformennoi Rossii* (Moscow, 1958), p. 321.

11. The census shows that 27.4 per cent of the Jewish labour force were employed in commercial pursuits and that 53 per cent engaged in craft production. Jung-Stilling, p. 31.

12. During the years from 1866–1870, 9.2 per cent of the ruble value of Russian foreign trade traveled through Riga, which was eclipsed only by St. Petersburg with 31 per cent and Odessa with 11.6 per cent. B.v. Gernet, *Die Entwicklung der Rigaer Handels und Verkehrs im Laufe der letzten 50 Jahren bis zum Ausbruche des Weltkrieges* (Jena, 1919), pp. 16–17.

13. Of the ninety "factories," twenty had less than ten workers apiece and another seventeen had less than twenty-five workers apiece. *Beiträge zur Geschichte der Industrie Rigas* (Riga, 1911–1912), I, 44–47.

14. Ibid., I, 45–46.

15. Ibid.

16. Ibid; BA. Sa R.: Bürgerverzeichniss, 1800–1899; *RAB* (1868/1869); *RS,* 1860, no. 3, p. 21; *RS,* 1866, no. 18, p. 176; W. Blackwell, *The Beginnings of Russian Industrialization, 1800-1860* (Princeton, 1968), pp. 69–70.

17. *Beitr. z. Gesch. d. Ind. Rigas,* I, 45.

18. Ibid., I, 46, BA. Sa R.: Bürgerverzeichniss, 1800–1899; *RAB* (1868/1869); Blackwell, pp. 69–70.

19. *Beitr. z. Gesch. d. Ind. Rigas,* III, 12; *RS,* 1874, no. 15, p. 133.

20. Established in 1843, the Kuznetsov firm was the largest porcelain manufacturer in the Russian Empire during this period. In 1864 it employed 251 workers. *Beitr. z. Gesch. d. Ind. Rigas,* I, 47; *Ocherki ekonomicheskoi istorii Latvii, 1860-1900* (Riga, 1972), pp. 124–125.

21. L.T. Hutton, "The Reform of City Government in Russia, 1860-1870" (Ph.D. Dissertation, University of Illinois at Urbana, 1972), pp. 10–11.

22. E.C. Thaden, "Nationality Policy in the Western Borderlands of the Russian Empire, 1881-1914," *American Contributions to the VIIth Congress of*

Slavists, Warsaw, 1973, III, *History,* (ed.) A. Cienciala (The Hague, 1973), p. 70; E.C. Thaden (ed.), M.H. Haltzel, C.L. Lundin, A. Plakans and T. Raun, *Russification in the Baltic Provinces and Finland, 1855-1914* (Princeton, 1981), pp. 15-6.

23. *Provinzialrecht der Ostseegouvernements* (St. Petersburg, 1845), part II, article 949.

24. Of the 182 surnames that appear on the magistracy membership list in the period 1650-1876, 27 per cent are repeated at least once and several as many as six or seven times. Of those who served in the magistracy from 1797 to 1876, 44 per cent were the sons of guild officers or magistrates. Böthführ, pp. 175-290.

25. *Provinzialrecht der Ostseegouvernements,* part I, article 5.

Chapter 2

1. J. Eckardt, *Die baltischen Provinzen Russlands,* (Leipzig, 1869), p. 398.

2. "Reformen in Russland," *BM,* I (1859), 474-480.

3. B. Hollander, "Dr. Julius Eckardt," *Baltische Geistesleben,* I (1929), 271.

4. J. Eckardt, *Juri Samarins Anklage gegen die Ostseeprovinzen Russlands* (Leipzig, 1869), pp. 175-176.

5. "Livländische Korrespondenz," *BM,* VII (1863), 190.

6. A. Bulmerincq, "Baltische Schragen," *BM,* VI (1862), 43.

7. L. Pezold, *Die Öffentlichkeit in den baltischen Provinzen* (Leipzig, 1870), p. 19.

8. P.A. Valuev, *Dnevnik* (Moscow, 1961), II, 426-427.

9. In 1859, for example, 451 nobles were resident in Riga. *RS,* 1860, no. 45, p. 384.

10. Lenz, *Die Entwicklung Rigas,* p. 4; W. Lenz, *Der baltischen Literatenstand* (Marburg, 1953), p. 11.

11. "Die deutschen Ostseeprovinzen Russlands," *Die Gegenwart,* 1848, no. 1, p. 495.

12. A. Bulmerincq, "Baltische Presse," *BM,* V (1861), 50.

13. E. v. d. Brüggen, "Unsere bäuerliche Verhältnisse im Jahre 1871," *BM,* XX (1871), 600.

14. Pezold, pp. 50 ff.

15. G. Berkholz, "Zur Nationalitätenfrage," *BM,* IX (1864), 574.

16. v.d. Brüggen, "Unsere bäuerliche Verhältnisse," p. 602.

17. Berkholz, "Zur Nationalitätenfrage," p. 569.

18. Ibid., p. 568; v.d. Brüggen, "Unsere bäuerliche Verhältnisse," p. 603; Pezold, pp. 48-52; R. Wittram, *Liberalismus baltischer Literaten* (Riga, 1931), pp. 82-83; R. Wittram, *Meinungskämpfe im baltischen Deutschtum während der Reformepoche des 19. Jahrhunderts* (Riga, 1934), p. 100.

19. G. Masing, *Der Kampf um die Reform der Rigaer Stadtverfassung* (1860-1870) (Riga, 1936), p. 127.

20. Ibid., pp. 52-56, 94-96.

21.   Ibid., p. 44.

22.   Berkholz, "Zur Nationalitätenfrage," p. 573.

23.   Ibid., p. 572.

24.   v.d. Brüggen, "Unsere bäuerliche Verhältnisse," p. 602.

25.   In 1865 alone, the St. Petersburg and Moscow press published ninety-eight articles attacking the Baltic Germans. Wittram, *Liberalismus*, p. 78. See also J.A. Armstrong, "Mobilized Diaspora in Tsarist Russia: The Case of the Baltic Germans," in *Soviet Nationality Policies and Practices*, (ed.) J. Azrael (New York, 1978), pp. 91–2; M. Haltzel, *Der Abbau der deutschen ständischen Selbstverwaltung in den Osteeprovinzen Russlands, 1855-1905* (Marburg, 1977), pp. 28–35; Thaden et al., pp. 125–6.

26.   "Livländische Korrespondenz," *BM,* IX (1864), 480.

27.   Eckardt, *Juri Samarins Anklage,* p. 176.

28.   Lenz, *Die Entwicklung Rigas,* p. 19; O. Grosberg, *Die Presse Lettlands* (Riga, 1927), p. 58.

29.   O. Kronwald, *Nationale Bestrebungen* (Dorpat, 1872), p. 16. For a conprehensive treatment of early Latvian nationalism see the contribution by A. Plakans in Thaden et al., pp. 207–26.

30.   Ibid., pp. 50–51. "O. Kronwald" was the German form of Kronvalds' name.

31.   M. Lindemuth, "Krisjanis Valdemars und Atis Kronvalds: Zwei lettische Volkstumpskämpfer," *Baltische Hefte,* XIII (1967), 94.

32.   Wittram, *Meinungskämpfe,* p. 104.

33.   "Livländische Korrespondez," *BM,* VI (1862), 590–591.

34.   A. Suvorov, "Rechenschafts-Bericht des Rigaschen Kriegs-, liv-, ehst- und kurländischen General Gouverneurs an den Kaiser Nikolai I," (ed.) M.v. Oettingen, *BM,* XLIV (1897), 526–527.

35.   "Livländische Korrespondez," *BM,* VI (1862), 374.

36.   Masing, p. 106.

37.   Ibid., p. 107.

38.   The *Rigasche Stadtblätter* was the organ of the Literary-Practical Citizens Association, a local philanthropic society whose membership was drawn chiefly from the local merchantry and literati, *RS,* 1861, no. 44, p. 393.

39.   G. Hernmarck, *Erinnerungen aus dem öffentlichen Leben eines Rigaschen Kaufmanns, 1849-1869* (Berlin, 1889), pp. 70–72.

40.   Masing, p. 21.

41.   Ibid., pp. 26–28.

42.   Ibid., pp. 58–61.

43.   "Zur Situation," *BM,* XIV (1866), 329.

44.   Masing, pp. 114–115.

45.   In addition, potential citizens were required to be Christian Russian subjects. Ibid., pp. 63–66.

46.   Ibid., p. 20.

47.   Ibid., pp. 63–6; Thaden et al., p. 51.

48.   Masing, p. 88.

49.   Ibid., pp. 102–104.

50. *ZSL*, 1894, no. 83.

51. M. Haltzel, "The Reaction of the Baltic Germans to Russification during the Nineteenth Century" (Ph.D. Dissertation, Harvard University, 1971), p. 113.

52. The report's authorship is not known, but it was found in the Valuev archive, and it is probable that Valuev himself had a hand in writting it. S. Isakov, *Ostzeiskii vopros v russkoi pechati 1860-kh godov* (Tartu, 1961), p. 179.

53. The activity of the Russian nationalist press was in part responsible for the growth of anti-German feeling, but it was not the only source. The high profile of conservative Baltic German nobles in the imperial government encouraged a tendency in Russian liberal and radical circles to identify Baltic Germans with everything that they found objectionable in the administration of public affairs. J.A. Armstrong has suggested that the anti-German mood may also be linked to the process of modernization in Russia. Ethnic Russians, beneficiaries of increasing opportunities for upward social mobility, often felt stymied by the disproportionately large presence of Baltic Germans (chiefly noblemen) in the senior ranks of the imperial service. Armstrong, pp. 83-4; Haltzel, *Abbau*, pp. 89-99, 157-62 passim.

54. See Valuev, *Dnevnik*, II, 421-434.

55. N. Carlberg, *Die Stadt Riga. Verwaltung und Haushalt in den Jahren 1878-1900* (Riga, 1901), p. xxxiv.

56. "Predpolozheniia mestnykh komissii o preobrazovaniiakh v obshchestvennom ustroistve gorodov Rigi i Revelia," *Materialy, otnosiashchiesia do novogo obshchestvennogo ustroistva v gorodakh imperii* (St. Petersburg, 1877-1883), VI, 101-109, 121-129, 146, 172-181, 200-270.

57. "Zhurnal komissii po predmetu primeneniia Gorodskogo Polozheniia 16-ogo iunia 1870 g. k. gorodam Pribaltiiskikh gubernii," *Materialy*, VI, 9.

58. Ibid., p. 14.

59. O. Greiffenhagen, ed., "Aus den Erinnerungen eines Revaler Justizbeamten," *BM*, ser. 2, LXI (1930), 461.

60. *Die Neue Städteordnung für die baltischen Provinzen* (Riga, 1877), pp. 13-14.

61. "Zhurnal komissii po obsuzhdeniiu predpolozhenii o primenenii Gorodskogo Polozheniia 16-ogo iunia 1870 g. k. gorodam Pribaltiiskikh gubernii," pp. 368ff.

62. H.v. Stein, "Die Centralschule für Handel und Gewerbe in Riga," *BM*, I (1859), 379-380.

63. Many of the goods exported from Riga were subject to *Waage* and *wrake*. The latter was a quality control requiring inspection and classification of certain exports. Its antiquity is betokened by the very word *"wrake,"* which is Low German, a dialect long extinct in Riga by the mid-nineteenth century. The *Waage* regulations required many exports to be weighed on a special scale, and, like the wrake, dated from the Middle Ages. These regulations caused delay and expense to the exporter, and some Russian merchants went out of their way to ship goods through Köngisberg in order to avoid them. Lenz, *Die Entwicklung Rigas zur Grosstadt*, pp. 15-16; Carlberg, *Die Stadt Riga*, pp. 77-80.

64. B. Hollander, *Geschichte der Literärisch-praktischen Bürgerverbindung in Riga, 1802-1927* (Riga, 1927), pp. 151-154; E. Hollander, "Der Gewerbeverein in Riga," *BM*, XIII (1866), 164.

Chapter 3

1. J. Eckardt, *Lebenserinnerungen* (Leipzig, 1910), I, 161.
2. A. Bucholtz, *50 Jahre russischer Verwaltung in den baltischen Provinzen Russlands* (Leipzig, 1883), pp. 287-289.
3. Eckardt, *Lebenserinnerungen* I, 78-80.
4. Publication of the book was not permitted in Russia.
5. C. Schirren, *Livländische Antwort an Herrn Juri Samarin* (Leipzig, 1869), p. 158.
6. Ibid., p. 159.
7. Ibid., p. 42.
8. Ibid., p. 110.
9. Ibid., p. 43.
10. Ibid., pp. 107, 192, 194.
11. "Georg Berkholz an Edith von Rahden. 20 Mai 1869," *Baltische Briefe aus zwei Jahrhunderten,* ed. A. Eggers (Berlin, 1918), p. 165.
12. R. Wittram, "Carl Schirrens Livländische Antwort," *Ostdeutsche Wissenschaft,* I (1954), 283.
13. Liberalism was not, however, extinguished among the Baltic nobility. There remained those among the nobles who advocated the reform of rural and provincial institutions of government as the best way to avoid the introduction of alien forms by the imperial authorities.
14. "Aus dem Briefwechsel zwischen Viktor Hehn und Georg Berkholz," ed. H. Diederichs, *BM*, XLIV (1897), 80.
15. "Georg Berkholz an Edith von Rahden. 29 Mai 1869," p. 165.
16. Wittram, *Meinungskämpfe,* p. 121
17. Ibid., p. 94. Bienemann moved the head office of the *Baltische Monatschrift* to Reval. It was returned to Riga after Bienemann resigned as editor in 1888.
18. In the first duma election, held in 1878, 5,212 persons were eligible to vote. This figure increased to 5,822 in 1882 and ultimately to 6,017 by 1890. *RT,* 1884, no. 66; *RT,* 1897, no. 57.
19. In absolute figures, Riga's population rose from 102,590 to 169,329 between 1867 and 1881. The 1881 census showed that 31.4 per cent of the population was born in rural, largely Latvian-speaking areas of the Baltic provinces. Only 37 per cent were born in Riga. *Ergebnisse der baltischen Volkszählung vom 29. December 1881* (Riga, 1883), pt. 1, I, 56-57.
20. Ibid., pt. 1, I, 52-53.
21. A comparison of the 1867 and 1881 censuses is a good index of the growth of this class. In the earlier census only three people listed as "professionals" claimed Latvian as their "customary language." By 1881 this number had

jumped to thirty-six. In absolute terms the increase is tiny, but it does indicate that retention of Latvian nationality had become a viable option for at least some educated Latvians. Ibid., pt. 1, I, 8-9.

22. In the early 1880's the *Rigas lapa*, which merged with the journal *Baltijas vestnesis (Baltic Herald)*, was joined by a second Latvian nationalist daily, *Balss (Voice)*.

23. *RZ*, 1881, no. 266.

24. *Ergebnisse d. balt. Volkszählung*, pt. 1, I, 1.

25. Cited in the *NZSL*, 1881, no. 293.

26. "Georg Berkholz an Edith von Rahden. 1 Mai 1877," *Baltische Briefe*, pp. 166-167.

27. *NZSL*, 1881, no. 289.

28. Ibid.

29. Wittram, *Meinungskämpfe*, p. 124.

30. Buchholtz, *50 Jahre*, p. 246.

31. *ZSL*, 1880, no. 35.

32. *ZSL*, 1881, no. 134.

33. *RZ,*, 1882, no. 19; 1881, no. 268.

34. E. Hollander, "Riga unter der neuen Städteordung, 1878-1882," *BM*, XXIX (1882), 461.

35. *RZ*, 1881, no. 268.

36. *NZSL*, 1881, no. 289.

37. *RZ*, 1881, no. 293.

38. *RAB*, (1877); BA. SaR.: Bürgerverzeichniss, 1800-1899; *RS*, 1878, no. 4, 8, 10.

39. *RZ*, 1881, no. 293.

40. BA. SaR.: Bürgerverzeichniss, 1800-1899; *RAB* (1877); *RAB* (1885); *RS*, 1878, no. 4, 8, 10; *RA*, 1887, p. 115; *RA*, 1891, pp. 106-107; *Album Academicum der kaiserlichen Universität Dorpat* (Dorpat, 1889); *Album Academicum des Polytechnicums zu Riga, 1862-1912* (Riga, 1912).

41. Wittram, *Meinungskämpfe*, p. 109.

42. In 1878, for example, 79.75 per cent of the eligible first class voters and 75.3 per cent of the eligible second class voters actually exercized their franchise. The figure for the third class was 65.11 per cent. E. Hollander, "Riga unter der neuen Städteordnung," pp. 467-468.

43. *Ergebnisse d. balt. Volkszählung*, pt. 1, I, 52-53.

44. Cited in the *ZSL*, 1886, no. 214, 225.

45. More than a quarter of those who claimed Judaism as their religion in the 1881 census claimed German as their "customary language." *Ergebnisse d. balt. Volkszählung*, pt. 1, I, 12-13, 52-53. See also *Russisch-Baltische Blätter. Beiträge zur Kenntnis Russlands und seiner Grenzmarken* (Leipzig, 1883), II, 47.

46. E. Hollander, Riga unter der neuen Städteordung," pp. 467-468; *RS*, 1882, no. 6-7; *ZSL*, no. 42, *Livländischer Kalender auf das Jahr 1891*, p. 72.

47. Carlberg, *Die Stadt Riga*, p. 495; BA. SaR: Bürgerverzeichniss, 1800-1889; W. Lenz, *Deutsch-baltisches biographisches Lexikon* (Cologne, 1970), pp. 369, 557-558.

48. "Aus den Verhandlungen der Rigaschen Stadtverordnetenversammlung im Jahre 1886," supplement to *RS*, 1887, p. 31; *ZSL*, 1887, no. 17.

49. *NZSL*, 1880, no. 126; *Livländischer Kalender auf das Jahr 1884*, p. 75.

50. *ZSL*, 1884, no. 127.

51. P. Gerstfeldt, "Zur Schulfrage in Riga," *BM*, XXXII (1885) 310.

52. *ZSL*, 1884, no. 127.

53. A. Bielenstein, *Ein glückliches Leben* (Riga, 1904), p. 142.

54. *ZSL*, 1880, no. 218.

55. *ZSL*, 1884, no. 127.

56. *NZSL*, 1880, no. 222.

57. The jurisdiction of the new justices of the peace, who were introduced in 1884, was restricted to petty civil and criminal matters.

58. E. Hollander, "Riga unter der neuen Städteordnung," p. 474.

59. "Aus den Verhandlungen der Rigaschen Stadtverordnetenversammlung im Jahre 1885," supplement to *RS*, 1886, pp. 26–31; *Bericht über die Verwaltung und Haushalt der Stadt Riga, 1885* (Riga, 1886), pp. 621–622.

60. Chaired by the provincial governor, this board served as an appellate instance in disputes between municipalities and other levels of government.

61. *Manaseina Revizija. Senators N. Manaseina zinojums par vina izdarito reviziju Vidzemes un Kurzemes gubernas no 1882 lidz 1883 gadam* (Riga, 1949), p. 141.

62. Arend Buckholtz, *Geschichte der Rigaschen Familie Schwartz* (Berlin, 1921), pp. 469–470; Lenz, *Die Entwicklung Rigas*, p. 32.

63. *ZSL*, 1880, no. 280.

64. *RZ*, 1880, no. 125.

Chapter 4

1. K. Pobedonostsev, *Pis'ma Pobedonostseva k Aleksandru III* (Moscow, 1925), II, 165.

2. E.C. Thaden, "N.A. Manaseins Senatorenrevision in Livland und Kurland während der Zeit von 1882 bis 1883," *Jahrbücher für Geschichte Osteuropas*, XVII (1969), 56–7; I. Depman, "O naznachenii Senatora N.A. Manaseina revizorom lifliandskoi i kurliandskoi gubernii," *Izvestiia Akademii Nauk Estonskoi SSR*, X (1961), 144–145; Haltzel, *Abbau*, p. 79; Thaden et al., pp. 56–7.

3. *Manaseina Revizija*, p. 140.

4. Ibid., pp. 155–167.

5. Ibid., pp. 80–215. Manasein's distaste for Dorpat stemmed in part from the student experience there of his brother, who had not found the "provincial" and "peculiar" environment to his liking. Thaden, "Manaseins Senatorenrevision," p. 52.

6. *Manaseina Revizija*, pp. 167–179.

7. N. Carlberg, *Die Stadt Riga*, p. 262.

8. *Bericht über die Verwaltung und Haushalt der Stadt Riga, 1885* p. 616.

9. R. Byrnes, Pobedonostsev: His Life and Thought (Bloomington, Indiana, 1968), p. 189.

10. S.M. Seredonin, *Istorischeskii obzor deiatel'nosti komiteta ministrov, 1802-1902* (St. Petersburg, 1902), IV, 225.

11. On the reforms as a function of modernization see Haltzel, *Abbau,* pp. 89-99, 157-62 passim.

12. The two von Oettingens were distantly related.

13. B. Schrenck, *Beiträge zur Statistik der Stadt Riga und ihrer Verwaltung, 1881-1911* (Riga, 1909 and 1911), I, 281-282.

14. S.V. Rozhdestvenskii, *Istoricheskii obzor deiatel'nosti ministerstva narodnogo prosveshcheniia* (St. Petersburg, 1902), p. 670.

15. *RT,* 1884, no. 128.

16. *ZSL,* 1886, no. 116.

17. Rozhdestvenskii, p. 670.

18. *RZ,* 1885, no. 214; *RT,* 1885, no. 216.

19. M. Werbatus, "Aus den Erinnerungen des Schuldirectors Pastor Werbatus," *BM,* LXVII (1909), 169.

20. Lenz, *Die Entwicklung Rigas,* p. 57.

21. Pobedonostsev, *Pis'ma,* II, 51-9; Thaden et al, p. 165.

22. W. Kahle, *Die Begegnung des baltischen Protestantismus mit der Russich-Orthodoxen Kirche* (Leiden, 1959), pp. 105-107.

23. Haltzel, "Reaction," p. 299.

24. A.v. Tobien, *Die Livländische Ritterschaft in ihrem Verhältnis zum Zarismus und russischen Nationalismus* (Riga, 1925 and Berlin, 1930), I, 154.

25. *RT,* 1887, no. 44.

26. *DZ,* 1903, no. 27; *RV,* 1903, no. 25.

27. B. Hollander, *Riga im 19. Jahrhundert* (Riga, 1926), p. 93; Joh. v. Eckardt, "Beiträge zur Geschichte des deutsch-baltischen Zeitungswesens," *Zeitungswissenschaft,* III (1928), 37.

28. *DZ,* 1889, no. 104, 110, 136.

29. Werbatus, p. 106.

30. *Russisch-Baltische Blätter,* IV, 61.

31. Ibid., I, 54.

32. Ibid., I, 56.

33. Werbatus, p. 106.

34. *Russisch-Baltische Blätter,* I, 46.

35. Werbatus, p. 162.

36. G. Schweder, *Die alte Domschule und das daraus hervorgegangene Stadt-Gymnasium zu Riga* (Riga, 1910), pp. 111-119.

37. *RA,* 1907, p. 85.

38. F. Demme, "40 Jahre Schuldients," *BM,* ser. 2, LVIII (1927), 262-263.

39. "Die Justizreform in den Ostseeprovinzen Russlands," *Unsere Zeit,* 1890, no. 1, p. 374.

40. Schweder, pp. 111-119; M. Boehm, *Die Krisis des deutsch-baltischen*

Menschen. Eine Studie zum Kulturproblem der Ostseeprovinzen Russlands (Berlin, 1915), p. 10.

41. A. Buchholtz, *Deutsch-Protestantische Kämpfe in den baltischen Provinzen Russlands* (Leipzig, 1888), pp. 404-404.

42. Ibid., p. iii.

43. E. Seraphim, "Die baltischen Provinzen in der zweiten Hälfte des 19. Jahrhunderts," *Deutsche Monatschrift für Russland* (1912), I, 579, 588.

44. E. Seraphim, *In neuen Jahrhundert: Baltischer Rückblick und Ausblick* (Riga, 1902), p. 36.

45. *DZ,* 1902, no. 47.

46. *DZ,* 1901, no. 295.

47. *DZ,* 1900, no. 294.

48. *DZ,* 1901, no. 295.

49. *DZ,* 1902, no. 9.

50. Seraphim, *In neuen Jahrhundert,* p. 50.

51. *DZ,* 1902, no. 47.

52. Seraphim, *In neuen Jahrhundert,* p. 56.

53. B. Hollander, "Erinnerungen an den Jahren 1902-1905," *Baltische Blätter für allgemein-kulturelle Fragen,* II (1924), 112.

54. G. Kroeger, "Die Deutschen Vereine in Liv-, Est- und Kurland, 1905/06-1914," *Jahrbuch des baltischen Deutschtums,* XVI (1969), 40.

55. B. Hollander, "Erinnerungen," p. 114.

56. Seraphim, *In neuen Jahrhundert,* p. 35.

57. H. Schaudinn, *Das baltische Deutschtum und Bismarcks Reichsgründung* (Leipzig, 1932), pp. 174-202 passim; G. Bocke, *Von Niederrhein ins Baltenland: Erlebnisse und Beobachtungen eines deutschen Schulmeisters* (Hannover, 1925), p. 97: Lenz, *Die Entwicklung Rigas,* p. 20.

58. *RR,* 1901, no. 221.

59. *RR,* 1898, no. 201.

60. E. Seraphim, *Baltische Schicksale* (Berlin, 1935), p. 148; Seraphim, "Die baltischen Provinzen," p. 594.

61. *DZ,* 1901, no. 295.

62. B. Hollander, "Erinnerungen," p. 115.

Chapter 5

1. Between 1866 and 1905 the traffic in goods (measured by weight) between the Russian hinterland and Riga increased nearly ninefold. Flax exports doubled during this period and wood exports more than tripled. Gernet, pp. 31, 51, 96-97, 100-103, 105-111.

2. Grain exports rose from an annual average of 3.3 million puds in the period 1866-1870 to an annual average of 10.7 million puds from 1871-1875. Thanks to the closure of Black Sea ports during the Russo-Turkish War, Riga grain exports doubled again during the period 1876-1880, but then fell back to

an annual average of about 10 million puds for the rest of the century. The annual average export of eggs jumped threefold after the completion of the Trans-Siberian, while butter exports skyrocketed from an annual average of 34,000 puds in 1896–1900 to more than a million puds after 1901. Ibid., pp. 27, 40–42.

3. The importation of raw materials increased, but the increase was not as dramatic as was the case for export commodities. The only real exception to this was the importation of coal and coke, which increased constantly, the annual average import figures for these commodities during the period 1901–1904 being eight times as great as those in the period 1866–1870. Imports of steel, iron wares and machinery grew steadily until the implementation of a prohibitive tariff in 1891. Ibid., pp. 57, 59, 63 and 66.

4. *Beitr. z. Gesch. d. Ind. Rigas*, III, 96–97; *Ergebnisse der Rigaer Gewerbezählung, veranstaltet im April, 1884* (Riga, 1889), pp. 74–78; *Rigaer Handels-Archiv*, II (1875), 286–292.

5. *Rigaer Handles-Archiv*, II (1875), 286, 289; *Ergebnisse d. Rig. Gewerbezählung*, pp. 2, 14–15.

6. *Beitr. z. Gesch. d. Ind. Rigas*, I, 46; *Pervaia vseobshchaia perepis naseleniia Rossiiskoi imperii, 1897 g.* (St. Petersburg, 1903), XXI, 140–141.

7. *Och. ek. ist. Lat., 1860–1900*, pp. 113–115; *Beitr. z. Gesch. d. Ind. Rigas*, I, 45–46; *Ergebnisse d. Rig. Gewerbezählung*, pp. 14–15.

8. *Beitr. z. Gesch. d. Ind. Rigas*, I, 46; Carlberg, *Die Stadt Riga*, p. 104; *Perv. vseobschch. perepis' Ross. imp.*, XXI, 140–141.

9. *Beitr. z. Gesch. d. Ind. Rigas*, I, 47; Carlberg, *Die Stadt Riga*, p. 104; *Perv. vseobshch. perepis' Ross. imp.*, XXI, 140–141.

10. *Perv. vseobshch. perepis' Ross. imp.*, XXI, 2; Lenz, *Die Entwicklung Rigas*, p. 69.

11. Given the nature of the available census materials for Riga during this period, it is impossible to gauge the proportionate numerical decline of the German community with complete precision. Each of the three censuses taken in the late nineteenth century used a different method of measuring nationality. The 1867 census used "customary language." Consequently, the size of the German community was probably somewhat overestimated at the expense of the Latvians. In spite of the tendency of many Latvian speakers to Germanize and feel themselves fully German, it is safe to assume that some Latvians who had not fully Germanized claimed German as their "customary language" either because of its social prestige or because they used it at their place of employment. The 1881 census also asked for "customary language," but added "nationality" as a separate category which was intended to measure ethnic origin. Finally, the all-Russian census of 1897 used "native language" as the sole criterion of national differentiation, a circumstance which inflated the size of the Latvian community relative to the German. Many people who were fully Germanized were counted as Latvians because Latvian was their native language, although they may have considered themselves German.

12. Language is not an effective measure of the size of the Riga Jewish community, thanks to the Germanization of many upwardly mobile Jews.

Much more useful is a breakdown of the city population by religion. In 1867, 5.1% claimed Judaism as their religion; in 1881, 12.4% and in 1897, 7.8%.
13. The most important other groups were Estonian, Polish and, by 1897, Lithuanian.
14. Merchants listed in the first guild of the local tax community were men of considerable substance and in all likelihood were engaged in international commerce. *FRSR*-1883.
15. *PFGR*-1891.
16. *RS*, 1901, no. 23, p. 181.
17. *Jung-Stilling*, p. 28.
18. Lenz, *Die Entwicklung Rigas*, p. 36.
19. The figures are based on "customary language" for 1881, because that year's census did not offer a breakdown of occupation by "nationality." *Ergebnisse d. balt. Volkszählung*, pt. 1, I, 8–9; *Perv. vseobshch. perepis' Ross. imp.*, XXI, 160–161.
20. Lenz, *Die Entwicklung Rigas*, p. 11.
21. The board of the Riga-Dünaburg Railroad Corporation included former magistrate and journalist Alexander Faltin; Hermann von Stein, a local merchant who served as secretary to the Chamber of Commerce and as a duma representative from 1878–1890; former magistrate August Hollander; merchant and industrialist E. Mertens; and Bernhard von Schubert, an engineer and industrial entrepreneur who sat in the municipal duma after 1893. The directorate of the Riga-Mitau Railroad Corporation comprised Alexander von Heimann, a merchant, banking executive and duma representative; duma member and former magistrate Eugen Barclay de Tolly; Konrad Bornhaupt, likewise a duma member and former magistrate; Otto von Scheubner, a Baltic noble. Similarly, among the directors of the Riga-Tuckum Railroad Corporation were Alexander Faltin; C. Zander, a local industrialist and banker who served both as alderman of the merchant guild and as a duma member; and Carl Taube, a merchant and banker who was both duma representative and merchant guild elder. Friedrich Bonfeldt, the final member of the Riga-Tuckum Corporation directorate, cannot be precisely identified, as adequate biographical information is lacking. *Alb. Ac. d. Polytech. zu Riga; Alb. Ac. d. k. Univ. Dorpat; Album Fratrum Rigensum, 1823-1910* (Riga, 1910); *RA*, 1890, p. 130; *RA*, 1891, pp. 106–107; *RA*, 1893, pp. 123–126; *RAB* (1885).
22. Beginning in 1850 the Chamber of Commerce, using local commercial capital to finance its operations, engaged in several projects aimed at deepening and widening the mouth of the Dvina, which was in danger from silt. The Riga-Bolderaa telegraph enabled local merchants to gather information about sea conditions and incoming and outgoing commercial traffic from the port of Riga. A.K. Biron, "Portovoe stroitel'stvo v Latvii vo vtoroi polovine XIX i nachale XX v.," in *Ekonomicheskie sviazi Pribaltiki s Rossiei* (Riga, 1968), pp. 248–249; L. Ia. Sotnietse, "Rashirenie Rizhkogo porta vo vtoroi polovine XIX veka," *Izvestiia Akademii Nauk Latviiskoi SSR* (1969), pp. 17–21; Hernmarck, pp. 2–5, 10; Lenz, *Die Entwicklung Rigas*, pp. 11, 14; B. Hollander, *Riga im 19. Jahrhundert*, pp. 43–45.

23. The nationality of the owners of two of the sawmills cannot be determined. *Beitr. z. Gesch. d. Ind. Rigas,* III, 92–94; *Och. ek. ist. Lat., 1860–1900,* pp. 120–121, 175, 186–187, 396; *RAB* (1868/69); *RAB* (1877); *RAB* (1885); *RAB* (1901); BA. SaR: Bürgerverzeichniss, 1800–1889; *FRSR-1883,* pp. 6, 9–11, 21; *PFGR-1891,* pp. 80, 82, 84, 87, 98–99, 101, 107, 112, 119; *RS,* 1901, no. 33, p. 261; *Livländischer Kalender auf das Jahr 1860,* pp. 82–83; Iu. Netesin, "Ob inostrannom kapitale v obrabatyvaiuschei promyshlennosti Latyshkogo kraia," *Izvestiia Akademii Nauk Latviiskoi SSR,* (1964), p. 17.

24. *Beitr. z. Gesch. d. Ind. Rigas,* II, 32–36, 37; *FRSR-1883,* pp. 4, 14, 22, 29, 48; *PFGR-1891,* pp. 78, 87, 95, 99, 102, 105, 110, 120; *RAB* (1868/69); *RAB* (1877); *RAB* (1885) *RAB* (1901); BA. SaR: Bürgerverzeichniss, 1800–1889; *ZSL,* 1884, no. 174; *RR,* 1901, no. 192; *Rigaer Handels-Archiv,* II (1875), 290; Lenz, *Die Entwicklung Rigas,* p. 16; *Och. ek. ist. Lat., 1860–1900,* p. 133.

25. *Beitr. z. Gesch. d. Ind. Rigas,* II, 49, 53; BA. SaR: Bürgerverzeichniss, 1800–1889; *RAB* (1877); *RAB* (1885); *RAB* (1901); *FRSR-1883,* pp. 2, 5, 8, 16, 19, 21, 24–25, 34, 40–42, 44, 48; *PFGR-1891,* pp. 76, 78, 81, 86, 91, 95, 97–98, 113, 115–116, 118, 120; *Rigaer Handels-Archiv,* II (1875), 288; 290–291; *Och. ek. ist. Lat., 1860–1900,* pp. 131–132; *Livländischer Kalender auf das Jahr 1865,* pp. 75–76; Netesin, p. 17; *RS,* 1871, no. 18, p. 153; *RS,* 1901, no. 33, p. 262; *RR,* 1901, no. 157; Schrenck, *Beiträge,* I, 167.

26. *Och. ek. ist. Lat., 1860–1900,* pp. 125, 182, 389; BA. SaR: Bürgerverzeichniss, 1800–1889; *RAB* (1877); *RAB* (1885); *RAB* (1901); *RR,* 1901, no. 193; *FRSR-1883,* pp. 23, 45, 49; *PFGR-1891,* pp. 91, 95, 118, 121; Vilks, p. 115; *ZSL,* 1884, no. 159.

27. *Och. ek. ist. Lat., 1860–1900,* pp. 398–399; BA. SaR: Bürgerverzeichniss, 1800–1889; *RAB* (1877); *RAB* (1885); *RAB* (1901); *FRSR-1883,* pp. 7, 9, 21, 33, 49; *PFGR-1891,* pp. 80, 82, 93, 106, 121; *RR,* 1901, no. 155; *Rigaer Handels-Archiv,* II (1875), 287.

28. Netesin, p. 8.

29. J. McKay, *Pioneers for Profit: Foreign Entrepreneurs and Russian Industrialization, 1885–1913* (Chicago, 1970), p. 252.

30. *DZ,* 1902, no. 183.

31. *Beitr. z. Gesch. d. Ind. Rigas,* III, 49–53; Netesin, p. 15; *Och. ek. ist. Lat., 1860–1900,* pp. 177, 403.

32. *Beitr. z. Gesch. d. Ind. Rigas,* III, 16–17, 35, 37–39; Netesin, p. 15; *Och. ek. ist. Lat., 1860–1900,* p. 180.

33. *RAB* (1901); *Beitr. z. Gesch. d. Ind. Rigas,* III, 7; Netesin, p. 13.

34. *Beitr. z. Gesch. d. Ind. Rigas,* II, 41, 52; Netesin, pp. 13, 16; *Och. ek. ist. Lat., 1860–1900,* pp. 416–417; Vilks p. 114; E. Wallroth, *Die baltischen Provinzen und Litauen* (Lübeck, 1915), p. 46.

35. Netesin, pp. 12, 16; *Och. ek. ist. Lat., 1860–1900,* pp. 393, 417; Schrenck, *Beiträge,* II, 165; *RR,* 1901, no. 141.

36. Netesin, pp. 13, 15, 17; *Beitr. z. Gesch. d. Ind. Rigas,* III, 40–41; Schrenck, *Beiträge,* II, 166; *Och. ek. ist. Lat., 1860–1900,* pp. 382, 405; *RR,* 1901, no. 152; *RS,* 1901, no. 33, p. 261.

37. *Och. ek. ist. Lat., 1860–1900,* pp. 407–409; V.K. Iatsunskii, "Znachenie

ekonomicheskoi sviazei s Rossii dlia khoziakstvennogo razvitiia gorodov Pribaltiki v epokhu kapitalizma," *Istoricheskie zapiski,* XLV (1964), 113; Netesin, pp. 3–4; R. Pohle, "Riga," *Meereskunde,* XIII (1919), 29; Wallroth, p. 41; D.K. Ozoliniia, "O kommunal'nom khoziaistve Rigi v 90–kh godov XIX v.," *Problemy istorii,* VI (1962), 140.

38. The Riga Chamber of Commerce Bank was established in 1864 by the Chamber for the specific purpose of providing credit to local industry. The Chamber provided the bank's founding capital and directed its activity. The Riga Municipal Discount Bank was founded (in 1873) by the Riga estates and transferred to the duma during the 1880's. The Riga Bank of Commerce was a private institution founded in 1871 with capital drawn partly from the Riga merchantry, partly from investors in St. Petersburg, Warsaw and Moscow and partly from Germany. *Och. ek. ist. Lat.,* 1860–1900, pp. 408–409; Carlberg, *Die Stadt Riga,* pp. 76–77; Lenz, *Die Entwicklung Rigas,* p. 17; *RS,* 1871, no. 49, p. 416; E.v. Stieda, *Das livländische Bankwesen in Vergangenheit und Gegenwart* (Leipzig, 1909), pp. 188, 212, 227–228, 322, 344, 369.

39. Netesin, p. 8.

40. *Beitr. z. Gesch. d. Ind. Rigas,* III, 7, 12–15, 17, 34–36, 43, 57–58, 64–68; *Och. ek. ist. Lat.,* 1860–1900, pp. 148, 179, 379–384, 406–407; *RAB* (1885); *RAB* (1901); Netesin, p. 15; *RR,* 1901, no. 150; I. Skolis, *Riga: Ocherki po istorii goroda* (Riga, 1967), p. 119; A.I. Ivanov, "Vozniknovenie i razvitie predpriiatii sel'skokhoziaistvennogo mashinostroeniia Latvii v XIX i v nachale XX veka," *Izvestiia Akademii Nauk Latviiskoi SSR* (1967), p. 72; *DZ,* 1898, no. 194; *FRSR-1883,* p. 42; *PFGR-1891,* p. 118.

41. *Beitr. z. Gesch. d. Ind. Rigas,* II, 41, 52–56, 60–62; *FRSR-1883,* pp. 7, 20–21, 44; *PFGR-1891,* pp. 80, 93–94, 102, 110, 117; *Och. ek. ist. Lat.,* 1860–1900, pp. 128, 134, 398; *RAB* (1868/69); *RAB* (1877); *RAB* (1885); *RAB* (1901); BA. SaR: Bürgerverzeichniss, 1800–1889; *RR,* 1901, no. 157; *RS,* 1903, no. 20; Skolis, p. 119.

42. *Och. ek. ist. Lat.,* 1860–1900, pp. 416–417.

43. Ibid., pp. 404–405, 417; Netesin, p. 17.

44. *Beitr. z. Gesch. d. Ind. Rigas,* II, 43.

45. The total does not equal 440, because if an individual graduate pursued more than one career or worked in more than one place, he is counted once under each occupation and place.

46. The 1897 census is of no use in gauging the national composition of the artisan class. *Ergebnisse d. balt. Volkszählung,* pt. 1, I, 8–9; Jung-Stilling, p. 28.

47. BA. SaR: Bürgerverzeichniss, 1800–1889; F. Brunstermann, *Die Geschichte der kleinen oder St. Johannis Gilde in Wort und Bild* (Riga, 1902), p. 385.

48. Carlberg, *Die Stadt Riga,* p. 67; *Och. ek. ist. Lat.,* 1860–1900, p. 460.

49. *Ergebnisse d. Rig. Gewerbezählung,* p. 17.

50. BA. SaR; Bürgerverzeichniss, 1800–1889; *Beitr. z. Gesch. d. Ind. Rigas,* III, 7, 94; *RAB* (1877); *RAB* (1901); *PFGR-1891,* p. 98.

51. *Beitr. z. Gesch. d. Ind. Rigas,* II, 7–8, 41, 53, III, 14, 49–54, 64–66; *Och. ek. ist. Lat.,* 1860–1900, pp. 177–183, 378, 381–383, 386–389, 394, 403, 406,

426–427; *Ocherki ekonomicheskoi istorrii Latvii, 1900–1917* (Riga, 1968), p. 17; *RR*, 1901, no. 152. Netesin, pp. 14–16; *PFGR-1891*, pp. 82, 88, 105, 126; BA. SaR: Bürgerverzeichniss, 1800–1889; *RAB* (1877); *RAB* (1885); *RAB* (1901); *FRSR-1883*, p. 39, *RS*, 1876, no. 5, p. 57; *RS*, 1897, no. 48, p. 386; Vilks, p. 114; Wallroth, p. 46.
52.   *Och. ek. ist. Lat., 1860–1900*, p. 408, Stieda, p. 369.
53.   *Och. ek. ist. Lat., 1860–1900*, p. 144, 168–169; Wallroth, p. 43.
54.   *Och. ek. ist. Lat., 1860–1900*, p. 406.
55.   *RT*, 1900, no. 24.
56.   *RT*, 1901, no. 121.
57.   *RR*, 1901, no. 131.
58.   Eckardt, *Lebenserinnerungen*, I, 161–162.

Chapter 6

1.   B. Kalnins, "The Social Democratic Movement in Latvia," in *Revolution and Politics in Russia,* (ed.) A. Rabinowitch and J. Rabinowitch, (Bloomington, Indiana, 1972), p. 134; A. Plakans, "Peasants, Intellectuals and Nationalism in the Russian Baltic Provinces, 1820–1890," *Journal of Modern History,* XLVI (1974), 475; Thaden et al., pp. 255–7.

2.   "Baltische Chronik," supplement to *BM*, LV–LVI (1903), 27; Kalnins, pp. 135–136; Thaden et al., pp. 258–64.

3.   *RR*, 1897, no. 97, *ZSL*, 1893, no. 36.

4.   Lenz, *Die Entwicklung Rigas*, p. 42, Grosberg, p. 58.

5.   *RV*, 1891, no. 161.

6.   Cited in *DZ*, 1900, no. 212.

7.   Cited in *DZ*, 1901, no. 51.

8.   *RV*, 1891, no. 161; citation in *RT*, 1901, no. 180.

9.   *RR*, 1901, no. 127.

10.   Cited in *ZSL*, 1887, no. 73.

11.   *RR*, 1902, no. 222.

12.   *RR*, 1902, no. 52.

13.   *RR*, 1901, no. 221.

14.   *RT*, 1902, no. 157.

15.   *RR*, 1902, no. 52.

16.   Ibid.

17.   G.v. Pistohlkors, "Das Urteil Alexander Wäbers über das Scheitern der lettischen nationalen Bewegung und die Ursachen der lettischen Revolution von 1905–1906," in *Das Vergangene und die Geschichte,* (ed.) G.v. Pistohlkors, R.v. Thadden and H. Weiss (Göttingen, 1973), p. 242.

18.   Ibid., pp. 241–243; *RS*, 1893, no. 17, p. 135. The most prominent of the radicals nominated was Arnold Plates, editor of the "new current" journal *Mahjas veesis.*

19.   *RR*, 1902, no. 52.

20.   *RR*, 1901, no. 221.
21.   *RR*, 1897, no. 161.
22.   *RR*, 1902, no. 66.
23.   "Notizen," *BM*, LIII (1902), 143–144.
24.   The 1893 slate included among the Latvians a cab driver and a "Latvian trades" official, and among the Russians three merchants and the owner of a large chemical factory. In 1897 the Latvians nominated by the conservative committee included a cab driver and two merchants, and the Russians a chemical factory owner, a proprietor of a leatherware factory and a merchant. The 1901 Russian contingent comprised two factory owners, two merchants, a sawmill operator, a lawyer and a government tax collector. The occupation of one other Russian cannot be ascertained. The Latvian contingent that same year included three merchants, a lawyer, a physician, a cab driver, two artisans, the owner of a sawmill, and the owner of a brewery. See also Appendix II.
25.   Schrenck, *Beiträge*, I, 325–327.
26.   *RT*, 1899, no. 253; "Baltische Chronik," supplement to *BM*, LV–LVI (1903), 49.
27.   Cited in *DZ*, 1901, no. 64.
28.   T.v. Berent, "Nationale Kultur," *BM*, LXIII (1907), 343. G. Kroeger, "Zur Situation der baltischen Deutschen um die Jahrhundertwende," *Zeitschrift für Ostforschung*, XVII (1968), 628.
29.   v. Berent, p. 343.
30.   W. Conze, "Die deutsche Volksinsel Hirschenhof im gesellschaftlichen Aufbau des baltischen Deutschtums," *Auslandsdeutsche Volksforschung*, I (1937), 162.
31.   Bocke, p. 96.
32.   *RZ*, 1880, no. 266.
33.   Ibid.
34.   *RZ*, 1880, no. 220.
35.   *ZSL*, 1880, no. 95.
36.   *ZSL*, 1880, no. 138.
37.   Arend Buchholtz, *Gesch. d. Rig. Fam. Schwartz*, p. 472.
38.   *RS*, 1893, no. 17, p. 134.
39.   *RR*, 1898, no. 201.
40.   BA. SaR: Bürgerverzeichniss, 1800–1889.
41.   The 1901 figure for literati was somewhat higher (21.3 per cent) due to the inclusion of an unprecedented number of Latvians, many of whom were professional people, on the conservative slate. The decline of the literati was made all the more precipitate by their loss of special voting privileges (granted to them in 1877) after 1892. Under the 1892 municipal statute they had to meet the property qualification in order to vote. Even more striking is the decline of magistrates elected to the duma. Thirteen of them won election in 1878, but by 1901, a dozen years after the demise of the magistracy itself, only four former magistrates were in the duma.
42.   See Appendix II.
43.   Lenz, *Deutsch-balt. biogr. Lexikon*, pp. 17, 369.

44.   *RR*, 1904, no. 150. See also M. Hamm, "Riga's 1913 City Election: A Study in Baltic Urban Politics," *Russian Review*, XXXIX (1980), 449–50.

45.   *RA*, 1910, p. 99.

46.   *PSZ*, ser. 3, XII, 434.

47.   Ozoliniia, p. 144.

48.   Carlberg, *Die Stadt Riga*, p. 145.

49.   *Rigaer Handels-Archiv*, XIV (1887), 213–216.

50.   *RR*, 1894, no. 244.

51.   *RT*, 1897, no. 249.

52.   *Beitr. z. Gesch. d. Ind. Rigas*, I, 15.

53.   N. Carlberg, "Städtische Selbstverwaltung in den Ostseeprovinzen," in *Baltische Bürgerkunde* (Riga, 1908), pp. 216–218.

54.   *RT*, 1901, supplementary number.

55.   The best example of this school of thought is Reinhard Wittram's *Baltische Geschichte*, published in 1954 and still the standard history of the region.

56.   *RT*, 1892, no. 135.

57.   *ZSL*, 1893, no. 122.

58.   W. Wachtsmuth, *Wege, Umwege, Weggenossen* (Munich, 1954), p. 74. See also Thaden et al., p. 178.

59.   *RV*, 1894, no. 233.

60.   Lenz, *Die Entwicklung Rigas*, p. 61; *RA*, 1885–1893, 1905–1907.

61.   Cited in *RT*, 1901, no. 136.

62.   Byrnes, p. 303.

63.   Ibid., p. 191; Pobedonostsev, *Pis'ma*, II, 333–334.

64.   Byrnes, pp. 360–361.

65.   T. von Laue, *Sergei Witte and the Industrialization of Russia* (New York, 1963), p. 68; Thaden et al., pp. 55–6; S. Iu. Witte, *Vospominaniia: Detstvo, tsarstvovanie Aleksandra II i Aleksandra III (1849–1894)* (Berlin, 1923), pp. 334, 372–375.

66.   Thaden et al., p. 71; Witte, *Vospominaniia: Detstvo*, pp. 35–36, 128, 136–7, 272–3; S. Iu. Witte, *Vospominaniia: Tsarstvovanie Nikolaia II* (Berlin, 1923), I, 93–4, 97–8, 187–9, 220–1, 231.

67.   Witte, *Vospominaniia: Detstvo*, p. 276.

68.   Cited in *RT*, 1903, no. 133.

69.   M.A. Zinoviev, "Untersuchung über die landschaftliche Organisation des livländischen Gouvernements," supplement to *BM*, XXXIX (1895), p. ii.

70.   Ibid., p. iii.

71.   *DZ*, 1895, no. 275.

72.   "Baltische Chronik," supplement to *BM*, LV–LVI (1903), p. 9.

73.   *ZSL*, 1893, no. 292.

Chapter 7

1.   Land hunger in the Baltic provinces was a serious problem. The nobility, comprising two per cent of the rural population, owned, according to varying

estimates, between sixty and seventy-four per cent of the land, whereas many of the peasants were landless. L. Lundin, "The Road from Tsar to Kaiser: Changing Loyalties of the Baltic Germans, 1905–1914," *Journal of Central European Affairs,* X (1950), 231.

2. Schrenck, *Beiträge,* I, 163.

3. The Latvian left comprised both the Latvian Social Democratic Workers' Party and the Latvian Social Democratic Union, the political arm of the Riga Latvian Association. The two groups had virtually identical programmes save for the issue of minority rights. The nationalist Social Democratic Association specifically called for the establishment of an autonomous Latvia, whereas the internationalist Social Democratic Party voiced only general support for the concept of national self-determination for the proletariat of all peoples of the Russian Empire. M. Lindemuth, "Die lettischen Parteien 1905 und ihre Programme," *Baltische Hefte,* XV (1969), 82–86.

4. "Baltische Revolutionschronik," supplement to *BM,* LXV–LXVI (1908) p. 216.

5. In the Latvian-speaking areas of Livland province alone, eighty-two Germans lost their lives. Property damage was particularly severe in the countryside, where, in all three provinces, one hundred and eighty-four manor houses were destroyed. R. Wittram, *Baltische Geschichte, 1180–1918* (Munich, 1954), pp. 231–232.

6. M.v. Segeberg, "Die lettische Psychose," *Die Zukunft,* LIV (1906), 336. See also Lundin, p. 236.

7. This initiative came from Seraphim and other German nationalists, who were quite prepared to recognize the Latvian claim to nationhood and who had fewer illusions concerning the relationship between Latvian nationalism and social radicalism than did most Riga Germans. Seraphim, *Baltische Schicksale,* pp. 153–154.

8. "Aufruf und Programm der Baltischen Konstitutionellen Partei," *BM,* LX (1905), 372.

9. Lenz, *Die Entwicklung Rigas,* p. 74.

10. Ibid., p. 63.

11. *Erster Jahresbericht über die Tätigkeit des Deutschen Vereins in Livland* (Riga, 1907), p. 1.

12. Kroeger, "Die Deutschen Vereine," p. 44.

13. A conference aimed at the establishment of joint educational and cultural programmes with organizations representing German communities in Moscow, St. Petersburg, Odessa, Volhynia and the Volga region was planned to take place in Reval in 1908, but was prohibited by nervous government authorities. After this there was little in the way of constructive contact with Germans outside the Baltic region. E.F. Sommer, *Die Einigungsbestrebungen der Deutschen im Vorkriegs-Russland* (Leipzig, 1940), pp. 29–30.

14. Kroeger, "Die Deutschen Vereine," p. 42; Lundin, p. 226.

15. E.v. Stackelberg-Sutlem, *Ein Leben im baltischen Kampf* (Munich, 1927), p. 145. See also Lundin, p. 241.

16. "Literärische Rundschau," *BM,* LX (1905), 408.

17. v. Berent, pp. 337, 345.
18. E. Seraphim, "Literärische Rundschau," *BM*, LXXI (1911), 393.
19. Stackelberg-Sutlem, p. 127; E. Mensenkampff, *Menschen und Schicksale aus dem alten Livland* (Leipzig, 1944), pp. 313-314.
20. E. Seraphim, "Politische Revue," *BM*, LXXV (1913), 153.
21. Mensenkampff, pp. 247-248.
22. Wittram, *Baltische Geschichte*, p. 242; Kroeger, "Die Deutschen Vereine," p. 47; B. Raeder, "Praktische Berufe," *BM*, LXXI (1911), 289-290.
23. Lundin, p. 249.
24. Kroeger, "Die Deutschen Vereine," p. 47.

Appendix II

1. Some of the individual members who are listed here served beyond 1905, but the data given in this biography end in that year.

2. More precisely, Armitstead was Anglo-German. His family came to Riga from Britain, but married into the local German community and fully Germanized.

3. Dismissed in 1885 for resisting Russification.

4. Gustav Molien died in office in 1879.

5. Forced to resign in 1889 as mayor for resistance to Russification.

6. Dismissed by order of Governor Zinoviev in 1889 for resistance to Russification.

BIBLIOGRAPHY

I. Primary Sources

Filmed Archival Material in the Collection of the J.G. Herder-Institut

Baltische Archivfilme, Stadtarchiv Riga: Bürgerverzeichniss, 1800–1889.

Published Documents

Berichte uber die Verwaltung und Haushalt der Stadt Riga, 1885–1888, Four volumes. Riga, 1886–1889.

"Denkschrift des livländischen Adels-Convents," *Preussische Jahrbücher,* CXXIII (1906), 173–178.

Jahresbericht über die Tätigkeit des Deutschen Vereins in Livland. Riga, 1907 and 1909.

Manaseina Revizija. Senators N. Manaseina zinojums par vina izdarito reviziju Vidzemes un Kurzemes gubernas no 1882 lidz 1883 gadam. Riga, 1949.

Materialy, otnosiashchiesia do novogo obshchestvennogo ustroitstva v gorodakh imperii. 6 vols. St. Petersburg, 1877–1883.

Müller, Otto (ed.). *Die livländischen Landesprivilegien und deren Confirmationen.* Leipzip, 1870.

Die neue Städteordnung in den baltischen Provinzen. Riga, 1877.

Polnoe sobranie zakonov Rossiiskoi Imperii. Ser. 1, 45 vols. St. Petersburg, 1830. Ser. 2, 55 vols. St. Petersburg, 1884. Ser. 3, 28 vols. St. Petersburg, 1911.

Provinzialrecht der Ostseegouvernements. St. Petersburg, 1845.

Schirren, Carl (ed.). *Die Capitulationen der livländischen Ritter- und Landschaft und der Stadt Riga vom 4. Juli 1710 nebst deren Confirmationen.* Dorpat, 1865.

Shenshin, V. (ed.). *Sbornik tsirkuliarov po administrativnoi chasti Lifliandskoi gubernii za 1888–1895 gg.* Riga, 1896.

Newspapers and Periodicals

Baltische Monatschrift. 1859–1914.
Düna-Zeitung. 1889, 1893–1895, 1897–1904.
Livländischer Kalender. 1850–1855, 1857–1861, 1863–1866, 1868, 1874–1880, 1883–1885, 1889, 1891.
Neue Zeitung für Stadt und Land. 1880–1881.
Rigaer Handels-Archiv. 1874–1904.
Rigaer Tageblatt. 1882, 1884–1885, 1887, 1891–1895, 1897–1904.
Rigasche Rundschau. 1894, 1897–1904.
Rigasche Stadtblätter. 1855–1869, 1871–1872, 1874–1878, 1880–1882, 1884, 1886–1888, 1893, 1895–1898, 1900–1903.
Rigasche Zeitung. 1880–1882, 1884–1885, 1887.
Rigascher Almanach. 1860–1866, 1869–1873, 1875, 1878, 1880–1893, 1905–1907.
Rizhskii vestnik. 1891–1894.
Zeitung für Stadt und Land. 1880–1881, 1883–1887, 1892–1894.

Statistical Materials, Censuses, Address Books, Albums

Alabin, P. and Konvalov, P. *Sbornik svendenii o nastoiashchem sostoianii gorodskogo khoziaistva v glavneishikh gorodakh Rossii.* Samara, 1899.
Album Academicum der kaiserlichen Universität Dorpat. Dorpat, 1889.
Album Academicum des Polytechnicums zu Riga, 1862–1912. Riga, 1912.
Album Fratrum Rigensum, 1823–1910. Riga, 1910.
Album der Landsleute der Fraternitas Baltica, 1865–1910. Riga, 1910.
Annalen der Aeltesten der Kleinen oder St. Johannis-Gilde zu Riga. Riga, 1888.
Böthführ, H.J. *Die Rigasche Rathslinie von 1226 bis 1876.* Riga, 1877.
Brennsohn, J. *Die Ärzte Livlands.* Riga, 1905.
Ergebnisse der Rigaer Gewerbezählung, veranstaltet im April, 1884. Riga, 1889.
Ergebnisse der baltischen Volkszählung vom 29. December 1881, pt. 1. *Ergebnisse der livländischen Volkszählung, I. Die Zählung in Riga und im rigaschen Patrimonialgebiet.* Riga, 1883.
Firmenregister der Stadt Riga 1883. Riga, 1883.
Jung-Stilling, Friedrich (ed.). *Beiträge zur Bevölkerungsstatistik Livlands für die Jahre 1858–1863.* Riga, 1866.
———. (ed.). *Riga in den Jahren 1866–1870. Ein Beitrag zur Städte-Statistik.* Riga, 1873.
Perechen' firm gorod Rigi na 1891 g. Riga, 1891.
Pervaia vseobshchaia perepis' naseleniia Rossiiskoi imperii, 1897 g., XXI. St. Petersburg, 1903.
Rigasches Adress-Buch 1868/1869. Riga, 1869.
Rigasches Adress-Buch 1877. Riga, 1877.
Rigasches Adress-Buch 1885. Riga, 1885.

Rigasches Adress-Buch 1901. Riga, 1901.

Schrenck, B. *Beiträge zur Statistik der Stadt Riga und ihrer Verwaltung, 1881-1911.* 2 vols. Riga, 1909 and 1913.

Tobien, Alexander. *Statistiches Jahrbuch der Stadt Riga.* 2 Vols. Riga, 1891-1892.

Memoirs, Letters and Travel Literature

Berkholz, Georg. "Briefe an Edith von Rahden," in *Wir Balten.* Stuttgart, 1951, pp. 189-191.

Bielenstein, August, *Ein glückliches Leben.* Riga, 1904.

Bocke, Gustav. *Von Niederrhein ins Baltenland: Erlebnisse und Beobachtungen eines deutschen Schulmeisters.* Hannover, 1925.

Bosse, Heinrich (ed.). "Briefwechsel zwischen Arnold von Tiedeböhl, Redakteur der *Baltischen Monatschrift,* und K.P. Pobedonostsev, Prokureur des Hl. Synod," *Baltische Monatshefte,* III (1934), 571-577.

Bulmerincq, Wilhelm v. *Lebenserinnerungen des letzten deutschen Stadthaupts von Riga.* Wolfenbüttel, 1952.

Demme, Friedrich. "40 Jahre Schuldienst," *Baltische Monatschrift,* ser. 2, LVIII (1927), 251-268, 330-344, 401-414.

"Die deutschen Ostseeprovinzen Russlands," *Die Gegenwart,* I (1848), 472-498.

Dorneth, J.v. "Eine Reise durch Litauen nach Kurland und Riga," *Unsere Zeit,* No. 1 (1884), 60-8-, No. 2 (1884), 401-422, 530-554.

Eckardt, Julius. *Lebenserinnerungen.* 2 vols. Leipzig, 1910.

Eggers, Alexander (ed.). *Baltische Briefe aus zwei Jahrhunderten.* Berlin, 1918.

———. (ed.). *Baltsche Lebenserinnerungen.* Heilbronn, 1926.

Grieffenhagen, Otto (ed.). "Aus den Briefen Oskar von Riesemans," *Baltische Monatshefte,* I (1933), 522-529.

———. "Aus den Erinnerungen eines Revaler Justizbeamten," *Baltische Monatschrift,* ser. 2, LXI (1930), 439-477.

Hehn, Viktor. *De moribus Ruthenorum: Zur Charakteristik der russischen Volksseele. Tagebuchblätter aus den Jahren 1857-1873.* Stuttgart, 1892.

Hernmarck, Gustav. *Erinnerungen aus dem öffentlichen Leben eines Rigaschen Kaufmanns, 1849-1869.* Berlin, 1889.

Hollander, Bernhard. "Erinnerungen an die Jahren 1902-1905," *Baltische Blätter für allgemein-kulturelle Fragen,* II (1924), 111-125.

Hunfalvy, Paul. *Reise in den Ostseeprovinzen Russlands.* Leipzig, 1874.

Kohl, J.G. *Die deutsch-russischen Ostseeprovinzen.* 2 vols. Dresden, 1841.

Lange, Walter (ed.). "Rigische Studentenbriefe aus dem letzten Jahrzehnt des vorigen Jahrhunderts," *Baltische Hefte,* XXI (1975-1977), 198-234.

Leroy-Beaulieu, Anatole, *The Empire of the Tsars and the Russians.* 3 vols. New York, 1893.

Mensenkampff, E. *Menschen und Schicksale aus dem alten Livland.* Riga, 1943.

Pantenius, Louise. *Jugenderinnerungen aus dem alten Riga.* Hannover, 1959.

Pantenius, Theodor. "In Riga. Aus den Erinnerungen eines baltischen Journalisten," *Heimatstimmen,* V (1912), 5-48.

Pobedonostsev, Konstantin P. *Pis'ma Pobedonostseva k Aleksandru III,* 2 vols. Moscow, 1925.

Seraphim, Ernst. *Baltische Schicksale.* Berlin, 1935.

Turmann, Ernst. *Pickwa: Ein baltisches Leben.* Tübingen, 1975.

Valuev, P.A. *Dnevnik,* 2 vols. Moscow, 1961.

"V pribaltiiskom krae. Iz zapisok russkago chinovnika 1856-1876 gg.," *Russkaia starina,* XXXV (1882), 59-90, XL (1883), 553-572, XLI (1884), 1-14.

Wachtsmuth, W. *Wege, Umwege, Weggenossen.* Munich, 1954.

Witte, Sergei Iu. *Vospominaniia: Detstvo. Tsarstvovaniia Aleksandra II i Aleksandra III.* Berlin, 1923.

——. *Vospominaniia: Tsarstvovanie Nikolaia II,* 2 vols. Berlin, 1922.

Political Literature

Buchholtz, Alexander. *Deutsch-protestantische Kämpfe in den baltischen Provinzen Russlands.* Leipzig, 1888.

——. *50 Jahre russischer Verwaltung in den baltischen Provinzen Russlands.* Leipzig, 1883.

Eckardt, Julius. *Die baltischen Provinzen Russlands.* Leipzig, 1869.

——. *Baltische und russische Kulturstudien.* Leipzig, 1869.

——. *Bürgerthum und Büreaukratie: Vier Capitel aus der neuesten livländischen Geschichte.* Leipzig, 1870.

——. *Distinguished Persons in Russian Society.* London, 1873.

——. (ed. and trans.). *Juri Samarins Anklage gegen die Ostseeprovinzen Russlands.* Leipzig, 1869.

——. *Modern Russia.* London, 1870.

——. *Russia Before and After the War.* London, 1880.

——. *Zur Characteristik der Balten.* Hamburg, 1962 (first published Riga, 1863).

Freytag-Loringhoven, Axel v. "Die Krisis des baltischen Deutchtums," *Deutsche Monatschrift,* IX (1905-1906), 595-605.

Katkov, Mikhail N. *Sobranie peredovykh statei "Moskovskikh vedomosti."* 25 vols. Moscow, 1897-1898.

Kronwalds, Otto. *Nationale Bestrebungen.* Dorpat, 1872.

Pezold, Leopold. *Die Öffentlichkeit in den baltischen Provinzen.* Leipzig, 1870.

Russisch-baltische Blätter. Beiträge zur Kenntnis Russlands und seiner Grenzmarken. 4 vols. Leipzig, 1886-1888.

Samarin, Iuri. *Okrainy Rossii.* 6 vols. Prague and Berlin, 1869-1876.

Schirren, Carl. *Livländische Antwort an Herrn Juri Samarin.* Leipzig, 1869.

Segeberg, Meinhard v. [pseud.] "Die lettische Psychose," *Die Zukunft,* LIV (1906), 336-342.

Seraphim, Ernst. "Die baltischen Provinzen in der zweiten Hälfte des 19. Jahrhunderts," *Deutsche Monatschrift fur Russland,* I (1912), 577-595.

———. *In neuen Jahrhundert: Baltischer Ruckblick und Ausblick*. Riga, 1902.
Valdemars, Krisjanis. *Vaterländisches und Gemeinnütziges*. Moscow, 1871.

II. Secondary Sources

Aidnik, Erwin-Erhard. "Baltische Zunftgeist," *Baltische Monatshefte*, V (1936), 24–29.
———. "Zur nationalen und sozialen Lage des deutsch-baltischen Handwerkerstandes," *Baltische Monatshefte*, III (1934), 243–256.
Amburger, Erik. *Geschichte des Protestantismus in Russland*. Stuttgart, 1961.
Arbusow, Leonid. *Grundriss der Geschichte Liv-, Est-, and Kurlands*. Riga, 1918.
Armstrong, John. "Mobilized Diaspora in Tsarist Russia: The Case of the Baltic Germans," in *Soviet Nationality Policies and Practices*, (ed.), J.R. Azrael, New York, 1978, pp. 63–104.
Aschkewitz, Max. "Der Niedergang des baltischen deutschen Handwerks im 19. Jahrhundert," *Baltische Monatshefte*, VI (1937), 493–496.
"Bedrängnisse und Erfolge des Deutschtums in den Ostseeprovinzen Russlands," *Die Grenzboten*, LXV, pt. 1 (1906), 177–184, 240–251.
Beiträge zur Geschichte der Industrie Rigas. 3 vols. Riga, 1910–1912.
Bilmanis, Alfreds. "Grandeur and Decline of the German Balts," *Slavonic and East European Review*, XXII (1944), 50–80.
Bilmanis, Alfreds. *A History of Latvia*. Princeton, 1951.
———. "The Struggle for Domination of the Baltic," *Journal of Central European Affairs*, V (1945), 119–142.
Blackwell, William, *The Beginnings of Russian Industrialization, 1800–1860*. Princeton, 1968.
Blumenbach, Eugen. *Die Gemeinde der Stadt Riga in 700 Jahren, 1201–1901*. Riga, 1901.
———. "Zur Geschichte der Ehrenburger und Extemten und ihrer sozialen Lage," *Deutsche Monatschrift fur Russland*, III (1914), 522–528.
Bock. B.v. *50 Jahre des Technischen Vereins zu Riga, 1858–1908*. Riga, 1908.
Boehm, Max. *Die Krisis des deutschbaltischen Menschen*. Berlin, 1915.
———. *Die Letten*. Berlin, 1917.
Boehm, Max H. "Der Fall Schirren," *Jahrbuch des baltischen Deutsctums*, XVI (1969), 17–26.
Brunstermann, Friedrich. *Die Geschichte der kleinen oder St. Johannis Gilde in Wort und Bild*. Riga, 1902.
Buchholtz, Anton, *Geschichte der Juden in Riga bis zur Begrundung der Rigaschen Hebräergemeinde im Jahre 1842*. Riga, 1899.
Buchholtz, Arend. *Die deutschen Ostseeprovinzen*. Berlin, 1916.
———. *Geschichte der Rigaschen Familie Schwartz*. Berlin, 1921.
Byrnes, Robert. *Pobedonostsev: His Life and Thought*. Bloomington, Ind., 1968.

Carlberg, Nicolai. "George Armitstead als Sozialpolitiker," *Hefte der Gesell-schaft für kommunale Sozialpolitik in Riga,* VI (1913), 31–46.

——. "Stadtische Selbstverwaltung in den Ostseeprovinzen," in *Baltische Bür-gerkunde.* Riga, 1908, pp. 196–226.

Carlberg, Nicolai. *Die Stadt Riga Verwaltung und Haushalt in den Jahren 1878-1900.* Riga, 1901.

Conze, Werner. "Die deutsche Volksinsel Hirschenhof im gesellschaftlichen Aufbau des baltischen Deutschtums," *Auslandsdeutsche Volksforschung,* I (1937), 152–163.

Depman, I. "O. naznachenii Senatora N. A. Manaseina revizorom lifliandskoi i kurliandskoi gubernii," *Izvestiia Akademii Nauk Estonskoi SSR,* X (1961), 144–148.

Die deutsch-lettischen Beziehungen in den baltischen Provinzen. Leipzig, 1916.

Die deutschen Ostseeprovinzen Russlands. Berlin, 1915.

Dilevskaia, O.A. *Pribaltiiskii krai.* Moscow, 1917.

Dopkewitsch, Helene. "Die Grosse Gilde zu Riga," *Baltische Monatshefte,* V (1936), 8–23.

Dorneth, J. v. "Die Letten und ihr Anspruch auf nationale Selbständigkeit," *Unsere Zeit,* No. 1 (1883), 111–122, 290–307.

——. *Die Letten unter den Deutschen.* Berlin, 1885.

——. "Die Verdrängung des Deutschtums in den Ostseeprovinzen" *Unsere Zeit,* No. 2 (1887), 626–641, 748–763.

——. *Das Zerstörungswerk in den russischen Ostseeprovinzen.* Berlin, 1890.

——. "Zur Russificierung der Ostseeprovinzen," *Unsere Zeit,* No. 2 (1886), 317–335, 508–527.

Druzil, A. "Iz istorii revoliutsionnogo dvizheniia 70-80-kh godov v Latvii," *Istoricheskie zapiski,* XLV (1954), 201–207.

Eckardt, Johannes v. "Beiträge zur Geschichte des deutschen-baltischen Zei-tungswesens," *Zeitungswissenschaft,* III (1928), 20–51.

Eckardt, Julius. *Livland im 18. Jahrhundert.* Leipzig, 1876.

Ekonomicheskie sviazi Pribaltiki s Rossiei. Riga, 1968.

Elias, Otto. "Zur Lage der undeutschen Bevölkerung im Riga des 18. Jahrhun-dert," *Jahrbücher fur Geschichte Osteuropas,* XIV (1966), 481–484.

Englehardt, Alexis v. *Die deutschen Ostseeprovinzen Russlands.* Munich, 1916.

Evreinov, G.A. *Rossiiskie nemtsy.* Petrograd, 1915.

Gernet, Bruno v. *Die Entwicklung der Rigaer Handels und Verkehrs im Laufe der letzten 50 Jahren bis zum Ausbruche des Weltkriegs.* Jena, 1919.

Grosberg, Oskar. *Die Presse Lettlands.* Riga, 1927.

Haltzel, Michael. *Der Abbau der deutschen ständischen Selbstverwaltung in den Ostseeprovinzen Russlands 1855-1905.* Marburg, 1977.

——. "The Reaction of the Baltic Germans to Russification during the Nine-teenth Century." Ph.D. dissertation, Harvard University, 1971.

Hamm, Michael F. "Riga's 1913 City Election: A Study in Baltic Urban Politics," *Russian Review,* XXXIX (1980), 442–61.

Handrack, Hans. *Die Bevölkerungsentwicklung der deutschen Minderheit in Lettland.* Jena, 1932.

Handwörterbuch des Grenz- und Auslandsdeutschtums. 3 vols. Breslau, 1933–1940.

Hehn, Jurgen v. "Die Anfänge des lettischen Zeitungswesens," *Baltische Monatshefte,* VII (1938), 82–92.

———. *Die baltische Frage zur Zeit Alexanders III in Aesserungen der deutschen Öeffentlichkeit.* Marburg, 1953.

———. "Deutsche Kulturabeit und lettischer Nationalismus," *Jomsburg,* II (1938), 453–488.

Hein, Jurgen v. *Die lettisch-literarische Gesellschaft und das Lettentum.* Berlin, 1938.

Hollander, Berhnard. "Aus der Geschichte der 'Euphonie,'" *Baltische Monatschrift,* ser. 2, LVIII (1927), 168–177.

———. "Der Deutsche Verein in Livland," *Jahrbuch des baltischen Deutschtums in Lettland und Estlund,* 1931, pp. 107–113.

———. "Dr. Julius Eckardt," *Baltisches Geistesleben,* I (1929), 257–290.

———. *Geschichte der Literärisch-praktischen Bürgerverbindung in Riga, 1801-1927.* Riga, 1927.

———. "Die Gesellschaft 'Euphonie' in Riga," *Jahrbuch des baltischen Deutschtums in Lettland und Estland,* 1930, pp. 98–99.

———. *Riga im 19. Jahrhundert.* Riga, 1926.

———. "Vor 50 Jahren," *Baltische Monatshefte,* IV (1935), 544–560.

———. "Zur Geschichte der deutschen wissenschaftlichen Vereine in Lettland," *Der Auslandsdeutsche, VI (1923), 597–604.*

Hutton, L.T. "The Reform of City Government in Russia, 1860 1870." Ph.D. dissertation, University of Illinois at Urbana, 1972.

Iatsunskii, V.K. "K voprosu o razvitii promyshlennosti Pribaltiki vo vtoroi polovine XIX v.," *Izvestia Akademii Nauk Latviiskoi SSR,* 1953, pp. 48–70.

———. "Znachenie ekonomicheskoi sviazei s Rossii dlia khoziaistvennogo razvitiia gorodov Pribaltiki v epokhu kapitalizma," *Istoricheskie zapiski,* XLV (1954), 105–147.

Isakov, S. *Ostzeiskii vopros v russkoi perchati 1860-kh godov.* Tartu, 1961.

Istoriia latviiskoi SSR. 3 vols. Riga, 1952–1958.

Ivanov, A.I. "Voznikovenie i razvitie predpriiatii sel'skokhoziaistvennogo mashinostroeniia Latvii v XIX i nachale XX veka," *Izvestiia Akademii Nauk Latviiskoi SSR,* 1967, pp. 66–76.

"Die Justizreform in den Ostseeprovinzen Russlands," *Unsere Zeit,* No. 1, (1890), 357–376.

Kahle, Wilhelm. *Die Begegnung des baltischen Protestantismus mit der Russisch-Orthodoxen Kirche.* Leiden, 1959.

Kalnins, Bruno, "The Social Democratic Movement in Latvia," in *Revolution and Politics in Russia,* (ed.), A. Rabinowitch and J. Rabinowitch, Bloomington, Ind., 1972, pp. 134–156.

Katz, Martin. *Mikhail N. Katkov. A Political Biography, 1818-1887.* The Hague, 1966.

Kessler, Otto. *Die baltischen Länder und Litauen.* Berlin, 1916.

Kieseritzky, Gustav. "Die Entstehung des baltischen Polytechnikums und die ersten 25 Jahre seines Bestehens," in *Festschrift der Polytechnischen Schule zu Riga zur Feier ihres XXV-jährigen Bestehens.* Riga, 1887, pp. 1–137.

Knorre, Werner v. "Vom Wirtschaftsleben des baltischen Deutschtums," in *Wir Balten.* Salzburg, 1951, pp. 102–117.

Kroeger, Gert. "Die Deutschen Vereine in Liv-, Est-, und Kurland 1905/06–1914", *Jahrbuch des baltischen Deutschtums,* XVI (1969), 39–49.

——. "Die Reichsgrundung von 1871 und die baltischen Deutschen," *Jahrbuch des baltischen Deutschtums,* XVIII (1971), 22–28.

——. "Zur Situation der baltischen Deutschen um die Jahrhundertwende," *Zeitschrift fur Ostforschung,* XVII (1968), 601–632.

Kruus, Hans. *Grundriss der Geschichte des estnischen Volkes.* Tartu, 1932.

Larson, David. "Iurii Fedorovich Samarin and the Nationality Problem in Russia." Ph.D. dissertation, Indiana University, 1974.

Lenz, Wilhelm. *Der baltischen Literatenstand.* Marburg, 1953.

——. "Der Bervölkerungswandel einer baltischen Kleinstadt," *Baltische Monatshefte,* IV (1935), 537–543.

——. (ed.). *Deutsch-baltisches biographisches Lexikon.* Cologne, 1970.

——. *Die Entwicklung Rigas zur Grosstadt.* Kitzingen am Main, 1954.

——. *Umvolkungsvorgänge in der ständischen Ordnung Livlands.* Posen, 1941.

——. "Volkstumswechsel in den baltischen Ländern," *Ostdeutsche Wissenschaft,* III–IV (1956–1957), 181–200.

Liashchenko, Peter. *History of the National Economy of Russia.* New York, 1949.

Lincoln, W. Bruce. "The Russian State and its Cities: A Search for Effective Municipal Government, 1786–1842," *Jahrbücher für Geschichte Osteuropas,* XVII (1969), 531–541.

Lindemuth, Margarethe. "Krisjanis Valdemars und Atis Kronwalds: Zwei lettische Volkstumskämpfer," *Baltische Hefte,* XIII (1967), 84–107.

——. *Das lettisch-deutsche Verhältnis vor dem Weltkrieg auf Grund der lettischen Presse.* Heidelberg, 1939.

——. "Die lettischen Parteien 1905 und ihre Programme," *Baltische Hefte,* XV (1969), 75–88.

Livshits, R.S. *Razmeshchenie promyshlennoisti v dorevoliutsionnoi Rossii.* Moscow, 1954.

Lundin, Leonard. "The Road from Tsar to Kaiser: Changing Loyalties of the Baltic Germans, 1905–1914," *Journal of Central European Affairs,* X (1950), 223–255.

Masing, Gerhard. *Der Kampf um die Reform der Rigaer Stadtverfassung (1860–1870).* Riga, 1936.

——. "Riga und die Ostwanderung des deutschen Handwerkers," *Deutsches Archiv für Landes- und Volksforschung,* IV (1940), 36–51, 235–253.

McKay, John. *Pioneers for Profit: Foreign Entrepreneurs and Russian Industrialization, 1885–1913.* Chicago, 1970.

Mertens, O. *Das Zufuhrgebiet Rigas.* Riga, 1890.

Mettig, Constantin. *Baltische Städte.* Riga, 1905.

——. *Geschichte der Stadt Riga.* Riga, 1897.

Netesin, Iu. "Iz istorii proniknoveniia germanskogo kapitala v ekonomiku Rossii," *Izvestiia Akademii Nauk Latviiskoi SSR,* 1960, pp. 33–45.

——. "Ob inostrannom kapitale v obrabatyvaiushchei promyshlennosti Latyshkogo kraia," *Izvestiia Akademii Nauk Latviiskoi SSR,* 1964, pp. 3–20.

Ocherki ekonomicheskoi istorii Latvii, 1860–1900. Riga, 1972.

Ocherki ekonomicheskoi istorii Latvii, 1900–1917. Riga, 1968.

Oettingen Arved V. "August von Oettingen," *Baltische Monatschrift,* ser. 2, LVIX (1928), 114–149.

——. "Die Gebrüder von Oettingen," *Baltisches Geistesleben,* I (1929), 348–528.

Ozoliniia, D.K. "O kommunal'nom khoziaistve Rigi v 90-kh godov XIX v.," *Problemy istorii,* VI (1962), 137–164.

Page, Stanley. "Social and National Currents in Latvia, 1860–1917," *American Slavic Review,* VIII (1949), 25–36.

Pistohlkors, Gert v. "Führende Schicht oder nationale Minderheit?," *Zeitschrift für Ostforschung,* XXI (1972), 601–618.

——. Gert v. *Ritterschaftliche Reformpolitik zwischen Russifizierung und Revolution. Historische Studien zum Problem der politischen Selbsteinschätzung der deutschen Oberschicht in den Ostseeprovinzen Russlands im Krisenjahr 1905.* Göttingen, 1978.

——. "Das Urteil Alexander Wäbers uber das Scheitern der lettischen nationalen Bewegung und die Ursachen der lettischen Revolution von 1905/06," in *Das Vergangene und die Geschichte,* (ed.), Gert von Pistohlkors, Rudolf von Thadden and Hellmuth Weiss. Gottingen, 1973, pp. 232–271.

Pistohlkors, Harry v. *Livlands Kampf um Deutschtum und Kultur.* Berlin, 1918.

Plakans, Andrejs. "Peasants, Intellectuals and Nationalism in the Russian Baltic Provinces," *Journal of Modern History,* XLVI (1974), 445–475.

Pohle, Richard. "Riga," *Meereskunde,* XIII (1919), 1–40.

Rashin, A.G. *Naselenie Rossii za 100 let, 1811–1913.* Moscow, 1956.

Rauch, Georg v. "Die nationale Frage in den russischen Ostseeprovinzen im 19. Jahrhundert," in *Der Ostseeraum im Blickfeld der deutschen Geschichte.* Cologne, 1970, pp. 165–181.

——. "Der russische Reichsgedanke im Spiegel des politischen Bewusstseins der baltischen Provinzen," *Ostdeutsche Wissenschaft,* I (1954), 183–208.

——. *Russland: staatliche Einheit und nationale Vielfalt.* Munich, 1953.

Redlich, Friedrich. "Haltung, Sitte und Brauch im Leben der Grossen Gilde zu Riga," *Baltische Monatshefte,* V (1936), 1–7.

——. "Der Pole in den baltischen Landen," *Deutsche Wissenschaftliche Zeitschrift im Wartheland,* II (1941), 71–108.

Der Rigasche Borsen-Comite in den Jahren 1866–1872. Riga, 1873.

Rohland, W. v. *Das baltische Deutschtum.* Leipzig, 1906.

Rothfels, Hans. "The Baltic Provinces: Some Historic Aspects and Perspectives," *Journal of Central European Affairs,* IV (1944), 117–147.

——. *Reich, Staat und Nation im deutschbaltischen Denken*. Halle, 1930.

——. "Russians and Germans in the Baltic," *Contemporary Review*, CLVII (1940), 320–326.

Rozhdestvenskii, S.V. *Istoricheskii obzor deiatel'nosti Ministerstva Narodnago Prosveshcheniia, 1802–1902*. St. Petersburg, 1902.

Ryndziumskii, P.G. *Gorodskoe grazhdanstvo doreformennoi Rossii*. Moscow, 1958.

Schaudinn, Heinrich. *Das baltische Deutschtum und Bismarcks Reichsgründung*. Leipzig, 1932.

Schiemann, Theodor. *Viktor Hehn: Ein Lebensbild*. Stuttgart, 1894.

Schroeder, Herbert. *Russland und die Ostsee*. Riga, 1927.

Schweder, Gotthard. *Die alte Domschule und das daraus hervorgegangene Stadt-Gymnasium zu Riga*. Riga, 1910.

——. "Das deutsche Schulwesen in den Städten der Ostseeprovinzen," in *Baltische Bürgerkunde*. Riga, 1908, pp. 255–276.

Seraphim, Ernst. *Baltische Geschichte im Grundriss*. Reval, 1908.

——. "Ist eine Germanisierung der Letten und Esten möglich gewesen?," *Baltische Blätter*, XIII (1930), 717–725.

Seredonin, S.M. *Istoricheskii obzor deiatel'nosti Komiteta ministrov, 1802–1902*. 5 vols. St. Petersburg, 1902.

Sering, Max. *Westrussland in seiner Bedeutung für die Entwicklung Mitteleuropas*. Leipzig, 1917.

Simon, Gerhard. *Konstantin Petrovich Pobedonostsev und die Kirchenpolitik des Heiligen Sinod, 1880–1905*. Göttingen, 1969.

Skolis, I. *Riga: Ocherki po istorii gorod*. Riga, 1967.

Sommer, E.F. *Die Einigungsbestrebungen der Deutschen im Vorkriegs-Russland*. Leipzig, 1940.

Sotnietse, L. Ia. "Rashirenie Rizhkogo porta vo vtoroi polovine XIX veka," *Izvestiia Akademii Nauk Latviiskoi SSR*, 1969, pp. 13–22.

Speer, H. "Zur Frage der Umvolkung in den baltischen Landen." Unpublished manuscript.

Spekke, Arnolds. *History of Latvia*. Stockholm, 1957.

Stegmann, Helmuth. "Graf P.A. Walujew zur baltischen Frage in der Zeit Alexander II," *Baltische Hefte*, XIII (1967), 59–83.

Stein, Hermann v. *Der Rigaschen Borsen-Comite in den Jahren 1816–1866*. Riga, 1866.

Steida, Eugen v. *Das livländische Bankwesen in Vergangenheit und Gegenwart*. Leipzig, 1909.

——, *Die Rigaer Börsenbank, 1864–1914*. Riga, 1914.

Strazdins, K. "K voprosu ob obrazovanii latyshkoi burzhuaznoi natsii," *Istoricheskie zapiski*, XLV (1954), 163–182.

——. "O mladolatyshkom dvizhenii 60-70-kh godakh XIX v.," *Voprosy istorii*, 1958, pp. 113–122.

Thaden, Edward. *Conservative Nationalism in Nineteenth Century Russia*. Seattle, 1964.

——. "N.A. Manaseins Senatorenrevision in Livland und Kurland während der Zeit von 1882 bis 1883," *Jahrbücher für Geschichte Osteuropas*, XVII (1969), 45–58.

Thaden, Edward. "Nationality Policy in the Western Borderlands of the Russian Empire, 1881–1914," in *American Contributions to the VIIth Congress of Slavists, Warsaw, 1973*. The Hague, 1973, III, 69–78.

Thaden, Edward C., ed., Haltzel, Michael, Lundin, C. Leonard, Plakans, Andrejs, and Raun, Toivo. *Russification in the Baltic Provinces and Finland, 1855–1905*. Princeton, 1981.

Tiesenberg, Ludwig. "Einiges über die St. Johannis-Guild zu Riga," *Baltische Monatshefte*, V (1936), 30–33.

Tobien, Alexander v. *Die Agrargesetzgebung Livlands im 19. Jahrhundert.* Berlin, 1911.

——. *Das Armenwesen der Stadt Riga.* Riga, 1895.

——. *Die livländische Ritterschaft in ihrem Verhältnis zum Zarismus und russischen Nationalismus.* 2 vols. Riga, 1925 and Berlin, 1930.

Transehe-Roseneck, Astaf v. "Das Agrarwesen der Ostseeprovinzen," in *Baltische Bürgerkunde*. Riga, 1908, pp. 277–330.

——. *Die lettische Revolution.* 2 vols. Berlin, 1906–1907.

Valeskaln, P.I. *Ocherk razvitiia progressivnoi filosofskoi i obshchestvennopoliticheskoi mysli v Latvii.* Riga, 1967.

Vigrab, G.I. *Pribaltiiskie nemtsy.* Iuriev, 1916.

Vilks, B. Ia. *Formirovanie promyshlennogo proletariata v Latvii vo vtoroi polovine XIX veka.* Riga, 1957.

Villebois, Arthur v. "Die Landvolkschule der Ostseeprovinzen," in *Baltische Burgerkunde*. Riga, 1908, pp. 240–254.

Die Volkswirtschaft der russischen Ostseeprovinzen: Ihre Jetzige und zukunftige Leistungsfahigkeit. Berlin, 1915.

Wachtsmuth, Wolfgang. "Der Rigaschen Burschenstaat bis zum Ersten Weltkrieg," in *Festschrift Fraternitas Baltica*, 1865–1965 Aschaffenburg, 1965, pp. 13–48.

Wachtsmuth, Wolfgang. "Von deutscher Schulpolitik und Schularbeit im baltischen Raum," *Deutsche Archiv für Landes- und Volksforschung*, VII (1943), 45–89, 351–396.

Wallroth, E. *Die baltischen Provinzen und Litauen.* Lubeck, 1915.

Walters, Mikelis. *Baltengedanken und Baltenpolitik.* Paris, 1926.

——. *Lettland: Seine Entwicklung zum Staat und die baltische Frage.* Rome, 1923.

Weiss, R. "Friedrich Bienemann d. Ä. und die Revaler Jahren der *Baltischen Monatschrift*," *Baltische Monatshefte*, IV (1935), 622–627.

Wittram, Reinhard. "1870/71 im Erlebnis der baltischen Deutschen," *Deutsche Archiv für Landes- und Volksforschung*, IV (1940), 29–35.

——. *Baltische Geschichte*, 1180–1918. Munich, 1954.

——. "Carl Schirrens Livländische Antwort," *Ostdeutsche Wissenschaft*, I (1954), 278–298.

——. "Deutsch und baltisch. Zum Verständnis der deutschbaltischen politischen Tradition," *Baltische Monatshefte*, II (1933), 187–201.
——. *Drei Generationen: Deutschland, Livland, Russland.* Göttingen, 1949.
——. "Die geistige Lage des baltischen Deutschtums in historischer Perspektive," *Baltische Monatshefte*, II (1933), 249–261.
——. "Liberal und konservativ als Gestaltungsprinzipien baltischer Politik," *Baltische Monatschrift*, ser. 2, LXI (1930), 213–233.
——. *Liberalismus baltischer Literaten.* Riga, 1931.
——. *Meinungskämpfe im baltischen Deutschtum während der Reformepoche des 19. Jahrhunderts.* Riga, 1934.
——. *Das Nationale als europäisches Problem.* Göttingen, 1954.
——. "Vomärzlicher Freisinn und ständische Reformpolitik," *Zeitschrift für Ostforschung*, V (1956), 481–499.
——. "Wandlungen des baltischen Nationalitätenproblems," *Baltische Monatshefte*, I (1932), 253–265.
——. "Wendepunkte der baltischen Geschichte," in *Wir Balten*, Salzburg, 1951, pp. 12–48.
——. *Zur Geschichte Rigas.* Bovenden, 1951.
Wolffen, A.v. *Die Ostseeprovinzen Est-, Liv- und Kurland: Ihre Vergangenheit, Kultur und politische Bedeutung.* Munich, 1917.
Wulffius, W. "Carl Schirren," *Baltische Monatschrift*, ser. 2, LVIII (1927), 1–35.
Zaionchkovskii, P.A. *Rossiiskoe samoderzhavie v kontse XIX stoletiia.* Moscow, 1970.
Ziv, V.S. *Inostrannye kapitaly v russkikh aktsionernykh prepriiatiiakh.* Petrograd, 1915.
Zur Geschichte der "Rigaschen Zeitung." Riga, 1907.

INDEX

Admiralty, 80, 112
Aksakov, Ivan S., 14
Albedinskii, Peter P., 21, 28
Alexander I, Tsar of Russia, 2
Alexander II, Tsar of Russia, 6, 9, 22, 45, 48, 51, 65, 101, 107
Alexander III, Tsar of Russia, 45–6, 47–8, 54, 99–101, 108
Alt, Eugen, 93
Armitstead, George, 95–6
Armstrong, John A., 187 n. 53
artisans, 1, 6, 8, 26, 36, 76–8, 90–1, 103–4, 114, 184 n. 10
Austria-Hungary, 74

Baerens, John, 10, 13, 20, 28
Baird, Charles, 73
Baltic Constitutional Party, 111
Baltic Governor-Generalship, 8, 23
Baltic Polytechnical Institute, 26, 72, 76–7, 80, 96
  Russification of, 50, 56, 98–9
Baltijas vestnesis, 86, 189 n. 22
Balss, 189 n. 22
Baltische Monatschrift, 9, 12, 25, 28, 31, 35, 57, 89, 93
Banks, 72, 74–6, 79, 196 n. 38
Barclay de Tolly, Eugen, 194 n. 21
Berent, T. v., 113–4
Bergwitz, Friedrich, 71
Berkholz, Georg, 9–10, 13–4, 16–7, 19, 28, 30–1, 33–4
Berlin, *see* Germany
Bielenstein, August, 39
Bienemann, Friedrich, 31, 55, 92
Bocke, Gustav, 91–2
Boer War, 59
Bohemia, 34, 113

Bolderaa, 70
Bonfeldt, Friedrich, 194 n. 21
Bornhaupt, Konrad, 194 n. 21
Bötticher, Theodor, 9
Brüggen, Ernst v. d., 13–4
Buchholtz, Alexander, 34, 42, 52, 55–7
Buchholtz, Arend, 55
Büngner, Johannes, 53
Büngner, Robert, 18, 38, 47–8, 54, 95–6

Capitulations of 1710, 6, 11, 23, 28–30, 33, 46
Carlberg, Nikolai, 97–8
Catherine II, Empress of Russia, 17
Censorship, 27–8, 52–3, 62, 100
Census, of 1867, 1–2, 68, 76, 183 n. 1, 184 n. 11
  of 1881, 32–3, 38, 68–9, 76–7, 188 n. 19, 194 n. 19
  of 1897, 68
Chamber of Commerce, 3, 18, 26, 66, 69–70, 97, 194 n. 22
Council of State, 19, 24
Crimean War, 9, 70
Czechs, 34

Dalton, Hermann, 100
Delianov, Ivan, 49–50
Demme, Friedrich, 55
Den', 14
Dettmann, Heinrich, 74
Dorpat, 10, 19, 30
Dorpat University, 2, 15, 18, 28, 30, 47, 57, 59, 190 n. 5
  Russification of, 50, 56
Doss, Matthias, 53
Dünaburg, 65, 70
Düna-Zeitung, 53, 57–9, 81, 86, 89, 103

215

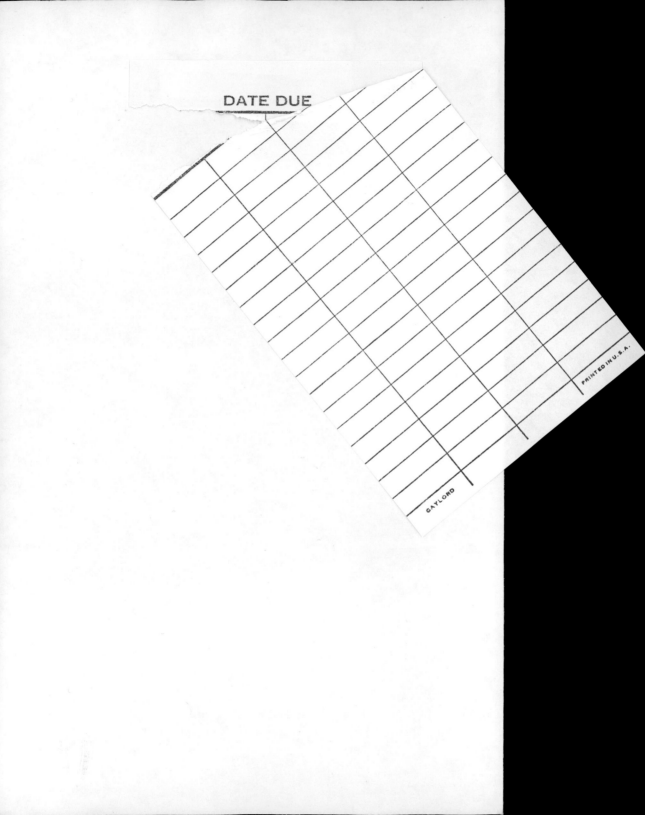

DATE DUE

GAYLORD   PRINTED IN U.S.A.